SOCIALIST RENEWAL

Urban Politics

Accommodation or Resistance?

Teresa Hayter

Spokesman
for
European Labour Forum

First published in Great Britain in 1997 by
Spokesman
Bertrand Russell House
Gamble Street
Nottingham, England
Tel. 0115 9708318
Fax. 0115 9420433

Publications list available on request

British Library Cataloguing in Publication Data available on request from the British Library.

ISBN 0-85124-606-0 paper

Printed by the Russell Press Ltd, Nottingham
(Tel. 0115 9784505)

Contents

Teresa Hayter has written six books, including *Aid as Imperialism* (Penguin 1971) — on the Penguin best seller list in the early 1970s — and *The Creation of World Poverty* (Pluto 1981 and 1990) — reprinted six times. She co-edited *The Factory and the City: The Story of Cowley Automobile Workers in Oxford* with David Harvey (Mansell 1993), as part of a campaign against the closure of the car plant. She wrote a 60-page chapter on 'Industrial Democracy: the GLEB Experience' in *A Taste of Power: the Politics of Local Economics*, edited by Maureen Mackintosh and Hilary Wainwright (Verso 1987).

She worked for the Greater London Council (1984-86) and the London Strategic Policy Unit (1986-88). She has been a research fellow at Oxford Polytechnic, Oxford University and South Bank University, research officer at the Overseas Development Institute, co-owner of a bookshop in Leeds, and a political activist since the 1960s. She is currently active in the Campaign to Close Campsfield.

Preface

This book was written while I was employed as a research fellow at South Bank University. Under a research programme entitled 'A Sense of Place', I was sent to do interviews on City Challenge in Brixton and North Kensington. I am grateful to have then had the opportunity to write a book on urban politics, and especially for the support of Irene Bruegel and Professor Mike Gibson.

The book was commissioned by Blackwells, who decided not to publish it because 'The readers' reports received on the book were, regrettably negative'. These reports included the following statements by two of the readers:

> 'The academy is very timid these days . . . and would not recommend a book as a main book if it included too much polemicising. OK for Pluto perhaps but not Blackwell. The book would be recommended as an illustration of one particular point of view perhaps . . .'

> 'The other problem is that the political preferences of the writer militate against the idea of a textbook. Textbooks should be as neutral as possible. . . . What is presented here is a personal account of politics of the 1980s from a hard left perspective which even modern socialists would find out of date and embarrassing. . . . The writer's 1970s style revolutionary socialist political beliefs are clearly revealed . . .'

I believe that books which proclaim themselves as neutral are virtually never so. They are in fact expressions of a particular political point of view, dressed up in language which makes it hard to discern what this point of view is, and they are therefore misleading. Currently what goes for 'neutrality' is, in any case, shifting further and further to the right. I have also a slight sense of *déja vu*, after the World Bank's attempt in 1969 to censor *Aid as Imperialism*. So it was good to hear from Spokesman that they want to publish a series of pamphlets and books to help keep alive socialist ideas in the face of a cautious attitude by other publishers, and I greatly appreciate their willingness to publish this book.

I should like to thank Di Parkin for her very helpful and supportive comments. Thanks also to Hilary Kean for help on banned councillors, to Jamie Gough for comments on parts of the manuscript, to *Index on Censorship* for permission to reproduce material on Campsfield immigration detention centre, and to all the people in North Kensington, Brixton and other places who gave time to be interviewed.

Introduction

Human beings now typically live in towns and cities. Increasingly, they live in vast conglomerations around these towns and cities, or urban sprawl. This is not a phenomenon merely of the so-called advanced industrialised countries. Half of the total population of the world now lives in urban areas, and the percentage is rising. By the year 2000, if something else does not happen and United Nations projections are to be believed, two thirds of the world's population will live in cities and towns. 23 cities will have populations of over ten million, compared to four in 1970 and ten in 1985. In 1975, the number of people in the Third World living in towns overtook the number in the industrialised countries, and now there are many more in the former than the latter.

Britain is one of the most urban of the industrialised countries. Even though the population of most of its big cities has declined over the past thirty or so years, nearly 90 per cent of the total population of 55 million people now lives in urban areas. Nearly a third live in seven conurbations, or 'metropolitan counties', around London, Manchester, Liverpool, Sheffield, Newcastle, Birmingham and Bradford. A further million live in Glasgow and Bristol. 12 cities, with a combined population of over 13 million, contain over 300,000 people. Many more people live in smaller towns and suburbs, sprawling extensions of cities. Many of those who now live outside cities and towns nevertheless work in them. While a little over 10 per cent of the population lives in rural areas, only one per cent work on the land, as farmers and agricultural workers. This is less than, for example, the numbers working in post and telecommunications.

In the world as a whole, virtually the whole of the human population now forms part of the system of economic organisation, or the capitalist world market, which originated with industrialisation and which created massive urban growth during the nineteenth and twentieth centuries. The people who still live in rural areas almost never live in isolation from the economy of cities. There are no more than a few, small areas of the world which are not integrated into this capitalist market. Many people move to and fro between cities and the countryside, on a daily or seasonal basis or at longer intervals, for jobs or other reasons. Virtually all of the people who live in rural areas consume the products of industries based in towns, and may sell their own products to towns. Rural self-sufficiency is an aspiration for some, but it is hardly anywhere a current reality. In the same way the problems of individual cities, however big they are, let alone areas within them, cannot be resolved in isolation. Their prosperity or otherwise is largely determined by economic and political forces which are outside the control of the people who live in them. In the world as it is, there are few purely local solutions, fashionable though the notion of 'localness' may be both on the left and on the right of the political spectrum.

Cities nevertheless of course differ from rural areas in many ways. Because most people come to cities to work in industry and in other organised waged employment, the periodic slumps of capitalism, such as the current one, which cause a large rise in unemployment, may hit them more directly and powerfully, and leave them with few alternative resources. Cities are places of excitement and creativity, but in decline they are desolate and, over large areas, ugly places. Homelessness, crime and riots seem to be features of cities, as well as cultural and other achievements. Cities are the product of migration, and they are the places where new migrants hope to find jobs. Many of the recent migrants to British cities have been black; they have become the butt of some white people's resentment at the loss of jobs and services, and they have been subjected to the prejudices and violence of racism. Because people are concentrated in cities, their problems are also concentrated and more visible, and they usually appear more threatening to the established order than they do in rural areas. And, also because of the concentration of people in urban areas, political movements and especially radical politics have flourished in cities.

It is particularly for the latter reason that governments have felt obliged to adopt policies intended to alleviate, or at least distract attention from, poverty in cities. Cities present a threat to the established order not merely because they are sites of concentrated poverty or even because of crime, but because they have been fertile ground for radical politics. Central governments, both Labour and Conservative, have responded, especially from the 1960s onwards, mainly by setting up special programmes directed at the supposedly specific problems of certain parts of what came to be called, in Britain, the 'inner cities'. Local government, which is often seen as remote, bureaucratic and unresponsive, has on the other hand, in Britain and elsewhere in Europe, at times pushed forward reforms and even embodied some of the radical and socialist ideas nurtured in cities. From 1979 onwards, Conservative governments therefore set out, with considerable success, to weaken Labour-controlled local government in inner cities.

After the second world war, capitalism had one of its periodic booms. But from the 1960s onwards the capitalist system began its latest lurch into decline, with a progressive loss of prosperity and jobs. The first political reaction to this phenomenon, while the sense of optimism of the 1950s and 60s persisted, was one of rebellion and radical anti-state politics. This phase culminated in the late 1970s and early 1980s with the entry of many radical left and community activists into urban local government, in particular the Greater London Council and other metropolitan authorities. The activists retained much of their radicalism while they held a portion of state power. The Thatcher governments, the first of which was elected in 1979, succeeded in reversing or undermining most of these gains for radical left politics. Because the GLC was both self-proclaimedly socialist and popular with Londoners, the second Conservative government abolished it and other metropolitan authorities in 1986. The Conservatives then proceeeded to curb the activities and spending of the remaining local authorities, which they saw as a possible countervailing or alternative source of power and as excessive spenders of public funds.

Labour-controlled local authorities have failed in any case to mount much of a resistance to Thatcherite policies. The late 1980s and the 1990s have been a period of political accommodation. Labour councils have adopted 'new realist' positions which differ little from those of the government at a local level. Rather than risking losing office and perhaps being surcharged, local councillors have on the whole set their budgets in line with the government's prescriptions and thus become the instruments for implementing cuts. Their compliance has not earned them a reprieve from the Conservative onslaught on local government spending, which continues much as before. They have in the process taken much of the blame for the massive deterioration in public services. Even community activists have allowed themselves to be incorporated, moving from a radical left political position to one of acceptance of government grants and programmes. At the same time trade unions have been weakened by a combination of unemployment and

Conservative legal attacks on the right to strike, and their leadership has pursued a politics of accommodation and new realism similar to that of the Labour local authorities and the Labour party. Trade unions have done little to support unemployed people, and they do not find it easy to recruit, organise and support people who are casually and temporarily employed in small service sector firms, whose relative importance has grown with the recession and Conservative policies. The threat of the withdrawal of labour remains, in spite of unemployment, potentially the most powerful means of bringing about change in the interests of the working class, both employed and unemployed, in cities and elsewhere. The strikes in France in late 1995 demonstrated this with force. But industrial action has been relatively little used in Britain since the mid-1980s and the defeat of the 1984 miners' strike.

Mirroring the decline of labour movement politics, much of the intellectual debate on urban politics, even among those who call themselves left-wing, has degenerated into theories of 'post-Modernism', 'localness', a 'sense of place' and so on. It has largely ceased to nurture and feed into any radical political activism. Instead, 'left' intellectuals, including many geographers and other students of local specificities, lend credibility to the notion, favoured over the years by both Labour and Conservative governments, that people could 'pull themselves up by their bootstraps', if only they developed a sense of local pride and took responsibility for themselves and their areas. 'Localities' and 'communities' are studied for their special advantages and cultural attributes and encouraged to compete against one another for jobs, investment and markets, in a zero-sum game that benefits mainly private capital (and the peddlers of public relations hype). Left intellectuals and community activists now seldom argue, as they did in the 1960s and 1970s, that the problems of inner cities require fundamental changes in the national and international distribution of wealth and the abolition of the capitalist 'free market'. The Marxist left, which continues to argue for socialism, has lost influence, and it too has made little attempt to work with the unemployed and the poor in cities. The people who suffer in cities are thus left largely unrepresented, and have become increasingly cynical about politics and politicians.

Their most powerful means of drawing attention to themselves is to riot. But riots, when they occur, have so far been spontaneous and unorganised, and have not moved beyond the deprived areas of the cities in which the rioters live. The typical government response to these

4

expressions of despair and alienation is to increase the levels of repression and police activity. Similarly, the response to crime is often merely to put up barricades and create ghettos, and to seek to explain inner city violence in terms of the pshychological weakness of individuals and the failings of parents (especially if the latter are single women). There may also be, after riots, some increase in the levels of funding for the areas where the riots have taken place. But the government's 'special programmes' for inner cities continue to be little more than palliatives, a giving back of a small part of what has been taken away from them in cuts in public services and above all in loss of jobs. The condition of cities and their people, meanwhile, deteriorates.

There is a danger that, in the absence of credible political opposition on the left, this void will be occupied not only by the growth of state repression and racism, but even by fascism. Some of the few political organisations active among unemployed young people are fascist ones, although they have not yet made large gains in strength and membership. One area of optimism in this bleak political scene is perhaps the growth of activism among young people mainly on green issues, such as opposition to road-building. Up to now, much of this activism has not related directly to the central problems of unemployment and poverty of the half of humanity who live in urban areas. The movement lacks overall objectives and, unlike Marxism, it has no clear view on the agency for change or the means of implementing it. It remains in its idealism and its willingness to challenge many aspects of establishment politics a potential source of hope.

CHAPTER 1

The growth and transformation of cities

Until the industrial revolution in Europe, and the more recent growth in mega-cities throughout the world, cities contained only a small fraction of the world's population. First in the Eastern Mediterranean, then in other parts of Asia and later in Western Europe, they were devoted mainly to the self-aggrandisement and military aggression of rulers and religious orders. Cities grew in a planned and orderly way, and were dominated by palaces, churches, barracks and law courts. The industrial revolution, in Britain and other European countries in the late eighteenth and early nineteenth centuries, brought growth of a different kind, and on a bigger scale than before. Manchester, for example, had about 6,000 people in 1685; in 1760 it had between 30,000 and 45,000; by 1851 its population was 303,382; the population of Greater Manchester, including surrounding towns and suburbs, is now nearly two and a half million. With the industrial revolution came disorder. Growth was unplanned and anarchic, responding to the requirements of a laissez-faire capitalism. Most cities and towns, apart from perhaps a core area of old buildings, are now ugly excrescences on the face of the earth. Even the core may have been destroyed to accommodate the motor-car and its fly-overs, office towers and shopping malls. Expanding away from the centre are huge desolate areas of soulless and often run-down housing, crumbling and often empty factories and warehouses, with the occasional out-of-town shopping centre and landscaped 'industrial park'. Beyond them, the rich may have escaped to their leafy suburbs.

Initially, cities were parasitic in obvious ways. Their creation and survival depended on their ability to extract tribute from surrounding rural areas. These purposes were promoted by an alliance between kings and priests; as Lewis Mumford, in his grand history of the evolution of cities, puts it: 'what brute coercion could not accomplish alone, the two were able to effect within the growing town by reciprocal understanding and joint action'; thus 'War and domination, rather than peace and cooperation, were ingrained in the original structure of the ancient city'. With the growth of European imperialism from the sixteenth century onwards, the field of exploitation of European cities widened. Their inhabitants looted and plundered in vast areas of what is now called the 'Third World'. They brought back spices and silks from Asia and gold and silver from America. They murdered the local people or set them to work in mines, sometimes with the same effect. In the Americas, in Africa and in parts of Asia they took the best land and used it to grow crops for consumption in Europe. Having exterminated populations, they stole new workers from Africa. As Professor H. Merivale put it in a lecture at Oxford University in 1840:

> 'What raised Liverpool and Manchester from provincial towns to gigantic cities?. . . . Their present opulence is as really owing to the toil and suffering of the Negro as if his hands had excavated their docks and fabricated their steam engines.'

As in earlier times, a religious gloss was put on all this, so that Europeans, and their foreign subjects, were led to believe that their imperialist exploits and colonial conquests were carried out in the cause of a sacred or 'civilising' mission. Before the Europeans came to Africa, say Africans, 'we had the land and they had the bible', but now: 'they have the land and we have the bible'.

In the early days of imperialism, the Europeans imported not only precious metals, agricultural commodities and other raw materials, but also manufactured goods from the more advanced civilisations whose wealth they aspired to. With the industrial revolution, Europeans themselves became manufacturers on an increasingly large scale. From then on they began to import mainly raw materials from the territories they dominated; they processed them in their own industries and sometimes re-exported them; to protect their new industries they destroyed industries in other parts of the world, and most notoriously the Indian textile industry, through tariffs and taxes and sometimes physically. The huge increases in urban population in Europe, from the late eighteenth century onwards, were the result of this industrialisation, which took place in capital cities and other towns, and created new ones. In London for example, as a result of the growth of mass production from the First World War onwards, by 1951 there were more than one and a half million people working in factories throughout London. Many of the new factories grew up alongside the docks to

7

process the raw materials shipped from Asia, Africa and America. By 1971, some 13,500 people were employed in the docks and wharves in the five docklands boroughs (Greenwich, Lewisham, Newham, Southwark and Tower Hamlets). For every job in the docks, there were three in dock-related activities. Much of this activity took place in South London, in the wharves and warehouses along the river from Southwark to Rotherhithe. The men worked on the river and their wives worked in food processing factories such as Peak Freans.

Cities are places of cultural enrichment, places where artists, writers, poets and others have congregated and learnt from each other. They are also places of excitement, places where people can experiment and break out of the rigid social, family and sexual constraints of rural and village life, places where racial, sexual and cultural differences are more likely to be tolerated or even celebrated. As Marx and Engels wrote in the *Communist Manifesto*:

> 'The bourgeoisie has subjected the country to the rule of the towns. It has created enormous cities, has greatly increased the urban popularity as compared with the rural, and has thus rescued a considerable part of the population from the idiocy of rural life.'

People who found themselves among many others in towns and in urban large scale industries joined together and developed trade unions and radical political movements. They were able to use their collective strength to improve their working and living conditions and win democracy and other reforms. Urban working class people are much more likely to vote Labour than rural workers are; since the early 1920s the Labour Party has had the overwhelming support of the working class in big cities. Television maps on election days show red cities in a surrounding sea of blue.

Cities were themselves transformed when new large scale industries were set up in or near them. Oxford, for example, was a university town with a tradition of subservience to the university and hierarchical relationships among those employed by it. When, from 1913 onwards, car manufacturing began in Oxford, culminating in a workforce of over 27,000 in the car plants in the 1960s, the town gradually acquired a strong and supportive tradition of working class militancy and of solidarity among workers both within and outside the car plants. The car workers not only succeeded in improving their own working conditions; they had a considerable effect on the conditions of others in the town, supporting hotel workers, hospital workers and others in their

8

struggles for unionisation and better wages (see for example the chapter entitled *Women Making Cars, Making Trouble, Making History*, in *The Factory and The City: The Story of The Cowley Automobile Workers in Oxford*). When car manufacturers set up new plants on 'greenfield sites' in semi-rural areas, they do so in the hope that if they also recruit green workers straight from the fields, untainted by urban working class militancy, they will avoid trouble in the factory. Thus Honda, rather than building its assembly plant at Cowley in Oxford, as would have been the logical consequence of its relationship with Rover, built it near Swindon, and made clear its preference for rural and ex-military recruits and that it would not recruit any of the Cowley workers who had lost their jobs in Rover's 1980s closures. (Honda's hopes of retaining deferential attitudes among its workforce may however be vain ones: Alan Thornett, one of Cowley's most effective militants and deputy convenor in the 1970s, was once a Conservative-voting agricultural worker).

Over the last twenty years, cities have lost their attractiveness for some. Material conditions have deteriorated. The growth of industry, and employment in industry, in the imperialist countries has been subject to the booms and slumps which are a feature of the capitalist system; thus a period of growth after the second world war has been succeeded, since the late 1960s, by decline and then the deep recessions of the 1980s and 1990s. Industries have closed and people have lost their jobs in large numbers. Unemployment, increasing poverty, and continuing cuts in public services have made cities dangerous, dirty and often unpleasant places to be. There has been an exodus of the middle classes and professional and skilled people, who have moved to quieter, safer and more prosperous suburbs, small towns, and even the countryside. In New York for example it is mainly the very rich, the artists, the young (in search of freedom and excitement) and the poor (because they have nowhere else to go) who live in Manhattan, originally the heart of New York. Something of the same phenomenon is occurring in British cities, although it has not yet taken such an extreme form. London is unusual in the continuing close juxtaposition of the rich and the poor in its central areas. In London, and also in other British cities such as Glasgow and Oxford, the poor have sometimes been driven out of older housing in the centre which has been gentrified, and relegated to peripheral estates. In Paris, sometimes taken as a model of successful urban development and planning, this process has been taken to great lengths; the elegance of the central areas was achieved partly through a policy of evicting the working classes and the poor to the grim housing estates of the 'red suburbs' which surround the city.

In Britain government planning policies in the 1950s had some direct responsibility for producing the dereliction and abandonment which now afflicts large areas near the centre of cities. After the second world war, during the period of boom and relative prosperity, British governments adopted a policy of dispersal, of both industry and people, from cities which were considered over-crowded to new towns and rural areas. This planned policy was in theory addressed to the needs of everybody in cities; the poor and the unemployed were to have the opportunity to move to new areas as well as the rich and middle classes. Part of the plan was to be the rehabilitation of the inner city areas whose population was reduced, to better environmental standards. But little of this second objective was achieved. Although 'slum clearance' took place on a large scale, this meant the destruction rather than the rehabilitation of much existing housing. The housing was partially replaced by high rise blocks of flats, which, although they had modern facilities and were initially welcomed by many of their new occupants, were built on the cheap and rapidly became justifiably unpopular. They are the source of much of the ugliness and suffering which exists today. When these effects were misinterpreted as the effect of dispersal outside cities, the policy was abandoned. Out-migration continued, but it was out-migration of the relatively well off, the young, the mobile and the skilled. Between 1966 and 1971, for example, according to the Labour government's 1977 White Paper *Policy for the Inner Cities*, only 15 per cent of net migrants from Birmingham were semi-skilled and unskilled workers; from Manchester it was 16 per cent. Overall, between 1966 and 1976, Glasgow lost 205,000 people (21 per cent of its inhabitants), Liverpool lost 150,000 (22 per cent), Manchester lost 110,000 (18 per cent), Inner London 500,000 (16 per cent), Newcastle 40,000 (12 per cent) and Birmingham 85,000 (8 per cent). Those left behind were increasingly deprived.

The so-called 'inner cities', the areas of poverty and dereliction near the centres of cities which have been partly abandoned or were never occupied by the middle classes, are now considered to be a problem which governments need to address. Both Labour and Conservative governments have set up and funded special programmes for the inner cities, while continuing to pursue policies, such as public expenditure cuts, which far outweigh any beneficial effects these programmes may have, and amount in effect to giving back a small proportion of what is being taken away. The problem of course is not a new one. The poor and underprivileged in cities have been exploited under capitalism, and before it, for centuries. There were poverty and riots in cities in Europe in the nineteenth as well as the early and late twentieth centuries, and politicians and writers complained of urban 'mobs'. Moreover the concern of governments about the 'inner cities' derives in part from their proximity to areas where the rich live and work. There are in addition vast urban areas, often estates which have been built on the outskirts of towns and cities when inner city slums were cleared or gentrified, in which there are minimal facilities to alleviate and provide some distraction from the burdens and miseries of poverty and unemployment. These areas remain hidden from most outsiders and are even more seriously neglected. They receive little attention from governments. They are areas of growing despair.

CHAPTER 2

Migration

Cities usually contain a large diversity of peoples, which is one of the reasons why they are exciting places to live in. In London, for example, people now speak nearly 200 languages and have come from all over the world. New immigrants have usually made big contributions to the economies and cultural achievements of the places they have migrated to. And in any case the inhabitants of cities are, necessarily, virtually all immigrants or the descendants of immigrants.

This is also the case for Britain as a whole. According to current historical belief, humans first developed in Africa, and spread from there gradually into Europe and elsewhere. The migrants to Britain came first as hunters, then as cultivators in search of land, as conquerors, as refugees fleeing persecution, later as workers in industry and services. Early humans are said to have reached Britain during the Ice Age, before the sea cut it off from the continent of Europe, but Britain was not continuously inhabited until about 15,000 years ago, when the climate improved and vegetation and animals could survive. In AD43, the Romans invaded Britain and soon after founded London and other towns; their soldiers and administrators were followed by tradespeople and others from Italy and elsewhere in Europe; Britons were exported as slaves. The Romans were followed by Saxon, Viking and Norman invaders. The Anglo-Saxons were mainly farming people, who came for land which they could cultivate. By the early 600s, London became a trading centre for people from many parts of the continent of Europe, and some of them settled there. From the 800s there were large Danish invasions and settlements, followed by the Norman invasion of 1066. Jewish people migrated to Britain soon after and were confined by restrictive laws to occupations such as medicine and money lending, in which they became useful to their rulers as a source of finance for their military adventures.

When cities began to develop new economic activities and eventually large scale industry, their population grew largely through migration from rural areas within Britain. From the fifteenth century onwards, 'enclosures' of common land and peasant evictions were carried out by landlords to increase the size of their holdings, and created large numbers of landless people who had, as Marx put it, nothing to sell but their labour power. At first there were few jobs for them; in order to force them into low paid work laws were introduced against 'vagabondage' and employers were supplied with what amounted to forced labour, in the form of vagabonds who could escape execution if they worked as virtual slaves. Laws against vagabondage and loitering, designed to keep the unemployed off the streets, persisted into the nineteeth century and included the 'Sus' laws (which were temporarily revived in the 1970s and widely used against young blacks; see below). From the eighteenth century onwards, the industrial revolution created a new need for workers. The existence of a displaced rural population was one factor which accounted for the early success of the industrial revolution in Britain. A large pool of workers was available for the new urban factories, as well as to build railways, power plants and other infrastructure.

In addition, in a practice which has a long history, workers and craftspeople were invited from overseas to remedy the absence of British labour and skills. Many came, from the Low Countries in particular, to establish industries to process the wool produced in quantity in Britain; others came in response to the desires of kings and noblemen for weapons, artefacts and adornments; from the sixteenth century onwards black slave servants were imported, much as Filippino maids are imported now. In the sixteenth and seventeenth centuries, Dutch people came to Britain in large numbers, partly to escape the persecution of Protestants on the continent; they set up textile, pottery and brewing industries. From the late seventeenth to the mid-eighteenth centuries, many Protestants, known as Huguenots, fled persecution in France; between 40,000 and 50,000 settled in England. Many of these immigrants settled in South London, whose relative availability as a place of residence for new immigrants, in addition to its geographical features, accounted for its growth into an important manufacturing centre. According to a massive work edited by H E Malden and published in 1905, *A History of Surrey*, referring to the contribution to manufacturing industry in Lambeth made by the 'huge immigrations' of Dutch, French and Scots:

'the later extension of this district, the multiplication of the industries carried on within it, and the various degrees of excellence which many of them ultimately attained, have been largely due to the influence of the foreign workmen who at successive stages of our history came to settle within our country.'

Migrants came to Britain from abroad not just to flee persecution, but also to seek economic betterment. From the early nineteenth century, people migrated to Britain from rural poverty in Italy and Ireland. The need for such migration increased as a result of imperialism, which not only undermined the economies of the areas the migrants came from, but also created employment in the new industries set up in the imperialist heartlands and funded, in part, from the proceeds of imperialism. Migration from Ireland on a large scale started with the potato famine, mainly caused by British rule, and grew with the continuing underdevelopment and oppression of Ireland by the English. The Irish in particular now form a large part of the workforce in British cities, especially in heavy manual jobs in construction and roadbuilding. The expansion of the British colonial empire into Asia, the Caribbean and Africa brought a new source of immigrants. As black migrants sometimes point out, 'We are here because you were there'. In the early years of imperialism some came involuntarily, as servants and slaves. By the twentieth century British rule had conferred British citizenship to the inhabitants of large areas of the world. Until 1962 'Commonwealth citizens' could enter Britain without controls and settle there; some of them did. Some came for education and perhaps excitement. Especially from the Caribbean and the Indian sub-continent, many came to escape from the economic hardship and dislocation which resulted from British rule. They settled almost exclusively in the big cities where there were jobs. Some were actively recruited. In the period of rapid post-war growth British governments worried about a 'labour shortage' pushing up wages and causing breakdowns in public transport and the health services. In 1946 James Callaghan (who thirty years later was Labour Prime Minister) declared:

'We ought now to become a country where immigrants are welcomed. We should break away from this artificial segregation of nation from nation . . . Who is going to pay for the old age pensions and social services unless we have an addition to our population, which only immigration can provide in the years to come?'

From 1945 British governments and employers turned first to Polish people, Italians and other 'displaced people', housed in camps around Europe, to work in industry and hospitals, then to recruitment drives in Ireland, especially for the construction industry, the National Health Service and the transport systems. With the needs for labour still unmet, they turned finally to their colonies and ex-colonies. In 1956 London Transport sent recruiting teams to Trinidad and Jamaica. The British Hotels and Restaurants Association and some hospital boards followed. The latter were encouraged by Enoch Powell, when he was Health Minister from 1960 to 1963, to continue their campaign to recruit doctors and nurses from the Caribbean, India and Pakistan, thus in addition benefitting from the resources devoted by those areas to their training; in the House of Commons on 8 May 1963 Powell commented on:

> 'the large numbers of doctors from overseas who come to add to their experience in our hospitals, who provide a useful and substantial reinforcement of the staffing of our hospitals and who are an advertisement to the world of British medicine and British hospitals.'

Workers were actively sought from India as well. A book published by the Museum of London, entitled *The Peopling of London: Fifteen thousand Years of Settlement from Overseas*, quotes a British manager as follows: 'After the war there was . . . a shortage of workers . . . we tried employing continentals and refugees, but it didn't work out . . . In 1950 we employed Indian workers'. In other cases potential employers, especially in hotels and catering, obtained work permits from the government and handed them to agencies, who then sold them to foreign workers already in Britain who recruited their relatives and friends from home; in this way, for example, the Moroccan community in Notting Hill in London, over 90 per cent of which is from Larache, a small rural town in Morocco, and which is as large as the Caribbean community in this part of London, was built up. In Bradford, Leicester, Coventry, East London and other places, a large part of the textile and clothing industry is dependent on workers from South Asia, as are numerous small engineering firms, in Birmingham for example. Many car-workers at Ford's plant at Dagenham in East London are from the Carribean. There was a brain drain of skilled people from the Third World, in particular from the Indian sub-continent, whose training was provided by their countries of origin but benefits Britain: doctors, nurses, accountants, computer operators and academics.

Others came to live in British cities in order to escape persecution and danger in their own countries. In the nineteenth century refugees and revolutionaries from political struggles in Europe and elsewhere came to Britain; they included Giuseppe Mazzini, Sun Yat Sen and Karl Marx. Between 1881 and 1914 Jewish people fled pogroms in Russia, Poland and Romania, and in the 1930s and 1940s they fled Nazi persecution; some were able to take refuge in Britain. In the 1930s refugees came from the Spanish Civil War and formed a substantial community in Notting Hill. More recently, refugees have come to Britain from the Third World, attempting to escape persecution by dictatorial post-colonial regimes. Many of these regimes were created and continue to be supported, with arms and money, by colonial and ex-colonial governments, by the United States, and by Western-controlled financial institutions such as the World Bank and the International Monetary Fund. The latter are also responsible for the harsh economic conditions which, in turn, lead to repression. In particular their attempt to transfer the burden of the international recession onto the poor in the Third World, and to extract debt servicing at exhorbitant rates of interest, has caused them to demand the implementation of austerity programmes including job cuts, cuts in public expenditure and big increases in the price of basic necessities including food, which have created severe hardship and sometimes riots and have meant that their governments have lost such political legitimacy as they previously had. In 1991 there were 44,800 applicants for political asylum in Britain; in 1993 the numbers were down to 22,370. Most of them are from former British colonies, attempting, often unsuccessfully, to exercise their rights to claim asylum under the 1951 Geneva Convention on Refugees. The refugees who succeed in travelling to Britain are generally skilled and well educated; their skills are nevertheless not used, and many find themselves in unskilled jobs or no jobs at all, living in material conditions greatly inferior to those they experienced in their own countries. Most refugees go elsewhere. The numbers coming to Britain are very small compared to those coming to Germany or other European countries, let alone the Third World. The British currently take in some 0.015 per cent of the world's refugees, in spite of having had the largest colonial empire.

Some migration from rural areas within Britain into urban employment continued in the twentieth century. The 1930s slump, accompanied by slum clearances and the development of new industries in the South and Midlands, caused large movements of population.

16,000 Welsh people moved to Slough in the 1930s, forming a quarter of its population. Others travelled, sometimes on foot, to work in the car factories in Oxford, and were followed by their relatives once they became established there. The 1980s recessions and industrial closures have produced a new group of internal migrants who have followed the advice of the Conservative former minister Lord Tebbitt to 'get on their bikes' in search of work. They have travelled in most cases from the North of Britain to cities in the South, including London and Oxford, where they hoped there would be work. Some have found work on building sites during the week, living in crowded lodgings, and travel back to their families at weekends. Others have found jobs in service industries such as cleaning, catering and hotels. Many have ended up homeless and forced to beg on the streets.

CHAPTER 3

Unemployment, low wages and poverty

Although people come to cities sometimes for refuge and sometimes for excitement, mainly they come, or came, to work. Much of this work has disappeared, perhaps for good. Without it, life in cities is harsh. People who are unemployed suffer not only severe material deprivation, but often psychological and other social problems as well.

Unemployment is of course not the only cause of deprivation and poverty. The nature of the available jobs has changed for the worse. Low wages, and part time and casualised work, have become another widespread phenomenon in cities in the 1980s and 1990s. The main direct victims of high unemployment in Britain and other European countries have been unskilled workers who were or would have been employed in the manufacturing industries which have closed down or disappeared. Most of these workers were or are men, who would have been paid relatively high wages. The loss of their wages has of course affected not only themselves and their families, but local businesses and others who supplied them with goods and services. The only jobs in which there have been some significant increases in numbers are low paid jobs in parts of the service sector, such as cleaning and catering, and, in London and with ups and downs, a smaller number of jobs in financial services. The former are usually casualised, part-time and/or temporary. Many of them are the sort of jobs which women have been expected to put up with. Two-thirds of job growth in Britain in the 1980s was in part-time work, and nine out of ten part-time workers are women. According to reports from jobs agencies, the bulk of new jobs on offer in the autumn of 1994 were temporary. As David Widgery wrote, in his book *Some Lives: A GP's East End*, in this new world of the de-industrialised inner cities:

'the proletarians, especially those among them who are poor, socially unattractive, sick or mentally ill are debarred from both production and

18

consumption. There are jobs, minus tiresome, old-fashioned things like unions, closing times and safety regulations, as cooks and nannies, waiters and drivers, cleaners and guards, entertainers and prostitutes. . . . But very little production in the great manufacturing districts which once shaped London's industrial physiognomy. . . . Ordinary Londoners, whose parents and grandparents built the capital and created its wealth, are increasingly in the way. Expensively in the way, consumers of the wrong things: not high-priced leisure products but hospitals, schools and social services.'

Much of this change in the nature of jobs has been the result of Conservative government policies since 1979. During Mrs Thatcher's first period as Prime Minister the destruction of manufacturing industry was more devastating in Britain than it was in other European countries. The Conservatives under Thatcher did not believe in protecting industry and employment, and they also did nothing to correct the high foreign exchange rate which resulted from British access to North sea oil and which hit manufacturing exports. Oil revenues were not invested, but were squandered on unemployment benefits and social security payments. Since 1979 there have been both big increases in income inequalities, and increases in poverty in real terms; the poorest, including those who are in work, have suffered not only relative but absolute declines in their incomes. The government has directly aggravated income inequalities through its attacks on trade unions and other forms of protection at work, its glorification of high salaries and 'incentives' and also its tax changes. Government enforcement of contracting out from public services, local authorities' attempts to increase 'efficiency' to try to win tenders and the now widely prevalent contracting out of services in private firms usually result in wage cuts, abolition of holiday and sick pay, casualisation and, in most cases, the loss of trade union protection. According to figures from the government's Below Average Incomes statistical analysis published in July 1994, the real incomes of the poorest 10 per cent of the population declined by 17 per cent between 1979 and 1991-92 (while over the same period average incomes increased by 36 per cent, and the incomes of the richest 10 per cent increased by 62 per cent). In 1979 the proportion of the population receiving less than half average income was 9 per cent; in 1991-92 it was 25 per cent. The number of people officially at poverty level rose from 4 million in 1979 to just under 11 million in 1993. Tax changes have contributed to this situation. According to a 1994 article by Chris Giles and Paul Johnson in *Fiscal Studies*, legislation since 1985 increased the after-tax income of the top tenth by 5.8 per cent and reduced those of the bottom tenth by 2.9 per cent; three-quarters of the money spent on tax cuts since 1985 went to the richest 10 per cent. In particular the changes in the tax system introduced by the John Major government in 1994 made the rich richer and the poor poorer, mainly as a result of the shift from direct taxes to indirect taxes such as VAT and excise duties.

Government-imposed cuts in local government services and spending, in particular on housing, further hit the poor in inner cities. One result of these and other government policies has been a massive increase in homelessness; much inner city poverty manifests itself in homelessness. The programmes of slum clearance initiated by Labour governments in the 1960s cleared out many of the worst slums and much reduced the number of houses without amenities such as hot water. But they not only replaced these houses with poorly built and much hated high rise blocks, they also increased the numbers of people without anywhere to live at all. The 1969 and 1975 Housing Acts changed this policy towards one of rehabilitating older houses. But by then much inner city terraced housing had been destroyed. In the 1970s the numbers of homeless people doubled. During the 1980s the situation worsened further. Homeless people sleeping out on the streets became for the first time since the war a common sight. In London, where the problem of homelessness is most acute, the January 1993 issue of *Big Issue*, the magazine for homeless people, recorded that there were 250,000 people living in squats, bed and breakfast hotels, hostels and sleeping rough. Conservative governments' housing policies have consisted of an obsession with home ownership and privatisation to the virtual exclusion of anything else. Government spending on housing dropped in real terms between 1979 and 1992 from £10 billion a year to £5.8 billion. Government-enforced cuts in local government spending on housing have reduced many council estates to desolate areas of dereliction and destruction. In addition, councils are obliged to sell their housing, usually in practice their best housing, to its tenants but are allowed to use only 25 per cent of the proceeds to build housing to replace these public sector losses. The bulk of the proceeds from sales of council houses and land, some £5 billion during the 1980s, have therefore remained frozen in council bank accounts or been used to service their debt. In the 1992 budget there was a slight relaxation of this ruling in respect of future sales (plus an allocation of £50 million to pay tenants for giving up their housing) but by then council house sales were dwindling. Local authority house building has almost completely stopped. Meanwhile, councils spend large sums on putting homeless families into bed and breakfast accommodation, an alternative which is not only much more expensive than building new housing, but grossly inadequate and de-humanising for those who are forced to put up with it. In London, for example, council spending on bed and breakfast accommodation in 1985 was £40 million; in 1992/93 it was projected to rise to £540 million.

There is little alternative low cost, or even high cost, housing for rent in the private sector. The Conservatives' attempts to increase the availability of private rented housing by de-regulating rents and introducing fixed term tenancies under the 1988 Housing Act have not worked; there was a decrease of 60 per cent in private rented housing during the 1980s. The Act has had negative effects in other ways from the point of view of those who need rented housing. Landlords can now evict tenants virtually on a whim. Much of the rented accommodation that remains has been converted from low rents to (very) high rents. It may be inaccessible in any case to homeless people, since most private landlords require a deposit and/or a month's rent in advance. Sir George Young, then Minister for Housing, told a reporter from the *Kensington and Chelsea Times* that if people had trouble paying their rent, they should spend their savings and then they could apply for housing benefit. Apart from the gross inhumanity of this suggestion, housing benefit itself has its problems. Although until recent cuts it covered the whole of private rents, it does so only after long administrative delays which many landlords will not accept; in the 1994 budget housing benefit was cut and in 1996 housing benefit rules were changed; rent officers now determine maximum rents and councils' housing departments may not exceed them even if this means that claimants' rents are not covered. The number of people in need of housing, and statutorily entitled to receive it from councils, has been increased by the closure of some long stay mental hospitals. But, since 1996, people defined as homeless no longer receive priority for council accommodation and are entitled only to one year's emergency provision. Housing associations, the government's preferred alternative for the provision of low cost housing, have not been able to fill the gap and meet the escalating demands for low cost housing. The government has cut their rate of subsidy, forcing them to obtain a higher proportion of their funding from the private sector and therefore to charge higher rents. They have moreover been increasingly unable to provide housing in ways that meet the needs of the homeless and the low paid in any satisfactory way. Thus for example a report by the Joseph Rowntree

Foundation, entitled *Building for Communities* and published in April 1993, argues that government policy is forcing housing associations to build large new estates in order to economise, and to allocate most of this housing to homeless families; as a result three out of four new tenants on recently-built estates are unemployed; the average income of housing association tenants has declined from 73 per cent of the national average in 1981 to 33 per cent on large new housing association estates; and the estates are prone to vandalism, litter and serious crime, with which housing associations are badly equipped to cope. Home ownership itself, for which there were large financial incentives during the boom of the 1980s, has since then become a burden for many people who suffer from 'negative equity', unable to sell their houses for enough money to cover the mortgage, or, worse, forced to abandon them because they cannot keep up the payments, perhaps because they have been made redundant. They then find themselves homeless or in desperately inferior private rented accomodation. Many former council tenants, who took up inducements to buy their council houses, have now lost both their existing council houses and any future rights to rehousing by the local authority. In the 1994 Criminal (In)Justice Act, the government criminalised squatting and made it yet harder for people to find their own solutions to homelessness by living in vans and lorries as 'new age travellers'.

Although some people become homeless as a result, for example, of problems with their families, the single most important cause of homelessness, as of other forms of poverty in the inner cities, is unemployment. Unemployment has been rising since the early 1960s. In 1966 it was 1.5 per cent. By 1971 it was 3.4 per cent. In 1977 it was over 6 per cent, and one and a half million people were unemployed. It reached two million by the end of the 1970s. The Conservatives won the 1979 general election in part with the slogan 'Labour is not working'. By 1982, unemployment had in reality doubled, and in the second Conservative recession in 1992 it was higher still. The official rate of unemployment understates this reality. According to the official figures, unemployment in 1993 was over three million; but if the figures were calculated on the same basis as they were before 1979, it would be four or perhaps five million. Since 1979 Conservative governments have made some thirty changes in the way in which official unemployment is calculated; in nearly every case these have reduced the officially recorded level of unemployment. The biggest of these changes has been the switch to counting unemployment on the basis, not of whether people want work, but of whether or not they are entitled to claim benefits. First married women were removed from the count and then, when they were denied benefits, 16 to 18 year olds, for whom official unemployment rates had previously been highest (for example in Lambeth, according to Lambeth borough council, 35 per cent of people aged 16 to 19 were officially unemployed in 1986; in February 1989, after they had been denied benefits, the official unemployment rate for this group was 0). Similarly, when factories employing mainly women close, the official unemployment figures may change little, because many of the women will be married and will not be entitled to claim benefits. In addition, many people, including male former industrial workers, have dropped out of the unemployment statistics and have become simply 'inactive', because of restrictions on claiming benefits, because some have gone onto sickness benefits or taken early retirement, because workers made redundant cannot claim benefits until they have spent their redundancy money, and even sometimes because people who have worked all their lives cannot accept the indignity of claiming benefits. In a small survey of workers who lost their jobs at the Cowley car plant carried out by the Oxford Motor Industry Research project in 1990, we found that, among the third who had not found new jobs, over three-quarters were not claiming benefits, and were therefore not officially unemployed. According to a pamphlet by Edward Balls and Paul Gregg, entitled *Work and Welfare: Tackling The Jobs Deficit*, between 1977 and 1991 male *employment* in Britain fell by two million, reducing the proportion of men of working age with jobs from 91 per cent to 82 per cent, but only half of this drop showed up in the official unemployment figures:

'By 1991, 1.3 million jobless men were actively seeking work and included in the unemployment statistics. But another 1.8 million were out of the labour force and excluded from the unemployment count. Over the period 1977 91, the male unemployment rate rose from 5.1 per cent to 9.4 per cent of the active labour force. But the non-employment rate — the percentage of working age men without jobs — rose from 9 per cent to 18 per cent.'

These high rates of unemployment and non-employment are concentrated in the de-industrialised inner cities. They are also concentrated in particular areas. For example between 1979 and 1985 unemployment in Lambeth increased by 249 per cent, compared to a 154 per cent increase between 1979 and 1987 for London as a whole.

23

Even in the mini-boom of the late 1980s, when unemployment declined slightly in London as a whole, unemployment in many deprived areas of London, including docklands, continued to rise.

Employment has declined especially in manufacturing but also in the service sectors which depend on manufacturing, and in public services which governments have been cutting since the late 1960s. The loss of manufacturing jobs was not compensated for by a corresponding rise in service sector employment: all major sectors, including distribution, transport, construction and the public sector, but excluding a small rise in financial and professional services especially in London, lost jobs. But the losses were most dramatic in manufacturing. Manufacturing employment fell by a third between 1979 and the early 1990s. Between 1970 and 1987, the share of industrial employment in total employment fell by 15 per cent. In the North of Britain, since large areas were almost wholly dependent on industry, the devastation has been highly visible and destructive. The drop in industrial employment was even greater in London than in Britain as a whole: between 1978 and 1986 28 per cent of manufacturing jobs were lost nationally, and 34 per cent were lost in London. Between 1973 and 1982 the net loss of jobs in London was more than half a million. In the latest recession, the decline has been just as dramatic; in 1991 and 1992 300,000 jobs were lost in London, from financial and business services and also from a continuing decline in manufacturing. London now has the largest concentration of unemployment in the European Community.

The response of the free marketeers to this loss of jobs is to argue that people must 'price themselves into jobs', and that the main cause of unemployment is 'labour market rigidity'. The British and US governments have been the main official proponents of this view, especially under Reagan and Thatcher. The British government has promoted the aim of labour market deregulation with self-righteous tenacity against the arguments of other European governments, in spite of the latter's better economic records. Thus for example in its submission in 1993 to an EC review of competitiveness, the government stated:

'There has been an upward trend in EC unemployment from cycle to cycle since the late 1960s and an increasing proportion of long-term unemployed people. This is evidence of inflexibility in, and over-regulation of, labour markets. These factors deter employers from taking on new employees and damage job creation.'

In 1993 the British government opted out of the Social Chapter of the Maastricht Treaty (passed by the other 11 EU members to provide some minimum protections for workers). Like many governments in the Third World, it argued that Britain would attract more investment if it had a cheap and flexible workforce. It has attempted to make it easier for employers to sack workers by reducing their obligations to pay redundancy money. It has adopted various policies to force people into low paid jobs. It has denied state benefits to young people and has instead funded low paid so-called 'training' schemes, which effectively provide employers with cheap and subsidised labour, but frequently provide little or no training and are not followed by access to unsubsidised employment on normal wages. It has abolished wages councils which provided (weakly enforced) minimum wages for certain vulnerable categories of workers. It has promoted the 'contracting out' of work, especially in the public sector and in cleaning and catering, which has resulted in systematic wage cutting and casualisation (since this is the only way that private contractors can win contracts and cut costs). It has tightened the demands on unemployed people to prove they are looking for work and to accept any job on offer, obliging them to go on 'Restart' programmes or lose benefits. In 1996 it introduced the Job Seekers Allowance (JSA) which imposes further requirements for evidence of job seeking and enables officials to require claimants to take jobs, go on 'training' courses and/or 'improve' their appearance and to cut 100 per cent of benefits if they do not comply, providing incentives for the application of these measures through a system of bonus payments to officials. It threatens 'workfare' (see below). And it has weakened those who are in work, in particular through legislative attacks on the trade unions. According to a report by the Labour Research Department, *Bargaining Report No.90*, published in the autumn of 1994, British workers taking strike action are in a much weaker legal position than workers elsewhere in Europe; for example Britain is one of only three European countries in which workers have no statutory or constitutional guarantees for the right to strike, and in which employment contracts are deemed to be automatically broken by workers taking strike action, allowing employers to sack them. The Conservatives further weakened the position of striking workers by allowing employers to sack them selectively, as well as requiring ballots before strike action and forbidding 'secondary' action in support of other workers. Strikes have become increasingly difficult to organise in Britain unless unions are prepared to break the law, which so far they have not been.

It is in fact unclear whether the government does or does not consider unemployment to be a problem, since unemployment is itself a weapon used in the government's struggle to break the strength of the trade unions. Various ministerial statements have shown that it recognises this. Norman Lamont, British chancellor of the exchequer in 1993, stated for example that unemployment was a price 'well worth paying' for bringing inflation down. In *The Observer* of 21 June 1992 a former economic adviser to Mrs Thatcher, Alan Budd, was quoted as saying that increased unemployment in the 1980s 'was a very desirable way of reducing the strength of the working class', which 'recreated the reserve army of labour and has allowed capitalists to make high profits ever since'. The government and its supporters both seek to blame the unemployed for the fact that they are unemployed, and at the same time use and welcome high unemployment as a means of disciplining workers. It is possible that the British government's goal in pursuing labour market deregulation is thus not to reduce unemployment, but merely to cheapen labour and increase the profits of its supporters. In this case, arguably, it has been at least partly successful. But supposing that, as it claims, the government's aim is to increase employment, by making it easier and less risky for employers to hire new workers, then it has failed. Comparisons between unemployment rates in Britain and other European countries are misleading, because the latter's statistics on unemployment reflect more accurately the extent of non-employment (see above). If, instead, comparisons are made between the growth of employment, Britain comes out worse than many European countries with more protected labour markets. Over the period 1979-92, French employment, for example, grew by 3 per cent whereas British employment grew by 0.4 per cent, and Britain has had slower overall employment growth than the European average when its two recessions are included. It is true that in the USA, the other main proponent of labour market deregulation, employment grew in the same period by 19 per cent. But this growth was at the expense of drops in real wages which cause some disquiet even among mainstream commentators: in the USA the real wages of the poorest 10 per cent of workers have fallen by a third since 1970; and, faced with a denial of state benefits and/or wages below the poverty line, many people, especially young men, have turned to crime; a National Bureau of Economic Research survey in Boston in 1989 found, for example, that over two-thirds of young men believed they could make more money 'on the streets' than in a job, up from a third in 1980. Although both the USA and Britain have had faster growth than continental European countries in the employment of women, this growth has been overwhelmingly in part-time jobs, in the service sector and on low wages. And rates of unemployment among men of working age were actually slightly higher than they were in the more regulated continental European labour markets. According to Edward Balls, writing in the *Financial Times* of 6 November 1993, the growth in women's employment

'has co-existed with a sharp fall in male employment which is only partly reflected in the unemployment figures. The reason is that many jobless — or 'non-employed' — men have shifted from being counted as 'unemployed' to 'economically inactive'. On average, in the 1980s, 12.1 per cent of prime-age US males and 14.9 per cent of UK males were out of work compared to 9.1 per cent in France and 11.3 per cent in Italy. The claim that deregulated labour markets mean lower joblessness looks rather hollow.'

According to Balls' and Gregg's pamphlet, *Work and Welfare: Tackling The Jobs Deficit*, contrary to the assertions of the free market ideologues, this decline in employment 'has not been the result of a failure of wages to adjust — the relative wages of those at the bottom have fallen for the last fifteen years in the UK, leading to the widest pay inequalities since 1886'. On the other hand, 'Most European countries' (with their better record on male employment and their better economic records in general) 'have avoided this rise in wage inequality through relatively high minimum wages, more restrictive regulations on hiring and firing, more generous unemployment benefits, or by replacing private with public sector employment'. Moreover, since the US restricts unemployment pay to a maximum duration of 26 weeks, and Britain has begun to follow it along this path, 'The duration of benefits does not appear to affect total joblessness, only how that joblessness is allocated between unemployment and inactivity'.

While overwhelmingly the pressures from business in Britain reinforce the opinions of the government's free marketeers, some recognise there might be problems. Thus for example the *Financial Times* of 10 June 1994 published an article by Robert Bischof, chairman of Bosch Group, a fork lift truck maker recently bought from receivership by a German company, which largely dismissed the argument of the British government that 'Europe's labour and social costs have become too expensive and its labour laws are too inflexible, they give employees too

27

many rights and too much job protection', arguing instead that Germany, which has 'some 80 per cent higher labour costs per hour than Britain', 'still has a very healthy trade surplus with the world and the UK shows a huge deficit', and that 'Competitivesness depends on capital investment, R&D, processes, management qualities, work force attitude and skills, rather than on wage rates . . . British companies believe they can compensate for their lack of investment by focussing on labour costs', but: 'A link between low wage cost, international competitiveness and long-term success seems to me at best unproven and at worst to be more likely the reverse'.

Although the British government appears to believe that Britain should compete with the Third World in cutting wages and destroying working conditions, there is clearly little future for the British economy in any attempt to undercut labour-intensive producers of the Third World, quite apart from whether this is a socially or politically feasible or desirable project. It is true that part of the explanation for the collapse of demand for unskilled industrial workers has been 'globalisation', or competition from new manufacturers outside Europe and North America, above all Japan, but also more recently in smaller Asian states and city states and to some extent in Latin America and South Asia. Some multinational companies based in Britain·and elsewhere have shifted production to sources of cheaper labour in the Third World, and in some cases local manufacturers in the Third World have succeeded in building up industries, such as ship-building, steel-making and clothing, which produce similar products more cheaply because wages are lower. The share of Third World countries' products in industrialised countries' imports of labour intensive goods has grown from 9.8 per cent in 1965 to 18.7 per cent in 1989. However Third World countries' exports still account for less than a tenth of the manufacturing imports of industrialised countries and for only 3 per cent of their total consumption of manufactured goods.

Much more powerful causes of job losses in manufacturing have been the use by manufacturers within existing industries in the industrialised countries of new technologies and production processes; the shift towards white collar employment within those industries; the pressures on the remaining workers, weakened by the threat of unemployment and the legal restrictions on trade union activity, to work at an ever more intensive pace; and the fact that employers prefer to increase overtime rather than hire new workers. The jobs that remain in the much reduced manufacturing sector are increasingly skilled, white collar jobs. Employers prefer to invest in machinery to replace their less skilled and potentially troublesome workers rather than investing to increase production. Workers of all kinds are under heavy pressure to increase the speed and intensity at which they work; the fashionable Japanese model, for example, though promoted as a means of enhancing job satisfaction and skills, in reality involves an effort to ensure that workers work at an unrelenting pace, with every second of their time precisely planned so that they use all of their strength all of the time. In addition, rather than hiring new workers even on a temporary basis, manufacturers prefer to make their existing workforce work more overtime. David Savage, West Midlands area director with the Engineering Employers Union, was quoted in the *Financial Times* of 25 January 1995 as follows: 'Employers are increasing overtime rather than recruiting more staff because they are still unsure whether they are experiencing only temporary increases in demand'. In 1992 British workers worked the longest hours in Europe: an average of 43.4 hours a week, compared with 39.7 hours a week in France and Germany and an average of 40.3 hours in the European Union as a whole. Although overtime is usually not compulsory and is often welcomed by workers as the quickest way to supplement their wages, in Jaguar in October 1994 it was temporarily made compulsory, and at Honda compulsory overtime is part of workers' contracts. Thus in Britain, although there was a big growth in productivity in the 1980s, most of this increase in the quantity of goods produced per worker was a result of cutting jobs rather than increasing output. Fewer and fewer workers are required to produce the same quantities of goods.

The current resumption of growth in most of the advanced capitalist countries, if it continues, may or may not produce a return to something like full employment. There is much talk of 'jobless growth'. Sir Graham Day, used by the Thatcher government as hatchet man first for British Shipbuilders and then for the Rover Group, speaking at a South Bank University Business School inaugural lecture in November 1993, predicted as some incontestable fact of life that in the twenty-first century there would be a diminishing core of secure and relatively well paid wage earners, surrounded by a 'wadge' of unemployed people who would probably also be semi-literate and unemployable, and who would live at 'subsistence levels'. Similarly apocalyptic visions were produced by another business boss, Mr Percy Barnevic, president of ABB (the world's largest power engineering group) and reported in the *Financial Times* of 4 January 1993, who 'believes the problem is not rooted in recession, but in inexorable advances in productivity', forecasts a halving of the proportion of people employed in manufacturing and more cuts in public spending, and 'reckons the result will be a shake-out comparable to that in agricultural employment earlier this century':

'If anybody tells me, wait two or three years and there will be a hell of a demand for labour, I say, tell me where. What jobs? In what cities? Which companies? When I add it all together, I find a clear risk that the 10 per cent unemployed today could easily become 20 to 25 per cent.

'If you look at service industries, there are highly paid people, like lawyers and investment bankers, and then there are the cleaners and guest workers who earn a third or half as much as skilled factory workers. So we end up either with permanent unemployment or under-employment, or with two classes of differently paid people. Both are social dynamite. . . .

'If I knew the answer, I should probably win Nobel prizes in several subjects.'

These fatalistic pronouncements by businesspeople and others may turn out to be wrong. There is no inherent reason why employment should not rise in the next capitalist boom, and in even imperfectly 'socialisist' countries there is usually virtually no unemployment. The reasons for unemployment have much to do with the ideology of those in power. Most governments and other supporters of capitalism currently absolve themselves from responsibility for unemployment with the comforting notion (to themselves) that any decrease in unemployment (under capitalism) would only lead to higher wages and a rise of inflation and therefore in the long run to more unemployment. At a meeting of central bankers from 19 countries in Kansas City, reported in the *Financial Times* of 29 August 1994,

'Heads nodded piously in the audience as Professor Paul Krugman of Stanford University said that it was now all but universally accepted among academic economists, though still suspect to politicians and journalists, that there was a "natural" rate of unemployment. A central bank could expand demand and push the actual rate of unemployment below this level, but only at the expense of accelerating inflation.'

Most of the US participants appeared to agree that the USA had got it about right, and was near to its 'natural rate of unemployment', although there might be some scope in Europe for some relaxation of restrictions on spending. The British Labour Party, whose 'modernist' leadership seems reluctantly to have incorporated full employment into its current policy goals, is chided as clinging to a 'pipe dream'. The statement by Conservative right-wing maverick Keith Joseph that 'Full employment is not in the gift of Government. It should not be promised and it cannot be provided', appears now part of the conventional wisdom.

Unemployment nevertheless seems to have risen nearer the top of governments' concerns, in Europe at least, largely because of its potential for causing social disorder in cities. At the end of 1993 unemployment in the European Union was forecast to rise to 18 million people by 1994, the equivalent of the combined populations of Belgium, Denmark and Ireland. Jacques Delors, president of the European Commission, produced a White Paper on employment, growth and competitiveness, and there has been much debate in Europe between the promoters of labour market deregulation, wage restraint and curbs on trade unions, led by the British government, and the defenders of labour protections, 'social partnership' and the gains of the post-war welfare states on the continent of Europe, especially in Germany and France. Although the former are gaining ground, and their views were reflected in Delors' White Paper to an extent that surprised them given Delors origins in the French Socialist Party, there is nevertheless some dawning recognition that deregulation might not be enough. Even Samuel Brittan, himself a free marketeer, wrote in the *Financial Times* of 3 October 1993, that economists gathered at Salzburg, 'unlike some market economists',

> 'admitted that forces such as globalisation and technical change had an adverse effect on unskilled workers, which showed itself in unemployment in Europe but in low pay in the US.'

Delors' White Paper also floated the idea of vast European investments in 'information highways', roads, rail and telecommunications, and research. In similar vein, a few lone Keynesians continue to argue for growth, public spending increases and agreements between governments, business and trade unions to control wages. But few people any longer believe that unemployment can be reduced and capitalism saved through Keynesian policies of increasing demand and promoting growth, for example by expanding public expenditure.

Governments' concern over unemployment, to the extent that they have any, tends to translate into proposals for more training. In Britain, as in similar ways elsewhere, there is a growing consensus between the government, the Confederation of British Industry, the Labour Party and others that the unemployed should be trained. But training schemes do not create jobs; any success by an unemployed person in obtaining a job does not increase the total number of jobs but merely makes that particular job unavailable for somebody else. Training schemes may, on the other hand, give people the impression that they are themselves to blame for their unemployment: if they try harder they will get jobs, at the expense, of course, of others who have not tried so hard. At most the schemes may increase the number and motivation of suitable candidates competing for the available jobs, and their consequent usefulness to business. If training is paid for by the state rather than by private employers, this is then another subsidy to the latter and has the effect of increasing the size of what Marx called the 'reserve army of labour', and therefore the cheapness and docility of labour. But often the schemes are merely window-dressing. They reduce the official unemployment statistics. They may be in effect compulsory; in Britain and France for example young people can get no unemployment benefit (or, as it now called in Britain, contributions-based JSA) until they have been offically employed, and they can only get income support (income-based JSA in Britain) after a certain age. Up to then, their only certain source of state support is a training scheme. The training schemes themselves have a notoriously low success rate in getting people into jobs.

There is also an increased recognition that a 'poverty trap' exists. In Britain the welfare system is set up in such a way that if people, or their spouses, take jobs they immediately have any amount they earn above £5 deducted, pound for pound, from their welfare benefits; and they may lose housing benefit. This, together with the prevalence of low wages and casualised, insecure and often part-time jobs, means that, for many unemployed people, there is little or nothing to be gained from taking the few jobs that are on offer, unless they work 'off the books' and continue, illegally, to draw benefits. Some people, behaving in the income-maximising manner prescribed in neo-classical economics text-books, may therefore choose unemployment and the dole rather than low paid work (although many others, imbued with the work ethic, do not). This is no doubt why, for example, the Confederation of British Industry (CBI) proposed in October 1994 that welfare benefits should not be cut, or not be cut to the same extent, for people taking low paid and part-time work; in other words employers were asking the government to pay them a subsidy to enable them to attract workers while offering wages otherwise too low to be worth working for: 'There is a growing consensus', Mr Howard Davies, director-general of the

CBI was quoted as saying in the *Financial Times* of 30 November 1994, in a comment on the budget, 'that there is a problem in the interface between work and benefits'; and Mr Kenneth Clarke duly proferred a few measures to 'provide incentives to come off benefits'.

The free market right, or at least parts of it, continues to argue, in spite of its tacit admission that unemployment is an inevitable fact of life under capitalism, that the unemployed could 'price themselves into jobs' if only they were willing to work for even lower wages (although wages would probably have to fall to below subsistence levels in order for employers to be willing to employ all of the people who are currently unemployed, or even most of them). The view that the unemployed are to blame for the fact that they do not have jobs is widely prevalent on the right. Unemployed people are falsely stereo-typed as a welfare-dependent 'underclass', said to be both 'work-shy' and unemployable. Yet probably the vast majority of unemployed people search desperately for jobs, and moreover either had jobs before the capitalist crisis or would easily obtain them if levels of employment returned to what they were before the crisis. Many unemployed people write dozens or even hundreds of job applications, and many are highly skilled and previously earned good money.

The government, when it is criticised for its failure to resolve the problems of unemployment, in the inner cities in particular, continues to point to the continued existence of what it calls the 'safety net' of universal state benefits. However not only are these benefits diminishing, but they are increasingly subjected to tests and the compulsion of 'Restart' interviews and training schemes. The introduction of the JSA has led to increasing numbers of people being denied benefits altogether (and thus contributed to an 'improvement' in the unemployment statistics shortly before the 1997 election). In addition, the threat of cancellation of benefits for the long-term unemployed, and their substitution with workfare, continues to be raised, both by the government and by the Labour leadership. As Major put it in a speech to the Carlton Club, reported in the *Financial Times* of 4 February 1993:

'I increasingly wonder whether paying unemployment benefit, without offering or requiring any activity in return, serves unemployed people or society well.

'Of course we have to make sure that any conditions imposed improve the job prospects of unemployed people and give good value to the country. But we have already introduced this principle, for example through Restart, in a limited sense for the long-term unemployed. I believe we should explore ways of extending it further.'

'NO WORK, NO DOLE' crowed the *Daily Mail*'s banner headlines on the same day. For the government and others, workfare would have a number of potential benefits: it would keep potential members of the 'underclass' off the streets and out of trouble, it would provide employers with an extremely cheap workforce, it would force more people to adapt to low wage employment, and it might even reduce public spending if enough people opted for the alternative of losing benefits. However, some members of the government oppose the scheme on the grounds that any topping-up of benefits would be expensive. US experience is that workfare and training schemes have not, on the whole, enabled people to get better jobs; their function has been mainly 'to enforce the work ethic'. Often, far from being a means of social control, the cancellation of benefits has achieved exactly the opposite of the government's intention. As a leader in the *Financial Times* on the following day put it:

> 'Yet proponents of compulsion must ensure that their schemes have the intended effect. Here the US experience spins a cautionary tale. While workfare has been the chosen method for encouraging welfare mothers back to work, unemployed American men without children receive little or no welfare support at all after the first six months of unemployment. The consequence is not a markedly higher employment rate among US men than in those European countries where unemployment benefits last indefinitely. Instead a growing minority of US men, particularly young blacks with poor educational qualifications, have chosen black market activities or crime over poorly paid employment.
>
> 'Nor has the UK been immune from the effects of rising crime and drug use among the young as their relative wages have fallen and access to state benefits has been restricted. Linking benefits to participation in public works schemes for a nominal financial reward risks pushing more young British men out of legal society into crime.'

None of these proposals does anything to alter the harsh realities of the absence of jobs under capitalism. Meanwhile, many millions of people are marooned in the cities and former industrial areas of Britain and other European countries, with no obvious place to go, and in increasing immiseration. While some of the prosperous middle classes have fled the cities, the poor and the unemployed cannot easily escape. Few people have the opportunity to go 'back to the land' or any other such solution.

Unemployed and homeless young people who try to take matters into their own hands and, like the 'New Age travellers' in Britain, attempt to discover a simple way of life outside the cities, find themselves increasingly harried, and subjected to new repressive legislation in the Criminal (In)justice Bill. Even those people who migrated from the Third World with the idea of making some money to buy themselves land back home have nearly always found themselves trapped, apparently indefinitely, in British cities. While they had jobs, they perhaps had enough money to live at subsistence levels in Britain, to send remittances to their families, and to make savings towards buying land at home. But unemployment puts an end to such ambitions. Recently Bernie Grant, black Labour MP for Tottenham, caused an outcry from people who felt that he was playing into the hands of the far right supporters of repatriation by suggesting, at a Labour conference fringe meeting to mark the twenty-fifth anniversary of Enoch Powell's 'Rivers of blood' speech, that Caribbean people would 'go home' if they were offered money to do so. In an interview in *The Observer* of 10 October 1993, he was reported as saying:

'The bulk of my speech was about the causes of the [British National Party victory in Tower Hamlets]. I added that some black people are frightened. Some have no faith left in British society. They believe they are no longer wanted in this country. They have been asking me whether it might be possible to negotiate with the Government for them to be given grants to go home. I said at the meeting that I didn't know which side I would come down on.' [brackets added].

He added that:

'I would guess that 40 per cent minimum would want to go. The Jamaican High Commissioner says the number of people going home has increased by 66 per cent in the past three months. Similar numbers have been recorded by other Caribbean High Commissions. I personally know dozens of people who have recently sold their houses and left, saying, We can't take this any longer.'

There is undoubtedly much despair and disenchantment among Caribbeans, among others, who see little prospect of being able to work again or of being able to lead any reasonable sort of life in the increasingly desolate and run-down areas of British inner cities and towns. But few see much alternative and many, despite all the problems, continue to appreciate the advantages and cultural opportunities of a

metropolitan way of life to which they have, themselves, greatly
contributed.

People who have to live on the dole for any length of time cannot eat
enough and cannot keep warm, let alone clothe themselves and their
children adequately, pay their bills and replace any non-functioning
appliances. Not surprisingly, the physical health of unemployed people
tends to be worse than that of employed people, and there is a high
incidence of suicide among the unemployed. Any study of inner city
poverty is full of quotes such as the following (in Paul Harrison's study
of life in Hackney, *Inside The Inner City*), from a woman with three
children:

> 'There's one hundred per cent no way I could ever manage on social security
> without a little side job . . . We're getting low now. We've got food for today,
> but there's none for tomorrow. Last week we ran out of money for the
> electric meter. We had to hunt round the house for pennies to make up
> 50p. I make sure the kids eat all right, they get fish fingers and beefburgers,
> and if we're lucky once a week we'll have mincemeat. I just have one meal
> a day, sometimes I don't eat at all, sometimes I have soup or boil up potatoes
> and put cheese with them. I've had to get the little ones out of nappies — I
> couldn't afford them any more. For my ulcer, the doctor told me to eat
> boiled fish, eat this, eat that, but I couldn't afford it. . . . We're going steadily
> downhill. This week I started thinking of things I could sell to get a bit of
> money together. I don't like working and claiming. I'm not greedy: if I could
> get just two days' homework a week that would be enough. I don't want to
> get rich, just to feed my kids. I feel bad about it, I don't like doing it. If I
> could get a full-time job that would pay me enough to come off social
> security, I'd give my book back straight away . . .'

One strategy adopted by unemployed people is to engage in barter, to
exchange goods and services with other people in similar situations, and
otherwise to find ways of providing for themselves and their families
outside the regular money economy. Such activities tend to overlap with
crime and may or not be legal. One former new age traveller, for
example, claims benefit while earning cash in hand from fruit picking,
door to door newspaper subscription selling, painting boats and putting
on raves and other events. A film directed by Ken Loach called *Raining
Stones* begins with a hilarious sequence showing two northern city
dwellers struggling to catch a sheep on the nearby moors, trying and
failing to bring themselves to kill it in their back garden and then, having
taken it round to the butcher, failing to sell it wrapped in clingfoil in
pubs. They then take up the turf from a bowling green, load it into a

lorry and sell it down the street (many golf clubs now complain of the problem of losing their greens). One of these unemployed men, to his horror, discovers that his daughter, who he had thankfully thought had found herself a 'nice little job', is in reality in the business of selling drugs in night clubs. The other, in order to keep up appearances for his daughter's confirmation service, gets deeply embroiled in borrowing from one of the many individuals who make loans at extortionate rates of interest to people in such circumstances. Both they and their wives try desperately for anything legal in the way of work that might bring in a bit of money.

Whether because unemployed people lose their self-confidence and fall eventually into apathy, as some argue, or because of their inherent lack of power and problems of fragmentation and isolation from one other, they find it hard to organise effectively in order to improve their situation. Since they are a minority, they cannot vote out the Conservatives and they have little effect on the electoral politics of the Labour Party. In Britain trade unions have been notably unwilling to take action on behalf of the unemployed, including their own former members. They have also had little success in organising in the 'new' sectors into which many of those made redundant from well paid and well organised employment have been forced. In a situation in which many jobs are unskilled, temporary, casualised and insecure and many employers are small and well able to replace any troublesome workers, those who attempt to join a trade union and to organise to improve their wages and conditions are frequently sacked. In any case trade unions find it difficult to provide adequate support and to service their members in small and scattered workplaces. The far left, in its currently weakened state, has done little to organise unemployed people or recruit them to their campaigns, with the partial exception of the mass opposition to the Poll Tax. Claimants' Unions, Unemployed Centres and other organisations of the unemployed, some of them supported by trade unions and Labour-controlled local councils, struggle with limited success. The introduction of the JSA led to demonstrations and some direct action, with occupations of benefits offices; the staff of benefits offices themselves, most of them well aware that unemployment is not the fault of the unemployed, took some action against the introduction of the JSA. But one of the few means which unemployed people do have for making their demands heard, even though this may not be what they consciously intend, is to riot, engage in crime, or otherwise inconvenience the comfortable and complacent majority.

CHAPTER 4

Crime, drugs, riots and the police

Since 1979 crime, drug usage and unemployment have all risen fast, and there were inner city 'riots', or uprisings, in 1980 (Bristol), 1981 (Brixton, Liverpool, Manchester, North London, Birmingham, Sheffield, Nottingham, Hull and Slough), 1985 (Tottenham in London and Handsworth in Birmingham), 1991 (Cardiff, Newcastle and Oxford), 1992 (Wood End, Hartcliffe, Ordsall, Brackenhall Stoops and Hargher Clough), 1995 (Bradford), and elsewhere. Individual crimes against property force governments to pay attention, benign or otherwise, to the problems of inner cities. The outbursts of generalised and violent attacks on property that have taken place in large British and North American cities may have an even more powerful effect. An *Observer* article of 20 September 1987 points out that 'A riot makes a much bigger impact on government thinking than any amount of earnest and accurate research'. After a big riot in Los Angeles in 1992, a long article by Michael Prowse in the *Financial Times* on the various possibilities for improving the situation of the US urban poor concluded that the events in Los Angeles had for the first time provided some hope that some of the ideas might be implemented. Similar concerns no doubt prompted Mr Kenneth Clarke, then Home Secretary, in a speech to the Conservative Reform Group in November 1992, to state that the growth of an 'underclass' in decaying inner city areas was the most formidable challenge facing western democracies in the 1990s. 'Society', he said, 'cannot afford to alienate and exclude significant numbers of the poor, the black and the young'.

The link between unemployment, crime and riots appears obvious but is nevertheless much contested. The right wing likes to suggest that crime is caused, instead, by the psychological and behavioural problems of individuals, by prevailing permissive and liberal attitudes, by lack of parental discipline, by inadequate punishment of criminals and even by too much public ownership. Thus on 3 February 1993 the *Daily*

Express carried a double page interview with the Prime Minister of the day John Major in which, it said, the topic on which he expressed most passion was the need to address the rising levels of crime in inner cities, particularly crime against houses and cars by young people aged 8-18. Major is reported to have said that:

'(the Home Secretary) is working . . . to make sure they go somewhere secure where they can be retrained, looked after and educated . . . The reason for dealing with them firmly is that otherwise they become institutionalised . . . it has got to be made clear to people from the very youngest age that society disapproves of (crime), and that when people break the law, society will strike back and punish them severely. I think that line has been blurred in the tolerant Sixties, Seventies and Eighties. In the Nineties we have got to be a little more intolerant about crime . . . That is not something you expected to hear from me.' (brackets added).

Asked by the *Daily Express* reporter whether unemployment might have something to do with crime, he replied: 'I think it is very unfair to the people who are unemployed to suggest that'. In a speech to the Carlton Club in London, reported in the *Financial Times* of 4 February 1993, he announced that powers would be taken to put 'persistent young offenders into secure accommodation'. And he blamed 'over-government' for the break-up of communities:

'It is not where the free market pervades that ties of community are under threat, but where the state owns and controls to the greatest extent. Look at our suburbs and small towns and villages — where people, by and large, own their own homes . . . The big problem lies elsewhere. It is from the inner cities, where the state is dominant, that businesses have fled.'

In Blackbird Leys in Oxford, young unemployed men have, at times, engaged in 'joy riding', or the taking of cars and the performance of displays of driving virtuosity, usually followed by the cars' destruction. The young boys who engage in this activity would almost certainly have found relatively well paid jobs in Rover's nearby car plant at Cowley, as many of their fathers and mothers had, if Rover had not closed two of its plants and virtually ceased to recruit new workers after it was privatised in 1988. However when, apparently in response to the phenomenon of joy riding, riot police invaded Blackbird Leys in 1991, there was a chorus of official denials of any link between job losses and 'hotting'; thus, according to a chapter by Ann Schofield and Mike Noble in *The Factory and The City*:

'Government ministers, for example, immediately defined the clashes as a "law and order" problem and condemned, in the words of John Patten (MP for Oxford West and Abingdon and then Minister at the Home Office), "the mindless hooliganism and yobbery" of a small criminal element among the young. There was, he said, "no excuse for such behaviour". Oxford City Council also insisted on treating the events as a law-and-order problem, and refused to relate them to closures and job losses.'

The authors comment that, instead of people's needs and interests being 'treated as economic and employment issues' and responded to by focusing on 'the structural issues of managing the local economy', they are 'treated as a psychological or criminal problem', and then: 'personalized remedial or policing action by professionals will be the typical response'.

Above all, the right loves to blame single mothers. Not only the right: virtually every official report and academic treatise on inner city problems, including those that would not consider themselves as right wing or illiberal, lists a high percentage of 'single parents' as one of the defining characteristics of deprived and problematic inner city areas. In the concluding paragraph of a feature on crime and morality in the *Financial Times* of 25 October 1993, Michael Prowse, its Washington correspondent, suddenly introduces the topic of children who are not 'properly nurtured', which apparently derives from the fact that 'a majority of American children are now expected to spend some of their formative years in single-parent households', and approvingly quotes a criminologist influential in the USA, Mr James Wilson of the University of California, as saying that this fact is 'at the core of our social problems'. A leader in the *Sunday Times* of 14 November 1993, entitled 'The Lone Parent Problem', asserts that:

'Ministers have rightly, if belatedly . . . begun to realise the link between the rise in single-parent families and the growth of the underclass, welfare dependency, crime and the sort of increasingly common unsocial behaviour that has given Britain an international reputation for yobbism.

'The liberal-left, of course, has a vested interest in trying to deny that the collapse of the nuclear family is at the core of so many social problems . . . it is the policies and lifestyles promoted by the liberal-left that are largely responsible for the breakdown of so many communities . . .

'The problem is not single-parent families; it is a particular type of single parent . . . the recent soaring of illegitimacy was the key cause of Britain's burgeoning underclass, with its attendant culture of welfare dependency, crime and social despair . . .

'The surge in illegitimacy since 1979 is no accident. It coincided with easier access to houses for single mothers and increasing welfare benefits. It is not that teenage girls sit down with a calculator and work out if they would be better off getting pregnant. What has happened is far more subtle: 40 years ago it was punishing, because of the social stigma and lack of welfare, if a young unmarried woman got pregnant. Today the stigma has gone and the housing and benefit systems make it at least possible. If life at home is miserable, it might even be a relatively appealing possibility; and since sex and babies are nice, many young women are enabled to do something they would naturally like to do. Our social mores and welfare benefits allow illegitimacy to flourish among the poorest; we have reaped an underclass as a result.'

A rather different perspective is put forward by Beatrix Campbell in her book *Goliath: Britain's Dangerous Places*, in which she describes the abdication of unemployed fathers and husbands from any attempt to provide for their families and their flight into criminal activities. The women are thus forced into a situation in which they attempt to hold together both their communities and their families, with little help from the men; communities' attempts to find solutions to their predicament are overwhelmingly led by women. Single parenthood, for the women, becomes the consequence rather than the cause of the men's criminal behaviour, which in turn is directly related to the fact that the men are unemployed and to their 'masculine' and macho reaction to their situation:

'If the New Right ventured into the estates and saw the streets captured by thin, pale boys, it did not see the menacing response by men to the abolition of work, nor the street megalomania of boys trying to be men; in short, it did not see a *masculine* response to an economic crisis — it saw instead the failure of the *mothers* to manage the men.

'. . . there is an economic emergency in many neighbourhoods where the difference between what women do and what men do with their troubles and with their anger shapes their strategies of survival and solidarity on the one hand, danger and destruction on the other.'

The connection between unemployment, together with the materialism, greed and individualism promoted by Thatcher governments in the 1980s and the low wages in the only available unskilled jobs, and the increases in the rates of crime is nevertheless taken for granted by many people — and not only by the far or middle left. A leader in the *Financial Times* of 23 February 1992, for example, praising the Prime Minister for

41

saying that more condemnation of violent crime is needed but criticising him for 'his corollary of less effort to understand the criminal' which 'is exactly what is not needed', listed some of 'the many factors' causing crime, starting with:

> 'unemployment, which has left pockets of deprivation in many large cities where crime is seen as the only way of acquiring material wealth.'

Other factors, it says, are poor education, 'the erosion of the nuclear family', violence in the media and 'the easy availability of drugs, trafficking in which offers financial rewards way beyond those possible at a time of few job opportunities for young people with no qualification'.

Riots, in particular, almost invariably take place in areas of industrial decline, where young male unemployment is at least 25 per cent. John Benyon, editor of *Scarman and After: Essays Reflecting on Lord Scarman's Report, The Riots and Their Aftermath*, gives some figures. Unemployment in Brixton at the time of the 1981 riots was 13 per cent; unemployment among blacks was over 25 per cent, and 'For black males under 19 the figure was an estimated 55 per cent'. According to the 1981 census, 33.8 per cent of all men in the Granby (Liverpool 8) area of Liverpool were out of work at the time of the Toxteth riots; in Moss Side the figure was 27.1 per cent. Of the 4,000 people arrested in July and August 1981, about half were unemployed (and 66 per cent were under 21). In a study carried out in Harmondsworth a couple of months after the 1981 riots there, 43 per cent of the sample said unemployment was a major cause of the riot, and another 22 per cent said it was 'boredom'; among those who admitted active participation in the riots, 63 per cent were unemployed. Moreover, as the Blackbird Leys 'hotters' (all of them unemployed) who were interviewed on Channel 4's programme *Free For All* pointed out, they were 'hit from all sides' with advertisements for high-performance Rover cars; they also needed to relieve boredom and acquire the status and social networks which they would otherwise have obtained by having jobs.

As for more punishment being the answer, there is little evidence that this is the case. Crime levels seem to be correlated, if anything, with high rates of imprisonment of convicted people. Crime rates in Britain and the USA are higher than they are in any of the other EC countries; according to a report on *Criminal Victimisation in the Industrialised World*, produced in early 1993 by the Netherlands Justice Ministry and the British Home Office, Anglo-Saxon countries head the crime league, with some types of offense being twice as high in England and the USA as in countries such as France and Germany. The prison population of Britain is the highest in the EC, and in the USA it is, with Russia's, the highest in the world. As the *Financial Times* of 19 September 1994 put it, 'If more executions and more people in prison were the anwer, then the US would already be one of the safest places in the world' — while clearly the opposite is the case; a recent survey found that tourists were in greater danger in Miami than anywhere else in the world. On the other hand high crime levels in the USA and Britain do coincide with deregulated labour markets, casualised and insecure jobs, low wages and the relative absence of secure well paid jobs for unskilled men (see above). They are also the countries where the ideology of the free market has been most rampant, while public ownership, decried by the Prime Minister as one of the causes of crime, is higher in most continental European countries than it is in Britain or the USA.

Whatever its causes, crime, drugs and intermittent violence and looting are problems from which many people suffer inconvenience, and worse. Many women and old people have ceased to walk about, or even travel on public transport, at night. Women living in the pockets of bourgeois housing among the desolate estates of inner London and elsewhere do not return home, except in their cars or accompanied by men, after 6.30 in the evening, while men themselves, especially young men, are, according to most surveys, the most frequent targets of 'mugging'. Insurance rates on property and cars have climbed, and the sales of tempting 'hot' hatchbacks have declined. In the centres of cities the numbers of beggars and homeless people sleeping rough on the streets have multiplied. Above all it is the people who themselves live on the estates and in deprived inner city areas who suffer most. Many of them are angry at being seen as the perpetrators or causes of crime when they are in reality its victims. All of the 'riots' have so far taken place within deprived areas, and they have affected mainly local shops, businesses and people. In some inner city council estates people can no longer obtain house insurance at any price because burglaries are so frequent. Crime is among the first concerns of many people on these estates, sometimes coming higher on their list of worries than unemployment. This is one reason why for example Tony Blair, elected leader of the Labour Party in 1994, felt that he could win votes by stealing some more of the Conservatives' clothes and turning the Labour Party into a yet more committed champion of 'law and order', 'tough on crime and tough on the causes of crime'.

Much of this crime is associated with drugs: people steal and wound in order to satisfy their need for drugs such as heroine, cocaine and, most devastatingly, crack. These drugs provide a means of instant escape from the hopelessness and squalor of much of what is on offer in the inner cities, but they have horrific and destructive effects on the lives and health of those who become addicted to them. In addition, as an alternative to dead end jobs or the dole, the most obvious source of immediate wealth is dealing in drugs. People can make small amounts of money in a relatively harmless way by dealing in marijuana, but much larger fortunes are available from dealing in the 'hard' drugs which cause severe and sometimes fatal damage. Drug dealing has been the ultimate manifestation of Thatcherite free enterprise, a logical consequence not only of unemployment but also of the Thatcherite (or Reaganite) promotion of entrepreneurialism and self help; free marketeers should, logically, recognise the parallels between the drugs trade and the British insistence on their right to import opium into China in the nineteenth century, and echo the British condemnation of the Chinese government's 'immorality' in attempting to impede free trade. Mike Davis, in his book about Los Angeles entitled *City of Quartz*, has a section headed 'The Political Economy of Crack', in which he says that:

> 'The specific genius of the Crips [a Los Angeles gang] has been their ability to insert themselves into a leading circuit of international trade. Through "crack" they have discovered a vocation for the ghetto in L.A.'s new "world city" economy.
>
> 'Peddling the imported, high-profit rock stuff to a bi-polar market of final consumers, including rich Westsiders as well as poor street people, the Crips have become as much lumpen capitalists as outlaw proletarians. If this has only underwritten their viciousness with a new competitive imperative, it has added to their charisma the weight of gold-braided neck chains and showy rings . . .
>
> 'The contemporary cocaine trade is a stunning example of what some political economists (after the MIT duo of Sabel and Piore) are now calling "flexible accumulation", on a hemispheric scale.'

The desperate attempts of Andean peasants to survive the disasters imposed by the capitalist crisis and international bank debt, together with the Colombian cartels' entry into production using wage labour, led to over-production of cocaine. In response, the drug cartels developed a much cheaper and more lethal version of the drug, and 'designated Los Angeles as a proving-ground for the mass sales potential of rock cocaine or crack'. Gang members became the 'small businessmen' of this organised trade (the higher levels of which were still controlled by Colombians); according to some police estimates, many thousands of gang members were involved in trading crack; as Mike Davis puts it,

> 'if Levant's estimate of 10,000 gang members making their livelihood from the drug trade is anywhere near correct, then crack really is the employer of last resort in the ghetto's devastated East side — the equivalent of several large auto plants or several hundred MacDonalds.
> . . .
> 'The appearance of crack has given the Crip subculture a terrible, almost irresistible allure. Which is not simply to reduce the gang phenomenon, now or in the past, to mere economic determinism . . . But the Crips and Bloods — decked out in Gucci T-shirts and expensive Nike airshoes, ogling rock dealers driving by in BMWs — are also authentic creatures of the age of Reagan . . . Across the spectrum of runaway youth consumerism and the impossible fantasies of personal potency and immunity, youth of all classes and colors are grasping at undeferred gratification — even if it paves the way to assured self-destruction.'

While in the early 1990s the local Los Angeles dealers were mainly black, new immigrants from Mexico and Latin America, whose poverty is increasing faster than that of any other urban group in the USA, may follow their example:

> 'While their parents may still measure the quality of life by old-country standards, the iron rations of Tijuana or Ciudad Guatemala, their children's self-image is shaped by the incessant stimuli of L.A. consumer culture. Trapped in deadend low-wage employment, amid what must otherwise appear as a demi-paradise for white youth, they too are looking for shortcuts and magical paths to personal empowerment.'

In their despair, some people believe that the introduction of crack and other lethal drugs has been a deliberate policy of the authorities, intent on destroying their people and their communities. Drugs appeared on a large scale in Jamaica at the time of the general elections which deposed Manley; many Jamaicans saw them as having been introduced by the CIA. In Grenada, hard drugs appeared for the first time with the US invaders; whether or not this was the intention, they had a powerfully demoralising effect on potential opposition to the US occupying force. And crack has come into Britain too, with the usual time lag. While other drugs have destructive and tragic effects on individuals and push them into crime, crack is potentially devastating. As one (Caribbean) woman, working with the tenants of a North Kensington housing association and with long experience of the area and considerable tolerance, for example, of ganja, said, 'until we can get rid of crack, we might as well forget all the rest'. A slogan on a wall in South London, urging passers-by to 'Make joints not war', has doubtful implications.

Intermittently the frustration and anger of the deprived inhabitants of inner cities takes more generalised and violent form, and erupts into what are usually called riots. Riots are not new in cities. In 1819, for example, in what became known as Peterloo, weavers met in St Peter's Fields in Manchester to demand improvements in their conditions, and were charged by mounted soldiers who caused hundreds of injuries and eleven deaths. There were 'riots' in the Rhondda in 1910, in Liverpool in 1911, in Cardiff and other towns in 1919 and in London and Birkenhead in 1932. In Notting Hill in 1958 local black people were attacked by fascists, and fought back. In the 1980s and early 1990s, inner city riots occurred in greater numbers and with more frequency; the age of Thatcherism became also the age of the riot. The riots were triggered by a variety of incidents, but have a common pattern of looting, arson and battles against the police, engaged in mainly by young unemployed men within the deprived areas in which they live. Although in some people's perception and in the media riots tend to be associated with race, the participants may be predominantly white as well as black, or a mixture, depending on the nature of the local population. According to Home Office statistics in their *Bulletin* of autumn 1982, of the 4,000 people arrested in the July 1981 riots, 2,762, or 70 per cent, were white; the others were described as West Indian/African (766), Asian (180), other non-white (292). The riots have, on the other hand, sometimes been triggered by or developed into racist attacks, especially on Asian shops and businesses. They have invariably taken place in areas with high unemployment. Some politicians and media reports have at times asserted, without evidence, that external agitators were in some way involved; thus for example reactions to the 1981 Brixton riots are described by John Benyon in *Scarman and After*, as follows:

'David Alton, MP for Liverpool Edge Hill, asked whether evidence of the involvement of extreme groups had come to light, and Eldon Griffiths suggested that the petrol bombs used by rioters "must have been

46

manufactured beforehand with malice aforethought". The Member for Streatham, Mr William Shelton . . . asked the Home Secretary whether he was aware

> "that evidence is mounting that what sparked off the business on Saturday night might have been a planned trap for the police?
>
> ". . . Does he realise that the vast majority of the community in Lambeth is sick and fed up with Left-wing agitators taking advantage of the genuine grievances of many youngsters to further their subversive aims?"

The conspiracy theory was put forward outside Parliament as well. A number of newspapers proposed it and Sir David McNee, Commissioner of the Metropolitan Police, was quoted on Sunday 12 April as suggesting that outside troublemakers might be behind the events. However Lord Scarman [in his official report on the riots] found that the riots "originated spontaneously. There was no premeditation or plan".'[brackets added].

Others asserted, again, that poverty and unemployment were not causes; as Benyon reports:

> 'In Parliament, Mr Ian Lloyd (Havant and Waterloo) asked:
>
> "Since . . . there is no necessary or convincing correlation between poverty and the rioting . . . should we not seek an explanation for those deplorable events in some of the seditious, sociological claptrap that is passed on in our schools as education?"
>
> The Prime Minsiter replied that she very much agreed with her Honourable friend and she refused to accept that poverty was a cause of the disorders . . .
>
> 'Ronald Butt, in *The Times*, blamed "mischief-makers and do-gooders", while the *Daily Mail* went after "the masked motorcyclists". Local figures and police chiefs spoke of "political motivation" and "agitators" while Mrs Shirley Williams revealed that the Militant Tendency was involved in riot areas.'

In July 1981, after the Toxteth riots, ITN's *News at One* asked the Home Secretary whether 'agitators were causing some of the riots?', to which he gave a provisional yes, citing Manchester's Chief Constable James Anderton who had claimed in an ITN interview the previous day that he could not 'believe that it is within the intelligence and capacity of even many of the older groups of the young people involved to plan and organise an operation of this scale', and he thought 'there must be other people involved'.

In fact one of the main features of the Thatcher riots is precisely that they have not been organised, at least by the left, political parties, community groups or other official or semi official organisations. The

47

organised left, for example, has completely failed, in fact has barely even attempted, to establish any contact or form any relationship with the unemployed young people who become involved in riots. In Brixton in particular there has been a marked lack of contact between the organised white left and local young Caribbeans; the former are dismissed by some locals as merely sellers of newspapers outside the Brixton tube station. This was not always the case. In the late 1960s and early 1970s there were links between, for example, the International Marxist Group and militant black organisations in Brixton, including the Black Panthers; the IMG organised a speaking tour for Black Panther members in cities in Scotland and the North of England and supported them in other ways. But these links have disappeared, partly no doubt because the British Black Panthers themselves disappeared as an organisation and young militant Caribbeans did not set up the type of political grouping that might be interested in forming alliances with the far left. Michael Nally, in a chapter in *After Scarman* giving an eye-witness account of the Moss Side riots, reports that one young woman, asked about any possible political motivation for her and her friends' participation in the riots and any involvement of political groups, responded as follows:

> 'They've been here all day, selling their stupid newspapers. They're all Commies, we think. No-one's taking much notice of them. We know how bad it is here. Half of us don't work, and some of us live in hellholes. We don't need to be told that, do we?'

The riots have moreover not produced any articulated demands for improvements in conditions, for jobs, or for anything else. At most, they have produced demands for the police to clear out and leave them alone. During the Brixton riots, community leaders conveyed to the police the rioters' wish that the police should reduce their presence, and John Clare, a journalist who gave an eyewitness account of the events in *After Scarman*, reports that a rioter first asked to talk to the press and then said to him:

> 'We want all the prisoners that have been nicked down here, we want them all released, and we want them down here, right? Number two, we want all those policemen to move off, go somewhere else, go about their business, you understand?'

These demands were not acceded to. The riots nevertheless cause the authorities to take some action; rioting in Brixton and on Broadwater

Farm estate in Tottenham, for example, was followed by the spending of many millions of pounds on improvements to the housing estates concerned (thus belying their assertion that riots have no underlying economic and social causes). In addition, the offical inquiry on the Brixton riots by Lord Scarman produced recommendations for changes in police behaviour and for race relations courses for the police (as well as for their arming with CS gas and plastic bullets).

Insofar as the riots were provoked by external agents, these were often the police. This was most clearly the case in the 1980s, in the Bristol, Brixton, Moss Side, Toxteth and Tottenham riots, where a long history of police harassment of local people had built up a situation of profound hostility towards the police. In one poll, for example, reported in *Scarman and After*, black people 'placed this factor second (33 per cent) after unemployment (49 per cent)' as an explanation for the riots. Police provocation, especially of black people, over the periods preceding the riots clearly played a direct role in creating disaffection and inciting violence, and in some cases (see below) their actions provided the immediate trigger for rioting. The Scarman report on the Brixton riots itself contained strong criticisms of the 'insensitivity' of the police on issues of race. For example Scarman wrote that:

'Whatever the reason for this loss of confidence, and whether the police were to blame for it or not, it produced the attitudes and beliefs which underlay the disturbances, providing the tinder ready to blaze into violence on the least provocation, fancied or real, offered by the police.'

The police of course denied that they were responsible, preferring to blame the inherent criminality of their victims; thus Kenneth Oxford, Chief Constable of Merseyside at the time of the 1981 Toxteth riots, blamed the violence on gangs of 'young black hooligans' or, later, 'a small hooligan criminal element hell-bent on confrontation', whose 'fight was with us, the police, a symbol of authority and discipline which is anathema to these people'. After the Brixton riots in 1981 Sir Kenneth Newman, then Commissioner of the Metropolitan Police and one of the founders of Scotland Yard's Community Relations Branch, was quoted in the US *Police Magazine* of January 1982 as follows:

'In the Jamaicans, you have a people who are constitutionally disorderly. It's simply in their make-up. They are constitutionally disposed to be anti-authority.'

More recently the police have been criticised, on the contrary, for their absence and their failure to protect people in deprived areas from crime. On the other hand when they do react, their reaction may be inappropriate to the problems as perceived by local people, may arouse their further, and justified, hostility, and in some cases, again, actually provoke rioting. In Oxford, for example, *The Factory and The City* suggests that 'The "joy-riding" of a minority became the excuse for an exercise of police and social control over a whole community already disaffected by job-losses in the car plant'; and the community reacted to what it considered to be threatening action by the police (see below). Beatrix Campbell in her book *Goliath* reports numerous complaints by people on deprived housing estates about the lack of interest by the police in protecting them against the frequent menace of break-ins and muggings. When, in response to some incident, the police did finally enter the estates, they did so too late to protect the victims of crime and violence, they came in intimidating numbers, they provoked more violence and looting, and they often arrested the wrong people.

The first major riot of the Thatcher period was in 1980, in the St Pauls district of Bristol. It was provoked by a police raid on a Jamaican cafe, the Black and White Cafe, in search of drugs which they did not find. Young men, both black and white, threw stones at police, burnt out one of their vans, and then attacked white-owned shops, Lloyds Bank and the post office. There were 132 arrests and six convictions. In 1981, the following year, there were riots in Brixton (in South London), Toxteth (in Liverpool), Moss Side (in Manchester), North London, Handsworth (in Birmingham), Sheffield, Nottingham, Hull and Slough and more minor 'disturbances' in Leeds, Bradford, Blackburn, Leicester, Derby, Aldershot, High Wycombe and Cirencester. The riots in Brixton in South London started on Friday 10 April 1981 and continued for three days. Perhaps more clearly than any of the other riots, they did have an objective, which was articulated during the riots themselves: to drive the police off the streets of Brixton. As George Greaves, then Principal Community Relations Officer of the Council for Community Relations in Lambeth, comments in *After Scarman*, 'There is no doubt in my mind that large sections, particulary of the black community, regarded the police as an oppressive force which disregarded their civil rights and dignity as human beings'. Greaves relates numerous causes for this sentiment; thus for example:

'It was in 1976 that I had the first real premonition that relations between the police and the black community of Brixton were approaching a point of violent confrontation. The incident which caused me to come to that conclusion involved the police and a black man in his late fifties. The man was on his way home along Railton Road, which forms part of "the front line", when he was stopped by police and questioned about a parcel of groceries he was carrying. He was man-handled, and his groceries scattered in the roadway. A pregnant young woman intervened but she was rebuffed with such force that she fell to the ground. The incident was witnessed by the young people who frequent the "front line". So intense was the anger generated in those who witnessed the incident that they marched as a body to Brixton Police Station to complain, and it was a spontaneous demonstration without any prompting from community leaders or community activists.'

The 1981 riots were preceded by 943 'stop and searches' in Brixton in the previous five days in their 'Operation Swamp '81'; on Saturday, before any violence started, there were 84 police officers patrolling the streets in Brixton and three police vans driving round and round in what seemed a menacing manner. The particular trigger for Friday's initial riots was the stopping of a black young man by the police. The events were the subject of a massive official inquiry conducted by a judge, Lord Scarman, who commented on the first day of rioting as follows:

'Nothing that happened on Friday could have taken the police by surprise — until they were stoned. Tension between the police and black youths was, and remains, a fact of life in Brixton. Young black people, as well as many local people of all ages and colours, lacked confidence in the police. The worst construction was frequently put upon police action, even when it was lawful, appropriate and sensible . . .

'. . . the crowd of black youths felt, with some reason, that they were being pursued. They turned and fought. Their action was criminal, and is not to be condoned. It was not, however, planned. It was a spontaneous act of defiant aggression by young men who felt themselves hunted by a hostile police force.'

Yet Scarman also indulged in a good deal of sensationalising purple prose, talking of 'horror and incredulity', a 'toll of human injury and property damage' on Saturday 'such that one observer described the scene as comparable with the aftermath of an air raid' and commenting that 'over that terrible weekend' the police 'stood between our society and a total collapse of law and order in the streets of an important part of our capital'. On Saturday, the following day, the riots were triggered by two young white policemen, part of the continuing 'Swamp '81 Operation', who searched a black mini-cab driver and his car. There followed nearly six hours of violence, arson and looting. Three or four hundred young people, most of them black, attacked the police, at times with stones, bricks, bottles and petrol bombs. They set fire to buildings, destroyed vehicles and looted shops. According to the Scarman report, on Saturday 82 people were arrested, 279 police officers and at least 45 members of the public were injured, 61 private vehicles and 56 police vehicles were damaged or destroyed and 145 premises were damaged, 28 of them by fire. Most of the rioters were young black men; some were white, including some who came in cars to take advantage of the opportunity to loot. On Sunday 165 people were arrested, 122 police officers and 3 members of the public were reported injured, and 61 police vehicles and 26 other vehicles were damaged or destroyed. On Monday there were a further 29 arrests. Over 7,000 police were involved in 'quelling the disorders'. Three months later, on 15 July, about 170 police broke into eleven houses on Railton Road, looking for petrol bombs and illegal drinking, neither of which they found. They wrecked the houses and destroyed much of their contents. More riots followed.

In July 1981 there was a further series of riots. On 3 July 1981 Asian people in Southall were attacked by white racists, and fought back; the police became involved, there were 20 arrests and about 130 people, including police, were injured. On the same night police set off a riot in Toxteth, in Liverpool 8, when they chased a young black man on a motorcycle. The rioting lasted for three days. Police were attacked with a variety of weapons and they used CS gas, newly issued following Lord Scarman's recommendation. Numerous buildings, shops and businesses were set alight. On one night 282 police officers were injured, of whom 46 were hospitalised. Both blacks and whites looted. Eleven days later there was more violence, and a disabled man aged 23, David Moore, was hit and killed by a police vehicle; two others nearly died, one hit by a police Land Rover.

On 7 July 1981 a riot started in Moss Side in Manchester. There is a detailed eyewitness account of these events by Michael Nally in *After Scarman*. Like Brixton and Toxteth, the riots in Moss Side were seen by many of the participants as a challenge to the police, an assertion of their right to have 'the run of the streets'. During the day before the riots started, a plain clothes policeman asserted that the police were 'tooling up'. The Chief Constable of Greater Manchester, James Anderton, was notoriously hard and much hated in areas such as Moss Side. The rioters attacked a police station; Nally quotes one of them as follows:

> 'I'm here to see the pigs get theirs. They've done this for years. Now they know what it's like to be hit back. We had the bastards in there shitting themselves. We nearly got hold of them before they shut up the shop and screamed for help.'

The fighting continued for some five hours after the attack on the police station. The following day the police 'swamped the district' with 'about thirty vans and numerous other vehicles', and there was no more rioting. The Greater Manchester Council appointed a panel of inquiry under Mr Benet Hytner QC, which was boycotted by the chief constable James Anderton; Hytner wrote that 'We were satisfied that for some time prior to the summer of 1981 a number of officers misused their powers to stop and search subjects . . . We were satisfied that on many occasions, particularly but not only on Moss Side, black youngsters have been racially abused'. Police provocation continued after the riots. In a letter to *The Guardian* of 9 December 1981, a group of community workers described '"the almost unbelievable behaviour" of some officers, who careered through the streets in vans, beating their truncheons against the sides of the vans and chanting slogans, such as "Nigger, nigger, nigger, oi, oi, oi!"'.

In 1985 there were more riots. On the Broadwater Farm estate in Tottenham, an estate of monumental brutalism, a riot was triggered by the death of Cynthia Jarrett when the police broke into her flat and knocked her over, looking for her son Floyd Jarrett. As elsewhere, the police were accused of acting in a provocative way, but failing to respond to the community's real needs for protection. After Cynthia Jarrett's death, the police surrounded the estate and there was a massive confrontation between them and the mainly black protesters; a policeman was killed and three black men were arrested and convicted on trumped up evidence; they spent five years in gaol before being released on appeal. Also in 1985, in Handsworth in Birmingham, an area which had suffered from severe de-industrialisation and where nearly half of young black men were unemployed, police had been active against drugs traders, but failed to protect Asian shops and businesses from attack. When, after one drugs raid, young men started to throw petrol bombs and burn and loot shops, there was a long delay before the police came in. Two Asian traders died when their post office was burnt down, after desperately but unsuccessfully appealing for police help.

In 1991 the riots recurred. One of the main complaints about the police, again, was that they had been absent from the estates where the riots occurred, failing to provide any protection against crime and violence to their beleaguered inhabitants. In Beatrix Campbell's book *Goliath* there are detailed accounts of the events in Cardiff and Newcastle. In the Ely district of Cardiff, in August 1991, the disturbances were triggered by antagonism between Asian-owned and white-owned neighbouring shops. The police were called in when the former was attacked by local white young men, but initially appeared unable to prevent the attacks on the shop and threats to burn it down, or to curb the racist taunts. Eventually the police, including riot police, came in in large numbers. The events then turned into a confrontation between the police and the young men on the estate. There were three days of fighting; several people who had come to see what was happening were arrested; some of them and others were brutally dealt with by the police. In Meadowell in Newcastle there were even more severe riots in 1991. As in other places, the police had been absent, at best making brief appearances in their Panda cars, when local people needed them for protection against their overwhelming experience of daily crime, in which their houses were repeatedly stripped of their few possessions and sometimes burnt, and not only shops but sometimes houses themselves were 'ram-raided'. Nearly 85 per cent of all crime in the borough occurred on the Meadowell estate. Long-term employment among men was the highest in the North East, and a quarter of young men up to the age of 24 were unemployed. However in 1991 the police were beginning to take action against what Beatrix Campbell in *Goliath* describes as a 'criminal fraternity'. In September 1991 two boys were killed as they were being chased in a stolen car by police. The Meadowell estate, where the boys lived, was then looted and burned, telephone wires were burned out, and young men fought to keep out the police and firefighters. They attacked, looted and burned Asian shops and the families living above them, meeting resistance only from a few women on the estate; the Asian shopkeepers and their families fled, and did not return. It was several hours before the police assembled enough force to respond to their and other people's desperate calls for help; when they finally did move in, in what resembled a military operation, the rioters were scattered in a few minutes. The riots at Meadowell were followed by more riots in Elswick, another impoverished area at the opposite end of Newcastle, where the empty Dodds Arms public house was burned down, and in Scotswood, a few miles away and also a former industrial area on Tyneside, where petrol bombers set fire to cars, community buildings and the Post Office, and where the main targets were not Asian traders but women who had tried to organise to improve conditions and fight crime in their community. In Blackbird Leys in Oxford, the more minor disturbances, also in 1991, were triggered by an invasion by police supposedly in response to the phenomenon of 'joy riding'. Although the significance and drama of this activity has been much sensationalised and has done little to undermine the relative peace and respectability of this estate of small houses with gardens, many local people had complained for some time about the noise and nuisance of joy riders, whom the police seemed incapable of stopping. When eventually, in the summer of 1991, the police did react, they did so, again, by sending riot police onto the estate in large numbers. Referring to their 'Operation Pentagon' on Channel 4's programme *Free For All*, a police superintendant from Thames Valley Police said 'the Leys has had it fairly easy this weekend, we're going to go down and hit them', and described the police invasion of Blackbird Leys as 'a fight to decide who controlled Blackbird Leys estate', which they called a 'jungle'. In *Goliath* Beatrix Campbell quotes a local resident as saying 'one day they're not here, the next day they're here *en masse*. It was frightening. They were everywhere, you couldn't breathe'. Some young locals responded by throwing petrol bombs at police cars. The police arrested 29 people, none of whom were 'hotters' but several of whom were black, including a young and law-abiding black student on his way to the local chip shop.

In 1992 there were more minor riots in a number of places, including Wood End, Hartcliffe, Ordsall, Brackenhall Stoops and Haigher Clough. But since then, although there have been warnings of more to come, there have been no further major eruptions of anger in inner city areas. The probable explanation is that people are despondent, fear the likely severity of police reaction, and feel, rightly or wrongly, that rioting will not achieve an improvement in their conditions.

Lord Scarman's inquiry has been, up to now, the only serious official attempt to examine the causes of the rioting. Yet it was a solitary job, unlike the Kerner Commission in the USA (the National Advisory Commission on Civil Disorders), set up by President Johnson in 1967, which consisted of eleven people including Democrat and Republican politicians, a civil rights campaigner, a police chief, an industrialist and a trade unionist. Although Lord Scarman stated that 'Any attempt to resolve the circumstances from which the disorders . . . sprang cannot therefore be limited to recommendations about policing but must embrace the wider social context', he felt himself to be limited by the terms of his inquiry from examining this context or making 'specific suggestions or proposals in the field of Government financial or economic policy'. His specific recommendations were mainly confined to questions of policing. They include the recommendation that more attempts should be made to recruit black policemen and to ensure that 'racially prejudiced' people are not recruited to the police. Scarman also recommended dismissal for racially prejudiced or discriminatory behaviour, and more training for the police, in particular 'human awareness' training and training in 'community relations' and 'race relations'. The police fiercely opposed dismissal for racial prejudice, claiming that the police were no worse than the rest of the community and should not therefore be penalised for their racism, and said they already carried out training and were happy to do more. They took up, it seems with some enthusiasm, the proposals for more training to deal with riot situations, for example introducing the concept of 'snatch squads', intensively trained teams who move in to arrest people who are considered to be leaders. After Scarman, the police used CS gas in Liverpool, and many police forces have obtained plastic bullets and water cannon. Scarman also advocated 'community policing', or the use of policemen on foot who were to obtain a knowledge of the local community and seek the community's 'active consent and support'. The police have traditionally regarded officers on the beat as second class officers who were unlikely to get promotion; this attitude was supposed to change, and police chiefs such as Sir Kenneth Newman in London and Kenneth Oxford in Liverpool appeared to favour such a change. The police, on the other hand, were opposed to any concept of greater political accountability. They cling tenaciously to the so-called 'independence' of the police, which means that police will not accept direction from any quarter about how they conduct their operations and believe themselves to be constitutionally answerable only to themselves and 'the law'. Thus Basil Griffiths, vice chair of the Police Federation until his retirement in 1982 and then a Conservative political agent, wrote in *After Scarman* that the police are 'an organised force of constables, each one individually responsible at law for his actions'; any accountability to national or local politicians would risk creating a 'politically controlled repressive force' and:

> 'It is worth remembering that Nazis were elected to power in Germany and those who advance the notion of police accountability as a libertarian cause might ponder that there are those in British politics who show a taste for totalitarianism.'

(The word 'totalitarianism' is a word sometimes used by the right to denote communism, or left-wing politics in general). Moreover, Griffiths said, the police could not expect to have the support of all members of the community:

> 'It may be very difficult for some people to accept that there exists and has existed since the days of the industrial revolution hard core urban areas where a positive hatred is maintained towards the police by a sizeable minority of the people who live there. And this hatred is matched by a belligerence displayed towards any form of authority. It is amongst such people — unemployed even in times of full employment — that crime and violence is a way of life. It may be that the simple explanation for the wave of rioting was that those criminal elements discovered, possibly inspired by the tactics of their Ulster counterparts, that by the use of of the petrol bomb their arch enemies — the police — could for the first time be shown as impotent to prevent widespread crime and disorder.'

In the same book, Kenneth Oxford, chief constable of Merseyside, wrote that Lord Scarman, in advocating increased consultation between the police and communities, had failed to consider the 'practical difficulties', such as the 'confusion' caused by 'the influence of party politics'. In another chapter Alan Goodson, chief constable of Leicestershire, wrote that:

> 'there is a feeling among some people about the arrogance of the chief constable. They think he is too powerful and are not really sure what legal controls can be exercised over him . . .
>
> 'Well, chief constables consult today more than ever before, they listen to the views of the community through a variety of channels and where appropriate revise their objectives in the light of what they hear. But we must be clear that the chief constable is, and must remain, independent in his enforcement of the law: he and he alone has this responsibility. He has this legal duty and not even the courts can intervene. . . . And so after all the consultation has taken place, and after the deepest consideration by the chief constable of all the views of the community, at the end of the day he

alone will decide upon the operational enforcement of the law — and untramelled by the advice of any committee of politicians. To do otherwise would change the impartiality of the law enforcement process and alter the fundamental basis upon which the British police system operates.'

The problem is that many people, and not just the 'sizeable minority' in 'hard core urban areas' referred to by Basil Griffiths of the Police Federation, distrust the police and do not believe that they are impartial. Griffiths, in the same chapter, does recognise that:

'It is these inner city areas that the respectable, the old and the weak suffer most as victims of the criminality of the minority. It is this majority . . . who look to the police as their only means of protection. A partial failure on the part of the police to fulfill that task, as evinced by the level of crime and violence in such areas, may be laid at the door of decades of neglect of policing needs.'

Yet he fails to recognise that hostility to the police is widespread in such communities. The police are believed to be deliberately uninterested in people's everyday suffering. Many people feel desperate for support, of almost any kind; as one inhabitant of a Newcastle estate, quoted in *Goliath*, put it: 'I've had half a dozen burglaries. I felt myself feeling so vulnerable that anything or anyone who will protect you is your friend. I was becoming a law and order freak'. Darcus Howe, television producer and editor of *Race Today*, when asked what he thought about the current attitudes and behaviour of the police in Brixton, said he was now more critical of them for what they did not do than for what they did; the police tended to be absent, on training courses, keeping away from what had become virtually 'no-go' areas. Nevertheless, the hostility towards the police for what they do do remains strong. While failing to protect housing estates against crime and trading in hard drugs, the police persist in harassing young people, especially black young people but also other young people they do not like the look of, for minor offenses such as possession of cannabis, they continue to discriminate against black people in general and above all they now routinely harry people whom they suspect may be illegal immigrants (in other words simply on the grounds that they are black — see below). Once in police stations, people are liable to be roughly treated. In addition, the police have been publicly shown to have concocted evidence, especially against Irish people but also against the three Caribbeans accused of murdering a policeman on Broadwater Farm, in a string of successful appeals which have resulted in people being released after many years in prison. For these and other reasons, Paul Boateng in *After Scarman* and others elsewhere have argued for changes in the law so as to give elected local authorities the right to concern themselves in matters of operational policing.

In some areas, the police are now prepared to criticise the government not only for its inadequate funding of the police themselves, but also for the government's failure to recognise the connection between unemployment, homelessness and poverty and the increase in crime rates. The Chief Superintendant of North Kensington, Mr Gilbert, has been particularly active in articulating such ideas. Putting them into practice, he became an active member of the North Kensington City Challenge board (see below) and seconded one of his officers to work in the City Challenge office. The latter was engaged in tenant consultation exercises, to determine what the tenants thought would be the most useful form of protection to be provided by the police, and to give advice on the usefulness of different security systems. Police attitudes in North Kensington had previously been characterised by brutal confrontation with the black community, in particular at Notting Hill carnivals, and the North Kensington police had been especially notorious for drug raids and harassment of the Mangrove cafe. In 1993 a member of the current governing body of the Mangrove Community Association however stated baldly that: 'I have no problems with the police in North Kensington'. The change has no doubt occurred to some extent in both parties, but is nevertheless startling. Whether this has any effect in improving security for the inhabitants of this deprived and crime-ridden inner city area is another question. In the view of one black resident of North Kensington, the police were merely using their criticism of the government as an excuse for their own inactivity and unwillingness to provide real protection for the victims of crime: 'it's a cop-out', he said. Moreover, one representative of the Moroccan community complained of the misuse of public money involved in continuing to send out the police to harass Moroccan young people on the estates, on the pretext that they might possess cannabis. While some parts of the police have recently started to argue for the legalisation of cannabis, others still appear happy to use its illegality as a means of getting at the people they do not like.

Meanwhile the rich have their own ways of dealing with the problem. Increasingly they shut themselves behind physical barriers. In Los Angeles this process, described by Mike Davis in *City of Quartz*, has already reached a high point. New housing for the rich is built in a fortress mode, with narrow entrances leading to internal privatised space, rather in the manner of Oxford and Cambridge colleges but with the barriers of wealth and class reinforced with heavy locked gates and protected by electronic devices and guns. Los Angeles may yet fulfill the futuristic scenario depicted in the film *Bladerunner*, in which the wealthy live high up in fortified buildings to which they have access from the air and descend, if at all, greatly at their peril into the filthy impoverished streets, inhabited mainly by people with brown and yellow skins, below. The cities of Britain are of course still far behind even the current reality of Los Angeles, and may take other directions. But increasingly their spaces are privatised and made inaccessible to ordinary people. New shopping centres are guarded by private security firms, instructed to exclude those who appear unlikely to consume in other than legally permitted ways, through the possession of money. The new business park at Cowley which occupies what was once a car plant employing many thousands of people from the neighbouring housing estates now boasts a sign which states:

> Oxford Business Park.
> Private Estate.
> *The Highway Act 1980 Section A1.*
> Oxford Business Park is Private Property.
> Path, road and amenity areas are not dedicated to the public
> Oxford Business Park Management Limited.

Anybody ignoring this notice is threatened, on another notice, with video camera surveillance. The elaborate ornamental pools have yet more warning notices which state that they are 'periodically treated with chemicals', so must not be drunk or bathed in. The plans for the estate are mainly car parks and the major works so far have been in building new round-abouts and flyovers. The jobs, if they ever come, will not be for local people.

The new government-subsidised developments in London's Docklands come nearest to echoing the Los Angeles reality, at least in physical and architectural terms. Conservative governments have poured many millions of pounds into their quango, the London Docklands Development Corporation (see below). The LDDC's success in promoting a spate of speculative new office development and, in particular, in altering the housing mix in Docklands' Isle of Dogs in favour of private ownership has produced particularly blatant juxtapositions of wealth and poverty. The opulent new buildings are on sites next to public housing which is visibly cracking up, and whose occupants are without jobs (or without adequate jobs). The new luxury housing blocks then, of necessity, become fortresses, locked away behind remote control-operated gates and surrounded by empty spaces, from which life has been driven away. As David Widgery writes in *Some Lives: a GP's East End*,

'Islanders encountered the LDDC when it was taking away their communities, closing down local firms, buying up homes and cafés by compulsory purchase, shooing them off their imposing buildings and knocking down their homes to build motorways no-one wants. The fortified wall which had once circled the docks was not so much torn down as rearranged as a series of fences, barriers, security gates and keep-out signs which seek to keep the working class away from the new proletarian-free yuppie zones . . . a group of high-income Dockneys (the yuppy Isle of Dogs residents' self-designation) . . . sued their private landowners because they failed to curb the "nuisance" of the indigenous neighbours who had a propensity for shouting and hanging out washing. But few of the luxury residential developments have even got the degree of organisation to complain. Their owners are either subletting or absent most of the time in their weekend homes, or living invisibly behind high security in their refuge-with-a-view, insulated from anything outside the front door. Children, if there are any, are packed away at boarding school, health problems sorted out by private subscription, and groceries bought over the phone or computer. It is the future if the world was to be ruled by estate agents. And it doesn't work.'

CHAPTER 5

Racism and immigration controls

In Britain and elsewhere, black people live overwhelmingly in cities. Since cities were where workers were needed, nearly all of the migrants from abroad have come to live in cities. Black people, who are often the most recent migrants, usually also live in the most deprived areas of cities. In some small parts of cities, they constitute a majority. They are among those who suffer most from the decline in the prosperity of cities.

In spite of the evidence that they make a considerable net contribution to welfare, black people are, in addition, sometimes blamed for the problems of cities. The problems of inner cities have become confused with problems of race. Many people appear to believe that urban problems would be alleviated if new immigrants were prevented from coming here, or even if people who are already here were expelled.

On 30 January 1978, in an interview on *World in Action* shortly before she became Prime Minister, Mrs Thatcher declared:

> 'People are really rather afraid that this country might be rather swamped by people with a different culture. . . . There was a committee which . . . said that if we went on as we are then by the end of the century there would be four million people of the new Commonwealth or Pakistan here . . . The moment the minority threatens to become a big one, people get frightened . . . We must hold out the clear prospect of an end to immigration.'

Thatcher may have hoped thus to win the votes of those who at the time were expected to vote for the neo-fascist National Front. She was also, of course, stoking up fears, and thus perhaps hoping to enlarge this potential vote, by playing the numbers game. The 'committee' in question, the Franks Committee, had predicted a population of 3.8 million black people by the year 2000 and the Centre for Population Studies subsequently revised this figure downwards to 3.3 million, on the basis of a fall in immigrant birth rates. What Mrs Thatcher referred to as a 'minority' which 'threatens to become a big one', by which she presumably meant the black population currently living in Britain, was less than 4 per cent of the total British population. The numbers argument is easy to refute, supposing one wishes to engage in it. For much of this century there has been net emigration from Britain among both whites and blacks, there are more white than black immigrants, and birth rates are falling among both white and black people. Numbers are not the issue. The concern expressed by Thatcher about 'people of a different culture' was not directed at the influence of the United States of America in the media, entertainment and food businesses. The argument is usually a racist one. And when, in the same programme, Thatcher talked of threats to 'the British character (which) has done so much for democracy, for law and done so much throughout the world', it is hard to know what she was referring to. Controls on immigration undermine democracy, the law, human rights, justice and freedom, values which one might suppose were considered important in most people's view of British cultural and political achievements. What Thatcher was in reality doing was giving respectability to racist prejudice and to the ideas promulgated by the fascists, in other words to ideas which are fundamentally opposed to freedom and democracy.

Thatcher, of course, was far from being alone in this. She was part of a long and ignoble tradition. The British have at times prided themselves on a liberal and tolerant attitude towards migrants and particularly towards political refugees and those who flee from persecution. But often they have shown prejudice against foreigners and believed, wrongly, that immigrants, by which they now usually mean black immigrants, represent a threat to their livelihood and amenities. Over the years, they have intermittently given violent expression to their prejudices, and a succession of foreigners have been attacked and harassed. Thus for example the persecution of Jewish people began almost immediately after their arrival following the Norman invasion, and has continued with varying degrees of intensity ever since. *The Peopling of London* gives an account of some of these attacks on foreigners, including 'an episode in 1517 which became known as "Evil May Day"': antipathy towards French, Italian and Spanish merchants and financiers became such that 'a large mob took to the streets, with the aim of attacking any foreigners they found and breaking into and ransacking [their] houses and workshops. . . . The City authorities, well aware of the economic benefits brought by the skills and capital of these foreigners . . . punished the ringleaders severely. Three hundred were arrested and fifteen were hung, drawn and quartered'. When there was a large influx of Protestant Huguenots from France in the seventeenth and eighteenth centuries, they were welcomed by some of the locals, because of their perceived industriousness and because of anti-Catholic sentiments, but others described them as 'the very offal of the earth' and resented the competition: 'weavers all may curse their fates/because the French work under-rates'. When rural people from Italy and Ireland came to Britain, they in turn were subjected to negative stereotyping and racist abuse.

However the prejudices of British people are currently directed overwhelmingly against black people, who are assumed, not always accurately, to be recent immigrants. Hostility towards immigrants is articulated by some people in terms of rational-sounding arguments. Thus immigrants have become, in their minds, scapegoats for high unemployment and declining social services, and they are blamed for high levels of crime and intermittent violence in inner cities. Yet unemployment was at similar levels in the 1930s, when there were few blacks living in Britain, and housing, health and other social services are still somewhat better than they were in the 1930s; unemployment and poor living conditions are caused, not by immigration, but by the failures of the capitalist system, and in particular by its inability to avoid recurring depressions and slumps. With cruel inconsistency, immigrants are blamed for being unemployed, castigated as 'social service scroungers', and they are blamed for taking local people's jobs; they are held responsible for poverty and for deficiencies in public services, whereas, without them, many hospitals, transport systems and industries would have difficulty in functioning. In reality the hostility towards immigrants has no rational basis, and is overwhelmingly a product of racist ideology. In addition to the general xenophobia of many British people, black people experience particular prejudice which results from colonialist rationalisations of their mistreatment under imperialism, and in particular of the slave trade. Although Europeans were at first full of awe at the often superior civilisations which they discovered on their colonial adventures, they gradually built up theories of racial superiority. They ended up convincing themselves that their colonial subjects were lucky to have them as masters and were lazy, stupid and in fact barely human, possessing 'duller nerves' than themselves. Such prejudices are deeply ingrained, even if they may no longer be so crudely expressed.

Blacks are also widely blamed for crime, violence and riots. Mainly because of discrimination against new immigrants, who tend to be forced to live in the most deprived neighbourhoods where housing is cheapest and unemployment is highest, there are concentrations of black people in some of the 'worst' areas of some cities. Nevertheless in some of the areas of highest unemployment, in northern Britain, in Scotland and in northern Ireland, there are few blacks. In the succession of uprisings or 'riots' which have taken place in cities in the 1980s and early 1990s, there has been no discernible racial pattern or cause; the main generalisations to be made about the participants are that they live in deprived urban areas and that they are young unemployed men (see above). Sometimes, in areas of high immigration, these young men are black. Elsewhere, as for example in the riots in 1991 in Newcastle's Meadowell estate, they are overwhelmingly white. Usually they are a mixture. Moreover although black people are disproportionately represented in prisons, this is evidence of racial discrimination in sentencing more than of their actual participation in crime. An international study on youth and crime, the British research for which was carried out by the Home Office research department, published in the Netherlands but not in Britain (but reported in *The Guardian* of 6 July 1994), concluded for example that, 'contrary to the over-representation in police statistics of young black offenders, the English research showed that there was either no difference or lower offending rates for ethnic minorities with [sic] their white counterparts in property crimes or violent offences'; and: 'The English study found one drug user in four among white youth, one in eight amongst blacks and one in 12 among Asians'.

In reality, of course, there is a problem of race, but it is a problem of white people's racism. Whereas black people are very definitely not the cause of the problem of the inner cities, they are often its victims. Black people suffer discrimination in job and housing applications. As a result they suffer higher rates of unemployment than whites. In Britain as a whole, unemployment for 'ethnic minorities' is two or three times that of whites. According to the government's 1985 Labour Force Survey, 34 per cent of non-white women between the ages of 16 and 24 were unemployed, while the average for this age group was 15 per cent. The situation for young black men is even worse; in some deprived inner city areas, as many of 70 per cent of them may be unemployed, when the average for young people as a whole is 30 per cent. In London, according to a government survey of Youth Training leavers reported in *The Observer* of 12 Februrary 1995, the average rate of unemployment for black men aged 16 to 24 is 62 per cent; for white young men of the same age the average is 20 per cent; only a quarter of the black trainees found jobs after their training, compared to a third of disabled trainees and half of whites. Lower educational attainment does not account for the gap between black and white unemployment. According to the 1985 Labour Force Survey, among people with higher education qualifications, 10 per cent of blacks were unemployed, while the average for all academically qualified people was 3 per cent. In deprived inner city areas, the educational qualifications of young blacks tend to be higher than those of whites, perhaps partly because many of the more skilled whites have abandoned these areas, but also partly because blacks are often the children of first generation immigrants who have failed to secure employment to match their abilities and push their children to achieve more. Whatever the reasons for black children doing better, they do so in spite of discrimination in schools. They tend to be put in the lowest classes, whatever their abilities, or excluded from grammar schools even when they pass their '11 plus'. Numerous surveys confirm that employment discrimination exists, particularly against black men, in spite of legislation against it. For example the *Financial Times* of 12 October 1994 reported that a study by the Nottingham and District Racial Equality Council had found that the chances of getting an interview were twice as high for white applicants as they were for black candidates:

> 'The study . . . submitted three fictitious applications for each of 281 job vacancies. The candidates, one white, one black and one Asian, were evenly matched in terms of job experience, qualifications, age and sex.
> 'In the 38 cases where only one applicant was offered an interview, 30 of the employers picked the white applicant, five chose the Asian, and one chose the black candidate.
> 'In another case letters of application were sent to a well-known insurance company seeking a sales representative.
> 'The white job-seeker received an application form on the first day of the month asking him to contact the company for the interview. The other two applicants did not receive the form until the 11th of the next month, a full six weeks after the white applicant. There was no offer of an interview with the forms. The company described itself as an equal opportunities employer.'

There had been no improvement since a similar survey was carried out in 1981.

Worse still, black people are subjected to harassment and violence. Some of these are the result of the activities of fascists and those who support them or are influenced by them. In 1958, fascists and others attacked the black population of Notting Hill and provoked what became known as the Notting Hill 'race riots'. In 1968 Enoch Powell, then a member of the Conservative cabinet, made a speech proclaiming that immigration, if not stopped, would lead to 'rivers of blood' and demanding the repatriation of the black population. His speech gave new courage and respectability to racists and fascist sympathisers who had previously been kept at bay, and some ugly incidents followed. For example in one factory in Southall, where some members of the white workforce had, as in many British factories, been determined to keep out black workers, fascist sympathisers gained an immediate boost after Powell's speech and carried out violent attacks on shop stewards who supported the right of Asian workers to work in the plant. In East London, some dockers organised a march in support of Powell (although the dockers who were most active on the picket lines in the 1970 dockers' strike considered their action shameful). The Sheffield organiser of the National Front at the time was quoted in a Socialist Worker pamphlet, *The Case Against Immigration Controls*, as follows:

'We held a march in Huddersfield in support of what Powell had said, and we signed eight people up as members that afternoon. Powell's speech gave our membership and morale a tremendous boost. Before Powell spoke, we were getting only cranks and perverts. After his speeches we began to attract, in a secret sort of way, the right-wing members of the Conservative organisations.'

Since then, racist attacks have mounted. Although the National Front did badly in the 1979 elections (possibly because the Thatcher strategy of adopting their language and policies worked from the Conservatives' point of view), there has been a recent growth of fascist activity. In 1993 a British National Party candidate, Derek Beackon, was elected in a by-election as a local councillor in Tower Hamlets in East London (he was subsequently dislodged after local people organised for the annual elections in May 1994). After the BNP candidate was elected, race attacks in Tower Hamlets quadrupled.

Attacks extend far wider, of course, than those associated with declared fascists or their supporters. Racism is widespread in the British white population. It may take the form of verbal abuse or of violent physical attack. There are few black people in Britain who have not experienced some form of actual physical attack by racists, either on themselves or on their friends and relatives, and probably none who have not suffered racist abuse of some sort. For example a recent study by Di Parkin of attitudes among street cleansing staff in Leicester found that *all* the black street sweepers and car park attendants referred to regular racist abuse by the public as they went about their work. During the Thatcher period, along with increases in crime and riots, racist attacks grew rapidly. Thus for example reported racial incidents doubled in the five years to 1993. According to a *Morning Star* report on 24 September 1994 of a conference organised by the Runnymede Trust, there were between 150,000 and 200,000 reported racial incidents in 1993, many of them 'vicious assaults'; and there were at least nine racial murders. Other reports list higher numbers of murders. For example *Jacattack*, the newsletter of the Birmingham-based Justice Alliance Campaign, published in its summer/autumn 1994 issue a memorial list of 16 named victims of racism, of whom 10 were murdered and two committed suicide as a result of their treatment by the state. One of the best known of these victims was Joy Gardner, a 40-year old Caribbean woman who died on 1 August 1993 when the police bound and gagged her in their attempt to deport her (on the grounds she was an alleged 'over-stayer'). Another victim, Saled Ahmed, died in April 1994 'from burns after family home was firebombed in Oxford after a campaign of harassment by local racists. His wife and eight children were in the house when it happened. No-one has yet been arrested'.

In addition, black people are harassed by the state. It now appears to be the accepted doctrine that immigration controls, imposed by the governments of nation states to limit the number of people entering their territory, are necessary and desirable. Those who argue against immigration controls tend to be viewed as irresponsible extremists. Yet until this century there were only very limited checks and restrictions on the entry of foreigners. The extremists were those who argued *for* controls. Whatever is said by the large body of liberal opinion which now argues for immigration controls which are 'fair' and 'non-racist', such controls are inherently racist; they keep out 'others' who are less privileged than the native citizens of the country concerned. The restriction on the freedom to travel is a clear violation of human rights, and its enforcement leads to further specific, and exceedingly harsh, violations (see below). Even now, horror tends to be expressed if people are not freely allowed to leave a particular country; it is only free entry *into*, mainly rich Northern, countries which is apparently unthinkable; the Carriers Liability Act, moreover, means that an airline will not even carry you *out* of Britain unless your passport is in order and unless it is certain that you will be allowed into the country of your destination.

Once painfully admitted into a country, immigrants usually have fewer rights than those of citizens. They are liable to be deported if they commit a crime or otherwise cause offense, their voting rights are less than those of the natives, their access to state services may be less. While the free movement of goods is promoted and campaigned for by the free market right, labour is only free to move within national boundaries. Bob Sutcliffe, in an article in *Index on Censorship*, comments as follows:

'On your bike, as Margaret Thatcher's minister Norman Tebbitt said, and you are a saint shining with neo-liberal virtues. On your ferry, and you are a demon against whom great European democracies change their constitutions in panic.'

Sutcliffe writes in conclusion:

'If there existed in the world a country in which various ethnic groups lived, and in which the richest and most powerful group divided the country into ethnic areas, forbade the poorer, less powerful groups to enter the privileged groups' areas, except under strict conditions where they had to carry passes and submit to constant and humiliating police controls, which would often result in forced removals, then there is a good chance that it would be declared a pariah by other nations for its denial of human rights. Such a country did, until very recently, exist: South Africa under apartheid. And it was universally — if, by some, hypocritically — condemned. Yet, viewed as a whole, the world is worse in these respects than South Africa under apartheid. On the right to move, and the right of migrants when they have moved, the world is a macrocosm of the country which all other countries found it impossible to accept. The freedom to migrate — an end to the world pass laws — would be an essential plank in an anti-apartheid movement for the world.'

In the late nineteenth century those who argued for controls on immigration, especially trade unions who argued that the influx of Jewish refugees from Russian pogroms was a threat to their jobs and wages, were in a small minority. It was not until 1905 that the British government introduced the Aliens Act, which obliged people to submit to examination before entering the country. It was followed by the Aliens Restriction Act of 1914, which required that aliens must register with the police, and the 1919 Aliens Act, which, until it was superseded by the 1971 Immigration Act, made entry at the discretion of an immigration officer, restricted the employment of aliens, and gave the Home Secretary powers of deportation. During the Second World

War, while some German Jews were admitted as refugees, many Germans, most of whom were either Jewish, socialists or others opposed to the Nazi regime, were interned in British camps.

The mainly black people of British colonies and ex-colonies were treated differently. At first they had more rights than other foreigners. In 1914 the British Nationality and Status of Aliens Act conferred the status of British subject on all inhabitants of the British Empire; the 1948 British Nationality Act confirmed and strengthened this dispensation. However subsequently they became subjected to increasingly severe restrictions, and it is now much harder to get into Britain for black people than it is for whites, including Europeans and also North Americans and Australians. Successive governments created and constantly expanded a whole new repressive apparatus of immigration controls. First Conservatives and then Labour ministers argued, as they still do, that the way to combat racism was to restrict the number of black people living in Britain. Thus for example Mrs Thatcher, in her *World in Action* interview, claimed that: 'If you want good race relations you have got to allay people's fears on numbers'. She then proceeded to do the opposite (see above). Quite apart from the fact that she, like others before and after her, actually inflated the numbers, any such arguments give false credibility to the argument that there are or might be too many immigrants, and they feed and give respectability to racist prejudice.

Controls on Commonwealth immigrants were first introduced, in 1962, under a Conservative government. During the 1950s the ruling Conservatives had themselves rejected pressures from the right wing of their party for immigration controls. But in 1962, under pressure from the racists inside and outside their party, a Conservative government introduced the Commonwealth Immigrants Act, which instituted a system of employment vouchers to restrict immigration from the 'New Commonwealth', in other words of black people, to those who had specific employers to go to. Subsequently such vouchers ceased to be available, and immigration was then restricted to visitors and those who could prove that they were the dependants or spouses of existing residents; the latter provision gave rise to increasing numbers of abuses by the immigration authorities, with families being denied the right to live together and wives and children being subjected to humiliating examinations, including blood tests and virginity tests. At the time the 1962 Act was introduced the Labour opposition argued against any immigration controls, and its leader Hugh Gaitskell maintained opposition to such controls in principle until his death in 1963. However when the Harold Wilson Labour government took office in 1964 it not only failed to repeal the 1962 Act but passed its own Act introducing more severe restrictions in 1965. In 1968, in response to the expulsion of Asian people from Kenya, a Labour government under rushed through an Act restricting the entry of UK passport-holders to those who had a parent or grandparent born in Britain, thus revoking the pledge of a right of entry previously given to Kenyan Asians. In 1971 the Conservative government, under Heath, introduced an Immigration Act which formalised the division of immigrants into desirable (mainly white) and undesirable (mainly black) by introducing the categories of 'patrials' (those who had British ancestors) and 'non-patrials'. It effectively abolished all primary or settler immigration from the countries of the black Commonwealth; family reunion was to be the only major criterion for settlement, and this was enforced in a way which caused great hardship to families. The 1971 Act also gave immigration officials the right to detain immigrants whom they categorised as illegal, pending their removal. The Labour Party, again, denounced this Act when they were in opposition, but failed to repeal it when they were re-elected. When Roy Jenkins was Home Secretary in 1976 he set up a committee to work out how to tighten immigration controls further against the 'threat' posed by Malawi Asians. In the 1980s, under the Conservatives again, the British Nationality Act defined non-patrial British citizens as Overseas Citizens, with no automatic right of residence in Britain, and thus rendered them stateless. In 1986, under the Immigration Rules, the government imposed visa restrictions on people from West Africa and the Indian subcontinent. The 1987 Carriers Act imposed fines on airlines and others carrying people who did not have the correct documentation. New restrictions on asylum seekers were introduced. In 1993 the Conservatives passed the Asylum and Immigration (Appeals) Act, designed to tighten procedures for admitting refugees and to speed up procedures and thus deportations; an appeals procedure was grudgingly included after many protests against the government's intention to leave it out. In 1996 the Conservatives introduced a new Asylum and Immigration Act denying rights of appeal in certain cases and introducing a 'white list' of countries from whom asylum seekers would automatically be excluded; it also legalised the government's decision to deny income support and housing benefit to some categories of asylum seekers, a decision which the High Court had previously pronounced illegal and a breach of any norms of civilised conduct. This was followed by a further court decision that asylum seekers denied benefits were destitute within the legal definition of the term, and they thus became the responsibility of the social services and a further call on much cut local authority funds.

The system of immigration controls has given rise to increasing human rights abuses. This response to the problems of people who are forced to migrate, to Britain and elsewhere, forms part of the increasingly repressive stance taken by Conservative governments and their supporters. It parallels their attitudes towards crime, homelessness and the other consequences of poverty in cities. It is, in a sense, symbolic of, and linked to, the dangers of right-wing extremism which exist in Britain today. The government feels quite able to ride roughshod over the objections of liberals and democrats, even when they are members of the political and financial establishment. It apparently has no qualms about undermining the gains in democratic rights and safeguards and the rule of law which are considered important by a large body of liberal opinion as well as by the left. Thus under the various immigration acts, immigration officers acquired large administrative powers, in particular to refuse admittance to and also to detain people who attempt to enter Britain, as visitors, students or refugees. Their right to detain such people under the immigration laws is not subjected to any form of judicial process, and immigration officers are not obliged to give reasons, written or verbal, for their decisions. Innocent people can be detained for an indefinite period without charge and without trial. They are liable to spend many months and occasionally years in 'detention centres' and prisons, with limited access to lawyers, and virtually no possibility of bail. They are thus treated worse than criminals in Britain.

Asylum seekers may subsequently be granted entry, or refugee status, or 'Exceptional Leave to Remain'; or they may be deported. The numbers detained have been increasing rapidly. By 1996 there were some 850 people imprisoned under the immigration and asylum laws at any one time, and the numbers continue to increase. Apart from a few East Europeans, they are all from the Third World, especially from Ghana, Nigeria, Zaire, Algeria, Ivory Coast, Angola and South Asia. Nearly half of those detained are in some 20 prisons around the country, which, in the case of asylum seekers, is contrary to a specific provision in the United Nations Convention on Refugees (adopted in Geneva in 1951 by the British and other governments). Others are in 'detention centres': at Harmondsworth, a decrepit set of buildings near Heathrow airport, first used as a detention centre under the immigration laws in

1970 and run by the private security firm Group 4; at Haslar near Portsmouth, a barracks converted in 1989 and run by the prison service; at various airports and ports; and in wings of prisons redesignated as detention centres. In November 1993 the government opened a new immigration detention centre at Campsfield House near Oxford with 200 places, also run by Group 4. Most of those detained at Campsfield House are refugees. The government claimed that it was opening Campsfield House in order to reduce the number of asylum seekers in prisons, but between July 1993 and March 1994 the number of asylum seekers detained, both in detention centres and in prisons, doubled.

The detention centres are in effect prisons, and have been described by some as more like concentration camps, supposedly alien to British traditions. The one advantage of detention centres, as opposed to prisons, is that the detainees are normally not locked into their rooms and can associate with each other inside the centres during the day. Visitors who have or obtain their names can visit them every day. But the detainees cannot, of course, leave, and in some other ways the 'detention centres' are worse than prisons. Apart from Haslar, they are run for profit by Group 4, whose low paid staff have two weeks' training and sometimes behave with arbitrary cruelty; there are no published regulations and the official response to requests to inspect the terms of Group 4's contract with the government has been that the dictates of 'commercial confidentiality' make this impossible. Medical facilities are minimal. In some cases detainees are tranferred to regular prisons on the grounds that they need medical treatment. There are cases of severe neglect or mistreatment of people who are seriously ill. One such case is reported, among many others, in the *Campsfield Monitor* (the newsletter of the Campaign to Close Campsfield — see below) of Nov-Dec 1994, as follows:

'A Ghanaian woman, Valerie Senoo, was removed from Campsfield House bound and gagged at 5am on 25th November, according to Campsfield detainees. She was deported to Ghana the same day. She has no family in Ghana and is both mentally and physically unwell following her prolonged detention.

'Ms Senoo had been detained in Campsfield House since 9th December 1993, and had been confined by ill health to her room for much of that time. She suffered from asthma which worsened in detention, and sickle cell disease which caused her great pain. Her state of health was significantly worsened by acute depression manifesting itself in symptoms such as chest pain and boils. She was prescribed anti-depressants. Detainees allege that she was taken from her room by eight men and two women, her legs tied, her hands bound behind her back and her mouth plastered, wearing only night clothes. They are extremely distressed at the incident in which they say a woman was treated "as an animal". Ms Senoo was greatly respected by other detainees . . .'

The detainees have access to telephones but no means of obtaining money to use them, even to contact their lawyers; telephone cards are obtainable only haphazardly, from visitors. There are virtually no educational classes or employment opportunities. Campsfield House, which is a refurbished youth detention centre, has had added to it new twenty foot metal fences, electronic gates, at least fifty video cameras inside and outside, and newer additions of rolls of razor wire, bars on windows and metal sheeting to obscure the view to the outside and reduce contact with demonstrators. Detainees suffer a barrage of tannoy announcements relayed into each room, frequent early morning 'fire alarms', and other more or less petty harassments. As the months pass, the prisoners at Campsfield and other detention centres and prisons, some of whom have spent many months or as much as a year in various forms of imprisonment, and who have no idea of how much longer they will be detained, lose their resilience, their ability to concentrate or to think of any useful way of passing the time, and their spirits.

This treatment is, to many people, particularly shocking in the case of refugees. People who have been persecuted for their political, religious or other beliefs in their country of origin have the right under the Geneva Convention to seek asylum in the countries whose governments have signed it, which include Britain. Many of those who are detained are not only 'genuine' in the sense that their cases fall clearly within the definitions used in the Convention, but have been imprisoned and even tortured in their own countries. They come to Britain and are shocked and bemused to find themselves in prison again, in the country in which they had hoped to find refuge and in whose reputation for democracy and respect for human rights they probably believed. According to the Home Office, about one in 75 asylum seekers is detained; the rest are given temporary admission, usually with the condition that they reside in a particular place, notify any change of address, and sign on several times a week at police stations. Of those detained, over half have gone straight into detention from their port of entry. Within a few days they must answer a long list of standard questions, with no right to the help of a lawyer, and perhaps with an interpreter; their answers are written down in English and may or may not be correctly recorded. After two or three months in detention, they are summoned to their port of entry, to be given the immigration officers' decision, normally (especially for detainees) a refusal of asylum; of the 22,370 people who applied for asylum in 1993, only 1,590 were granted asylum, while a further 11,125 were granted 'exceptional leave to remain' (ELR); these numbers themselves fell rapidly in the course of the year, so that by the fourth quarter of 1993 only 150 of the 5,650 applicants were granted asylum and 520 exceptional leave (down from over half to a little over 10 per cent). By the time this decision is given they mostly have solicitors or legal representatives, who can be paid under the legal aid scheme for preparatory work; legal aid is unavailable for representation. The asylum seekers are given seven days to appeal and the date of their flight back to the country they escaped from, which will be cancelled when they appeal. The appeal, which now usually takes place after two further months in detention, is heard in front of an Adjudicator, appointed not by the Home Office but by the Lord Chancellor's Office, who may or may not have legal training and receives no legal assistance at the hearing. The statements of Adjudicators and immigration officials sometimes display a crass ignorance which would be laughable if it were not tragic in its consequences. One African refugee was told, inaccurately, that he could not have escaped across a river because it was full of crocodiles. Another was told, in a written decision rejecting his appeal, that his story was not credible, even though his suffering in prison in Ethiopia might explain some of his apparent confusion; he was a Zairean, and had been in prison in Zaire; he had never been to Ethiopia. Some 10 per cent of the Adjudicators' decisions are different from those of the Home Office; the latter may appeal, and detention may continue. Or lawyers may appeal, on a point of law but not fact, to higher courts; detention, again, may continue. Those who eventually fail in this process are deported.

Bail is rarely achievable. Once asylum has been refused, bail can be applied for and is decided on by an Adjudicator. But there is no presumption in favour of bail, as there is in criminal cases, and the Home Office normally opposes it. At least two sureties are generally required; the going rate is the prohibitive sum of £2,000 for each surety; even so bail is often refused. Detainees are sometimes, unpredictably, granted 'temporary admission' by immigration officials and released. Immigration officials have the power to give or refuse temporary admission at any stage in the process, and no obligation to give reasons.

Detainees released on temporary admission are given a piece of paper stating that they are 'a person liable to be detained', and a considerable number have in fact been re-detained after they were released (in at least three cases after they had given interviews to the media). When immigration officials are asked why they refuse temporary admission, their usual answer is that they have reason to believe that the detainee would not comply with the conditions set and would 'abscond'. Asked for evidence for this belief, they may say they do not need to provide any: 'we are not a court of law'. In reality they usually have no grounds for suspecting that detainees would 'abscond' if they were released. More than half of those detained were detained at the airport and therefore had no chance to demonstrate whether they would or would not comply with restrictions. In a 1994 study by Amnesty International, *Prisoners Without a Voice*, nearly half of the 50 detainees interviewed were eventually released; not one of them absconded. Alternatively immigration officials may say that the detainee has no friends in Britain (even in response to a visitor who is offering to provide accommodation), or, as is frequently the case, that he or she arrived without documents (even though this is specifically excluded as grounds for imposing penalties in the UN Convention on Refugees). The only discernible pattern is that those detained tend to be of a nationality for which immigration officials systematically refuse asylum. Thus in 1992 both refugee status and ELR were refused for 99% of Zaireans and Angolans, 98% of Ghanaians, 97% of Indians, 95% of Pakistanis, all of whom are detained in large numbers. But even as between the nationals of particular countries, the detention decisions are arbitrary and incomprehensible, and may depend to a great extent on the state of mind of individual immigration officers, as well as on whether detention places happen to be available at the particular time when the asylum seeker arrived. A further indication of the arbitrariness of the system is that, as *The Independent* of 13 December 1994 reported, immigration officials have recently been given targets for referring foreign nationals attempting to enter Britain for interrogation and possible detention, and may lose incentive payments if their rates of referral are lower than the average for their port of entry; section one, clause seven of the criteria issued under their new appraisal system states that: 'The proportion of cases referred for further examination which result in refusal and/or asylum claim should reflect the port average'.

Immigration officials do have to supply written reasons for the refusal of asylum. These may include questioning of the refugees' identity or even nationality, or of their account of their escape. Refugees are systematically disbelieved. Both immigration officials and adjudicators look for 'inconsistencies' in their accounts of their experiences as a pretext for rejecting their asylum claims. When they have been misunderstood by interpreters or misrecorded by immigration officers, the latter accuse them of inconsistency and deception. Frequently they report their despair at the refusal of officials to listen to them or try to understand. But above all, the immigration officers' reasons for refusal consist of inaccurate assertions about the absence of political persecution in their countries. In one letter responding to a visitor's appeal on behalf of a Zairean detainee, Michael Howard, Home Secretary, told Douglas Hurd, Foreign Secretary, that assessment was based on information from '. . . our Embassy in Kinshasa where the Charge d'Affaires and her staff are well placed to provide objective assessments of political developments . . . although there are sporadic arrests of political activists there are in fact very few political prisoners and the widespread opposition to president Mobutu and his government is usually tolerated'. Apart from the fact that this is simply untrue, it does not explain the refusal of asylum to those who *have* been political prisoners in Zaire, and some of whom are now political prisoners in Britain. Whether the blanket rejection of certain nationals is primarily a foreign policy or a Home Office decision is hard to tell. It is no doubt partly based on the British government's wish to have good relations with particular African and Asian governments; there is considerable association between the refusal of particular nationalities' asylum claims and the state of Britain's arms sales to that country. In 1992 40% of those *granted* refugee status were from Iran, Iraq and Sudan, whose governments had poor relations with the British government at the time. On the other hand it could be that the Home Office, precisely because the persecution in certain countries might produce numerous refugees, has asked the Foreign Office to provide 'evidence' of its absence. In any case, as with the detentions, the decisions on refusals of asylum applications appear arbitrary. In addition, the fact that rates of refusal have considerably increased over the last few years indicates that something other than an objective assessment of individuals' cases is involved. Thus one adjudicator at first asserted that his job was to examine the merits of individual cases and then, later on in the same interview, asserted that the number of asylum seekers had become too great in 1991, that something had to be done to reduce these numbers and that perhaps the near halving of applications between 1991 and 1993 showed that 'our stricter policy' was working.

Because refugees are desperate at the treatment they receive, and perhaps also because they are political people who have resisted tyrannies elsewhere, they have at times rebelled. Early in 1994 ten Algerians at Pentonville prison went on hunger strike, and were eventually released on 'temporary admission'. They were followed by another ten Algerians, and one Indian, at Campsfield House. One of them, a woman, was transferred to Holloway prison; the others were subsequently transferred to a private prison near York. Campaigners and their lawyers succeeded in finding out where they had been taken, and all of them were, again, released. Immediately afterwards Group 4 broadcast over the tannoy at Campsfield House a warning to the remaining prisoners not to expect the same treatment. Nevertheless in March 1994 180 detainees at Campsfield, and others elsewhere, went on a mass hunger strike. The Campsfield hunger strikers issued a declaration stating that Campsfield 'is a prison', that 'we want to be free while our cases are going on', and suggesting that the British government should 'withdraw its signature to the Geneva Convention and refuse to accept asylum seekers at all rather than putting men and women through trauma and uncertainty that we are experiencing in detention'. Group 4 staff, some alleged, tried to push food down their throats; immigration officials made false promises of release if people ate; detainees were locked into their rooms and corridors; some visitors, phone calls and letters were stopped; medical attention, when it occurred, seemed more of a threat than a help. Between ten and twenty of the hunger strikers were transferred to prisons. The Home Office issued a press release accusing the latter of being 'ringleaders', causing *The Voice*, for example, to report, quite incorrectly, that the prisoners had become violent and 'smashed furniture'. They were as usual not charged, but were put in isolation on their arrival in Blakenhurst and Winson Green prisons. At least one of them was subsequently granted refugee status, after the Home Office had failed to find grounds for persisting in refusing it. Most of those transferred to prison were, however, among a group of 100 or so prisoners who escaped into a courtyard, climbed onto a roof and exchanged shouted communications with the demonstrators outside. The government sat out this strike, possibly willing for people to do permanent damage to their health or even die rather than contemplate large scale releases. Nevertheless in June 1994 the prisoners at Campsfield House rebelled again, this time in one night of protest which was triggered by the removal without warning, contrary to Home Office assurances, of an Algerian. First the Algerians and then many of the other detainees smashed some of the furnishings and then broke out into a courtyard. They obtained a Group 4 ladder and a dozen escaped. Group 4 and immigration officials lost control and locked themselves into their rooms. The police took several hours to assemble enough force to go into the centre; when eventually they did, they had dogs and riot gear. Soon after the police went in, the ambulances came out; the Home Office has never accounted for the numbers of people whom the media and others present observed, and recorded on camera, in the ambulances.

These actions by the prisoners themselves helped to lift some of the veil of secrecy surrounding the injustices they suffer, and brought about brief flurries of publicity. But the efforts of lawyers, campaigners and supporters to publicise these injustices are hampered by the extreme vulnerability of the detainees, who expose themselves to retaliation both by the Home Office and by their own governments if they allow their stories to be told in public. There have been for many years a number of organisations campaigning against the mistreatment of immigrants and asylum seekers or working for their welfare. They include for example the JCWI (Joint Council for the Welfare of Immigrants), Asylum Aid, the Campaign to Stop Immigration Act Detentions, the Stop the Detentions Action Group and several organisations of refugees themselves, most of them organised on a national basis and coordinated through the National Union of Refugee Organisations (NURO). In 1994 Amnesty International's British Section produced a report, *Prisoners Without a Voice*, written by Richard Dunstan, on the detention of asylum seekers, which states for example that 'Amnesty International has long argued that such practice is in violation of international human rights standards', and argued for much less use of detention and much greater judicial safeguards against abuse. In Oxford a campaign was set up to call for the closure of the Campsfield detention centre soon after it was opened in November 1993; the Campaign to Close Campsfield calls also for the ending of all detentions under the immigration acts and the repeal of immigration controls, and is promoting the setting up of similar groups to protest against detention in other centres and prisons. It organises, among other things, regular monthly demonstrations outside Campsfield. Because the detention of asylum seekers, and the circumstances in which they are detained, constitute such blatant injustice, the Campaign to Close Campsfield has had support from a wide range of opinion. For example, partly as a result of the campaign, a letter was sent to the Prime Minister in 1994 which was signed by over 100 senior members of Oxford University, including 25 professors and 11 current and former heads of colleges, which condemned the policy of detention as 'arbitrary', flouting 'the normal rules of evidence and conventions of civilised behaviour', stating their concern 'at what we consider is a dangerous undermining of democratic principles and the rule of law' and their fear 'that, if persisted with, it could open the way to further abuses', and appealing for the 'early release' of the detainees. The Conservative government is impervious to all this. Charles Wardle, then Home Office Minister in charge of immigration matters, dismissed the protestors as a 'motley collection of the far left and liberals', thus sweeping aside the concerns of weighty members of the establishment about the erosion of democratic rights under the guise of immigration controls.

These abuses do not affect only new applicants for entry to Britain. Existing residents, when they are black, are increasingly under threat of harassment, arrest and deportation. Black people have long been subjected to discriminatory treatment and unjust arrests by the police. Black parents accompany their children to school to protect them from the police as well as from other white thugs. In the late 1970s, section 4 of the 1824 Vagrancy Act, known in shorthand as 'Sus', which enabled police to arrest people merely on 'suspicion' that they might be intending to commit an offence, became particularly threatening to young black men, who constituted around three-quarters of those arrested for 'Sus' in 1977, 1978 and 1979. 'Sus' convictions could be gained merely on the corroborative evidence of two police officers; they did not need to present either a potential victim or a witness. In *Scarman and After* (see above) George Greaves writes:

> 'So apprehensive had some parents become that their children might be charged as suspected persons that they either kept them indoors, particularly after dark, or arranged for them to be escorted by an adult if they had to be out. For example, parents would take turns to meet a group of children and escort them to their houses from the youth club.'

The relevant parts of the Act were repealed in 1981. But black people's sense of vulnerability and insecurity in the face of the authorities remains, and random and intimidatory police arrests are again on the increase. Blacks are now liable, in an updated version of the 'Sus' laws, to be picked up for minor offenses or no offense at all and then to have their immigration status routinely questioned. Unless they can produce immediate proof of identity which can be checked, they may then end up in prison on 'suspicion' of being 'over-stayers' or of having infringed the immigration laws in some other way, such as getting part-time jobs if they are students. The health authorities and the social services, and now also employers, are required to check the immigration status of individuals before providing them with services or jobs, and thus become a further extension of the apparatus of immigration controls. In 1996 the employment or support of an 'illegal immigrant' was criminalised in the government's new Immigration and Asylum Act. Even if black people have been living and working in Britain without committing any criminal offense for many years, they may end up being deported. The numbers of deportations are growing fast. In 1991 more than 5,000 people were deported, more than twice the number deported in 1987. The immigration 'service' has thus developed into a massively overblown and repressive bureaucratic apparatus, designed to keep to a minimum new immigration, to deter potential asylum seekers, and even to reduce the existing numbers of black people in this country, with quite arbitrary powers of arrest, detention and deportation — a kind of state within a state.

The state, on the other hand, provides little protection against racism and racist attacks. For black people, the experience of calling the police for help when they are attacked and finding that, when the police come, they arrest them rather than their attackers, has become so common that they have given up asking the police for help; instead, for example in the East End of London, they have begun to organise their own defence. Among innumerable such cases, *Jacattack*'s summer/autumn 1994 issue describes the case of a Birmingham council employee, who:

'has been a victim of racist violence and intimidation from her neighbours, council tenants who moved in 2 years ago. In July 1992, there was an incident where Lorna attempted to rescue her daughter who was being attacked by the neighbours. Police were called and Lorna was arrested and taken into custody for 7 hours, while her children were left unattended despite police promises that someone would sit with them.

'Since then there have been other incidents where police have threatened to arrest Lorna or her visitors, but have made no such threats or warnings to the white neighbours who are causing the harassment.'

Moreover the Race Relations Acts, passed to protect black people from discrimination and incitement to racial hatred, have been little used in situations where they feel seriously threatened. The Acts' use in cases of discrimination at work has seldom produced any real redress and has more often merely enabled people such as the Home Secretary Michael Howard (quoted in the *Morning Star* of 24 September 1994) to accuse them of taking 'trivial' cases to tribunals and being 'over-sensitive': 'If the newspaper-reading public laughs at the judgement in one case, you can be sure they are also being invited to laugh at the idea that real discrimination exists anywhere'. Howard refused to incorporate into the Criminal (In)Justice Bill amendments, proposed by a number of campaigning and pressure groups, intended to create a new offence of causing intentional harassment, alarm or distress and to increase police powers against racist literature. Virtually nothing has been done to stop the actions of fascist organisations and when demonstrations take place against them, the demonstrators are, again, hounded by the police, penned in, for example, and then charged by mounted police, as happened in attempts to demonstrate against the headquarters of the British National Party in South London in early 1994.

CHAPTER 6

Inner city politics

Since poverty and its disturbing consequences are both most concentrated and most visible to politicians and researchers in inner cities, they have attracted much attention. As Sir John Gorst, a Conservative MP, said in the 1880s:

> 'Modern Civilisation has crowded the destitute classes together in the cities making their existence thereby more conspicuous and more dangerous. These already form a substantial part of the population, and possess even now, though they are still ignorant of their full power, great political importance . . . Almost every winter in London there is a panic lest the condition of the poor should become intolerable. The richer classes awake for a moment from their apathy, and salve their consciences by a subscription of money . . . The annual alarm may some day prove a reality, and the destitute classes may swell to such a proportion as to render continuance of our existent social order impossible.'

This quotation well illustrates why, from the nineteenth century onwards, governments and others have felt that 'something must be done' about 'those inner cities'. The problem is not merely one of crime and riots, although these are usually present as threat or reality (see above). Governments have also been concerned, at different times and to varying degrees, that the problems of inner cities might give rise to organised resistance of a variety that might be threatening to the established political order.

The latter type of threat was particularly present in the 1960s and 1970s. This was a period when the capitalist boom was coming to an end, and the long decline of employment was beginning, especially in manufacturing industries in cities. Yet, because of the earlier prosperity, the confidence and militancy of the working class, of its political and trade union organisations and of their allies and supporters were at a high point. The government and ruling classes experienced not merely the anxieties which have been prominent in the 1980s and 1990s (such as rising levels of crime, the break-up of communities and traditional methods of family and community control, the 'growth of an urban underclass' and 'race riots', for example in Notting Hill in 1958); there were also forms of organised resistance, both in the workplace and in communities, which were widespread, sometimes successful in their immediate aims, and radically opposed to the existing political and economic order, to a much greater extent than anything which exists today.

In the workplace there was a strong and militant shop stewards' movement, which succeeded in winning higher wages and much improved conditions for the workforce in many industries. There were trade union-led attempts to oppose closures through strikes, occupations and work-ins. At Lucas Aerospace and to a limited extent in other industries, workers put forward 'alternative plans' to save their industries, and there was some discussion of workers' control. Some trade unionists were recruited into left organisations such as the Socialist Labour League, the International Socialists and of course the Communist Party, and worked towards wider political goals. Workers who had made gains for themselves within their own workplace supported the struggles of other workers in a weaker position. For example in Oxford militant and well organised car workers supported strikes and struggles against closures in the health service and for trade union recognition in the hotel industry, organised against racism and did much to change Oxford from a rather conservative town with a largely subservient, service-based workforce into a town with a relatively high level of militant political activity. The Labour government reacted in 1969 with an attempt to introduce a bill to curb the shop stewards' movement, based on their document *In Place of Strife*, but abandoned the idea in the face of labour movement resistance. In 1972 the Conservatives passed an Industrial Relations Act, with similar aims. Since 1979, and especially since the defeat of the 1984 miners' strike, the combination of unemployment and Conservative legislation, against secondary action in particular, has gone far, for the time being, towards the suppression of resistance by workers and their trade unions. There have been strikes, for example, by Asian women at Burnsalls and the Hillingdon hospital and by dockers in Liverpool, but they have usually been defeated and have received little or no official trade union support. In Oxford the car plant union leadership refused to call for strike action to oppose closures in 1988 and actively opposed attempts to campaign against closures (see *The*

Factory and the City, especially chapters 8 and 9) preferring to hold private discussions with management on their plans for new models.

Outside the workplace there were parallels. Community action is of course more directly a response to problems of poverty and homelessness in inner cities. In the 1960s and early 1970s there were community-based campaigns, especially around housing issues, with the development of numerous tenants' and action groups, rent strikes and squatters' movements, which were radical and at times successful, and which operated quite independently of the local state authorities and in opposition to them. Government's response to these community-based movements was however different from their response to the threats from the workplace (possibly because the latter were ultimately more threatening and potentially more powerful, since workers have the ability to hit the capitalists where it directly affects their central activities, through the withdrawal of their labour). Rather than repressing the community-based groups and movements, governments have succeeded, on the whole, in buying them off and incorporating them (see below).

Radical community action

Notting Hill in the 1960s and 1970s provides an impressive example of effective radical protest based in the community. From 1966 onwards a series of often dramatic local actions compelled the Conservative-controlled Royal Borough of Kensington and Chelsea to curb the activities of private landlords and speculative developers and to do something to stop the evictions of working class people from their homes. It led to a massive growth in housing trusts providing low rent accommodation and even to some council house building in a Conservative-controlled borough. The council was forced to spend over one and a quarter million pounds on building council housing in North Kensington between 1967 and 1974. The share of 'non-profit' housing, including council housing and housing trust accommodation, in the two wards mainly affected, Golborne and Colville, more than doubled in the period 1966-74. In this way the protestors were directly responsible for ensuring that the North Kensington area, in which many working class and black people lived, was not taken over and gentrified by an invasion of the middle classes from South Kensington and elsewhere, but remained available as a place of residence to its existing inhabitants. A book by one of the activists, Jan O'Malley, entitled *The Politics of Community Action*, published in 1977, states for example that:

'In housing, the Council policy was opened up to public debate in the neighbourhood and nationally, and plans for two major areas of North Kensington were developed . . . These involved the spending of over £6 million of public money and massive shifts from private to non-profit ownership in the two areas for which the Council had no plans at all at the beginning of this period of struggle . . .'

The struggle moreover moved on from housing issues to wider ones; thus:

'Hundreds, even thousands of local people had been involved in a real debate about the principles at stake in the housing struggle, and they came to see the struggles as a struggle between systems and not just as an individualised struggle between each tenant and his landlord . . . The profit-seeking motivation of the private landlord had proved itself inadequate to meet the housing needs of the area . . .

'The whole idea of playspace was established in the area and space, resources and manpower were won for play for years to come. The bureaucracy controlling the motorway space was pierced, the non-decision to turn the space into a car-parking wilderness was effectively challenged, and a policy decision forced to use the space for community facilities . . .'

And so on. The book also gives a detailed description of the various direct actions by local people and organisations such as the People's Association which helped to achieve these victories. For example in one episode local councillors were locked into a building for the whole of one night, with the protestors demanding that the council should not evict a family, until they were finally released by police at 10 a.m. the next morning. There were recurring battles and occupations of local squares to secure them for the use of local people. And, as a book by Andrew Duncan on the history of the North Kensington Amenity Trust, *Taking on the Motorway*, recounts:

'At the official opening of the Western Avenue extension in July 1970, local residents expressed their feelings. Shouts of "Philistine!" and "Get us rehoused now!" met the arrival of Michael Heseltine, Parliamentary Secretary at the Transport Ministry. Arriving by lorry the wrong way up an "unopened" slip road and evading a police block, protestors from Walmer Road and Pamber Street advanced down the motorway causing total confusion among the procession of official cars. Some sang "uncomplimentary songs, especially composed for the occasion", according to the *Kensington Post* . . . residents had hung, "Get us out of this Hell — Rehouse Us Now" on a huge banner outside their windows.'

The protesters had a radical political perspective which is generally absent from current community groups. For example one conference of what Jan O'Malley calls 'neighbourhood agitators', which took place in June 1972, issued a statement which read as follows:

'We, as groups involved in community organising, are opposed to the capitalist system and the inevitable exploitation this brings.

'We organise in the areas where we live, and therefore are separated from the traditional area of political organising, the place of work. However, the contradictions we seek to bring to the surface are vital, complementary ones, in the reproduction of wage labour, e.g. in housing, education, health and social security, play and leisure, and the position of women.

'With the present intensification of the class struggle and the deterioration of the economic situation we believe the time is now right to intensify our activities in all of these areas, developing whenever possible new, collective forms of power and developing the political consciousness of those who have come to feel themselves politically powerless.

'We seek contacts with and support from other groups such as women, claimants, blacks, new left groups and new political parties which share these aims and are engaged in similar struggles.'

Those participating were concerned to ensure that their actions contributed to wider revolutionary struggles. Jan O'Malley quotes the Camden Community Workshop as follows:

'In a very crucial sense there is a tension built into community organising: the overall perspective is that of social revolution and yet the chosen site of activity, the localised neighbourhood, is far removed from such a possibility. This gives a provisional character to the Workshop as a form of political work . . .'

But the community activists justified their actions partly on the grounds that, as Jan O'Malley writes:

'working class struggle can and must be extended to include all those who are not at the point of production . . . in the absence of such community-based struggles as those experienced in Notting Hill, a huge section of the population would remain in a political wilderness, with no sense of what socialism could mean to them and so open to the insidious courting of the far right. As the crisis of profitability intensifies and redundancies increase, turning the waged into the wageless, it will become increasingly important that a theory of socialist struggle includes the wageless as well as the waged population . . .

'. . . this experience . . . can be seen to add a fresh dimension to the kind of positive spontaneity Rosa Luxemburg described as "a series of great creative acts of the often spontaneous class struggle seeking its way forward" and as "the active untramelled, energetic political life of the broadest mass of the people" . . .

'. . . local people gained a wide experience of confronting the authorities and of all that this entailed . . . It was this experience of fighting for control in one area of life which was a vital political education for all involved and could well act as a springboard for challenging the controls over the other parts of one's life . . .

'So what does all this mean for future socialist strategy? There are those Marxist groups which have concentrated exclusively on the weakness built in to community struggle — the fact that community struggle is removed from the work place and therefore lacks the real political muscle, the sanctions which are inherent in industrial struggle . . .

'One of the aims of this book has been to force socialists to take seriously the experience of community struggle described, and to see it as a fundamental way of expanding and enriching working class consciousness of their capacity to take action to challenge the different kinds of exploitation which determine their lives.'

All this, as Jan O'Malley recognised, was 'far removed from the . . . community development tradition' which seeks 'a local wholeness that includes all people, all factions': the community activists in Notting Hill 'fully recognise the class divisions and class conflicts within the present society'. Little of this radicalism, however, remains. In the 1980s and 1990s community groups became increasingly dependent on local authority funding and increasingly incorporated into the policy-making of the authorities. In Notting Hill this change is symbolised by the trajectory of the Mangrove Cafe and the organisations around it, which in the 1960s and 1970s were engaged in continual confrontation with the authorities and the police, but by the early 1990s had become largely a welfare organisation, with good relations with the police and participation in council programmes, including City Challenge (see below).

Local government and welfare

The subversive anti-state activities of community groups in the 1960-70s were directed as much against Labour governments and councils as they were against the Conservatives. For the Conservatives and their supporters, however, the propensity of the people of inner cities to vote Labour, together with the resulting Labour control of local authorities, have been an additional worry. Labour's influence in inner city politics grew in the period between the first and second world wars. The Labour Party began to move away from being mainly a trade union party and became active in developing local public services, building an urban infrastructure and making collective welfare provision. These activities partly account for the fact that, from the early 1920s onwards, the Labour Party has more or less continuously controlled the municipal authorities in cities. In the 1970s and early 1980s, moreover, some of these authorities took a quite militant anti-capitalist stance. In particular the Labour-controlled metropolitan authorities, especially the Greater London Council, were in danger, from the Conservatives' point of view, of giving socialism a good name — and were therefore abolished (see below). They also provided financial support to numerous community, anti-racist, women's, trade union and other organisations, a process which had problems as well as advantages from the point of view of some of these organisations since, in a sense, it constituted the beginning of their dependence, incorporation, and downfall.

The degree of financial and statutory control exercised by local authorities and their independence from central governments has itself varied over the years. Historically they have been the source of much welfare provision. From time to time, various welfare functions have been initiated by local government, removed from it or added to it. The much hated Poor Law system, which provided segregated accommodation for unemployed people in work-houses, began in the nineteenth century and was administered by local authorities until 1934. Supplementary benefits were administered by local government until 1940. In the 1930s 'municipal labourism', under the influence of Morrison, built up and consolidated a system of locally provided welfare benefits. Many of these were subsequently incorporated into a national system, the 1945 'welfare state', based on the Liberal politics of Beveridge. But although this meant that local authorities lost some powers, this did not, unlike the experience after 1979, constitute a conscious effort to undermine them. As Alan Cochrane says in *Whatever Happened to Local Government*, 'noone would suggest that the social security system proposed by Beveridge was principally aimed at undermining troublesome local authorities . . . its stress was clearly on the provision of universal benefits coupled with a commitment to full employment . . . rather than leaving it as a permissive patchwork . . . the issue was not how to restrict spending in these fields, but rather how it might more effectively be extended and institutionalised'. Local governments after

1945 also retained control over large parts of the welfare state, including public housing and schools which accounted for 60 per cent of local council spending in the 1950s. While Conservative policies have diminished local authorities' control over both housing and schools, as well as their ability to fund them, the administration of housing benefit has been transferred to them and the Conservatives now also expect them to take on additional responsibility and provide funding for 'care in the community'.

Local authority spending almost quadrupled between 1940 and 1970, and it rose from around 9 per cent of national income in 1950 to over 13 per cent at the end of the 1960s. But, when the economic decline began, local spending was progressively cut. After 1979 Conservative governments embarked on a systematic onslaught on local government spending, which was motivated both by the desire to cut public spending and by the desire to weaken Labour's control of urban policies. Central government controls on spending have progressively made a mockery of the local state's supposed independence and local accountability. A large proportion of local authority funding is provided by central government, through the Rate Support Grant (introduced by a Labour government in the 1960s, in theory so that resources could be directed towards the areas most in need). By the 1970s the Rate Support Grant amounted to over £6 billion a year, or well over half of local government expenditure. Since 1979 Labour-controlled local authorities have increasingly turned into instruments for the implementation of Conservative public expenditure cuts, while some Conservative-controlled authorities, such as Wandsworth and Westminster, have received more favourable treatment. The concept of local democracy has had diminishing force.

There were of course always limitations on what could be achieved by local authorities, however radical they were in their commitment to the improvement of the situation of their most deprived citizens. The fate of the people who live in cities is determined to a great extent by events which occur elsewhere. British governments, both Labour and Conservative, whatever their attitudes towards local government, have adopted policies at the national level which make the situation of the people who live in cities worse in numerous ways. Planning policies in the 1950s actively dispersed industries and people outside cities but did little for those who were left behind. Since 1979 the Conservatives have shown little concern about unemployment, and in fact have used it as a means of helping employers to control their workers (see above). Their attacks on trade unions and protection at work have driven down wages and conditions for those who are still in work, and their glorification of greed has bred increasing inequality. Although, for a brief period since 1945, the British national welfare state has provided a universal means of bare survival for unemployed people, free access to health care, and the right to low rent housing for some categories of people, these recent welfare gains are being weakened and undermined. The cuts began in the 1960s and 1970s, when both Labour and Conservative governments reacted to the growing crisis of the capitalist system with orthodox policies of public expenditure cuts and deflation. Since 1979 right-wing Conservative governments have taken pride in their ideological attachment to the notion that the state should be smaller. They have been actively and on principle committed to making cuts in public services. J.K. Galbraith's description of 'public squalor and private affluence', made in respect of the United States in the 1960s, now applies with force to the situation in Britain.

The deteriorating situation of the British economy is, in turn, to some extent outside the control even of governments, given that they accept their role as the instruments of capitalism. Capitalist governments have found no way of preventing or curing the recurrent crises of capitalism and its lurches from boom to slump. Keynesian solutions, on which many pinned hopes after the disasters of the 1930s, have proved unworkable. In capitalism's current phase of crisis and depression, industries have disappeared and many thousands of urban jobs have gone with them. High unemployment in turn reduces government revenues and makes cuts in public spending appear inevitable. The increased international mobility of capital and the rapid expansion of international trade has diminished the power of national governments to influence events and has exacerbated the crisis for existing industries in the advanced capitalist countries, including Britain, which are subjected to new competition from sometimes low wage industries abroad.

Special programmes for inner cities, 1968-77

Nevertheless, over the years, governments have persisted in the notion that locally-based initiatives, designed specifically to address the problems of inner cities, can work. For the last thirty years or so, governments' main method of dealing with what they see as the problems of inner cities has been to create a proliferation of 'special programmes' for them, which scratch at the surface of the problem.

Some are administered through the local authorities, some by central government, and some by both of them together. With varying degrees of fanfare, a confusing succession of small, fragmented, special initiatives for inner cities are set up. From time to time, yet more programmes are adopted to 'coordinate' these initiatives. They have one thing in common. The sums of money involved are so small that they can make only marginal differences, for good or bad, to the people and problems they are supposed to address. The cuts in local authorities' 'main programmes' of spending, for example on housing, education, transport and waste collection, dwarf any sums spent on special programmes for the inner cities, even in terms of local spending alone. Governments, at least in their public presentations, claim that significant improvements can be achieved locally, even with such small resources, in the situation of the people of the inner cities. These claims are often underpinned by theories which state, explicitly or otherwise, that poverty is somehow the fault of those who are poor, rather than the consequence of the operations of capitalism or the national policies of governments. But, in spite of the hype with which ministers surround the introduction of each new initiative, they cannot seriously have believed that the level of resources provided was likely to make much difference to the situation of people faced with unemployment and de-industrialisation in the inner cities. The 'poverty programmes' can perhaps better be understood as an attempt to address not so much people's suffering, as the problems which this suffering might lead to. The people of inner cities are supposed to feel that governments are doing something for them, and thus to have their anger abated, while community leaders have their time and energies occupied by the scramble for crumbs. Seen in another light, the special programmes of urban spending amount to governments giving back a small part of what they take away, with strings attached (rather as they do in their aid programmes in the Third World).

Part of the rationale for this behaviour was also that, from the 1960s onwards, theories began to be developed that poverty was concentrated in small 'pockets of deprivation' or 'areas of special need'. Rather than merely receiving nationally-determined services with universal coverage, deemed adequate for the great majority of the population, these small especially deprived areas were to benefit from 'positive discrimination'. In the 1960s there was a flurry of government reports and research on the problems of inner cities. The Seebohm Report on social services and community development expressed 'concern at the increase in officially recorded delinquency' and emphasised 'the need to concentrate resources and a belief that preventative work with families was of cardinal importance in this context'; the Plowden Report on education advocated extra spending on primary schools in deprived areas; the Skeffington Report advocated increased public participation in planning and the appointment of community development officers. All called for special provision for inner cities. Then, from 1968 onwards, first under Labour and then from 1970-73 under the Conservatives, the phenomenon of government programmes set up specifically for inner cities took off. These programmes involved several different government departments, usually working with the local authorities. A publication produced in 1977 by the Community Development Programme (see below), entitled *Gilding The Ghetto: The State and the Poverty Experiments*, gives a brief history of these programmes, from which much of the following account and quotations are taken. First there was the Urban Aid Programme, set up by James Callaghan, then Home Secretary. Its purpose, he stated in Parliament on 2 December 1968, was:

'to provide for the care of our citizens who live in the poorest or most over-crowded parts of our cities and towns. It is intended to arrest, in so far as it is possible by financial means, and reverse the downward spiral which affects so many of these areas. There is a deadly quagmire of need and apathy.'

The programme, according to the first Urban Programme circular, was to concentrate on education, housing, health and welfare in 'areas of special need', which meant areas with poor housing, 'family sizes above the average', persistent unemployment, 'a high proportion of children in trouble or in need of care' and perhaps 'a substantial degree of immigrant settlement'. Responsibility for the Urban Programme was located in the Community Relations Department of the Home Office, the department which also dealt with the Community Relations Commission (set up to provide some services for new immigrants). The money, as in many of the programmes that followed, was not additional money, but money taken out of the general Rate Support Grant and set aside for the purpose, thus giving central government a new form of control over how local authorities spent their money. The sums were, in any case, not large: around £4 million a year. At roughly the same time the Department of Education and Science and the Social Science Research Council were setting up the Educational Priority Area (EPA) action-research projects. These were experimental schemes for 'positive discrimination' in schools and were set up in Deptford, Balsall

Heath/Sparkbrook (Birmingham), Conisborough/Denaby (West Riding), Liverpool 8 and Dundee. They cost £175,000 and resulted in a five volume report produced by A. H. Halsey at Oxford University.

In 1969 the Home Office set up the national Community Development Project, again with the object of concentrating on small pockets of deprivation, immigration and 'multiple deprivation', and with the additional goals of improving the coordination of the local delivery of services and encouraging participation of local communities in their activities. The Home Office's press release of 16 July 1969, announcing the setting up of the programme, stated that:

> 'This will be a neighbourhood-based experiment aimed at finding new ways of meeting the needs of people living in areas of high social deprivation, by bringing together the work of all the social services under the leadership of a special project team and also by tapping the resources of self help and mutual help which may exist among the people in the neighbourhoods.'

The Home Office document *Community Development Project — Objectives and Strategy*, also published in 1969, listed five assumptions on which the project was based. The first was that deprivation tended to be concentrated in 'particular areas, such as those suffering from urban or industrial decay'; the second that existing overall social services provision was not enough; the third, 'closely connected' assumption was that:

> 'there are immobilised or untapped welfare and "self-help" resources in communities; and, if ways could be found to release them through appropriate social action, they might have a dramatic effect, far greater than their apparent value, in reducing dependency on the statutory services.'

The fourth and fifth assumptions were that there were gaps in communication and knowledge. In its summary, the document reiterated that the general aim was:

> 'to create a more integrated community . . . and to take some of the load off the statutory services by generating a fund of voluntary social welfare and mutual help amongst the individuals, families and social groups in the neighbourhood, supported by the voluntary agencies.'

This emphasis on saving money through mobilising self help within communities was common to many of the programmes. For example when an adventure playground was set up, the expectation was that there would be a 'multiplier effect', and the parents of the children who used it would go on to organise other suitable community activities such

94

as summer coach trips, fundraising for a community centre and so on. Thus for example an *Urban Programme Circular No.6* of 6 December 1971 stated that 'the cooperation of parents in the running of the project can be of considerable importance in helping to foster the community spirit. The potential here is as yet largely untapped, and its value should not be underestimated'. By 'parents' they usually, of course, meant mothers.

There were twelve separate Community Development Projects, or CDPs, established first in Coventry, Liverpool, Southwark and Glyncorrg and then in Batley, Birmingham, Canning Town, Cumbria, Newcastle, Oldham, Paisley and Tynemouth. They were described as 'action-research' programmes, with the action funded 75 per cent by the Home Office and 25 per cent by the local authorities, and the research wholly funded by the Home Office and based on local universities and polytechnics. They were to operate for five years and cost approximately £5 million.

In 1971, after their victory in the 1970 election, the Conservatives set up a new department in the Home Office, the Community Programmes Department, to administer the Community Relations Commission and research projects relating to immigrants, Urban Aid and CDP. It launched the Neighbourhood Schemes, billed as a 'parallel and cross fertilising experiment' for CDP. The schemes were intended to concentrate relatively large amounts of money on small areas and to be concerned with physical rather than social planning, with less emphasis on participation by communities. Of the ten schemes proposed, only two were set up, in Liverpool and on Teeside. The £150,000 which was redirected from the Urban Aid budget was entirely for capital projects, mainly buildings. Soon afterwards the Department of the Environment announced what it called a 'total approach' scheme, the Six Towns Studies. Peter Walker, then Secretary of State for the Environment, stated in the budget debate in 1972 that:

'In our approach to the environment, we have endeavoured . . . to make a switch of resources to bad areas . . . I believe that the next most important step for any department is to bring about a total approach to the urban problem. In the past the attitude has been a series of fragmented decisions not properly co-ordinated . . .'

The first three of these studies, later renamed Urban Guidelines Studies, took place in Oldham, Rotherham and Sunderland. They were undertaken by private consultants and were mainly about coordination. The second half, now renamed Inner Area Studies, were in Small

Heath, Birmingham, Stockwell in South London, and Liverpool 8. They were also carried out by consultants but had a wider brief, were described as 'action-research projects' and in other ways resembled CDPs. The government clearly attached importance to them. By 1977 they had cost £1.3 million. At about the same time the Department of Health and Social Security and its Minister Sir Keith Joseph embarked on a seven year programme of Cycle of Poverty studies, to cost £½ million, to examine the theory that deprivation was transmitted through families from generation to generation, rather than a product of circumstances external to the deprived. In a speech to the Pre-School Playgroups Association in June 1972 Joseph asked:

'Why is it that, in spite of long periods of full employment and relative prosperity and the improvement of community services since the Second World War, deprivation and problems of maladjustment so conspicuously exist?'

In 1973 the Department of the Environment came up with a new idea, the Quality of Life Studies. These were set up in Stoke-on-Trent, Sunderland, Clwyd and Dumbarton, designed to last for two years, with a budget of around £1 million. They were to encourage self help, especially in the areas of culture and sport, and employed professional 'animators'.

The government then, as on several subsequent occasions, became concerned about the proliferation of schemes and possible duplication of effort. So it set up a new unit inside the Home Office, the Urban Deprivation Unit. This, according to Robert Carr, the Home Secretary, speaking in Parliament on 1 November 1973, would be:

'a unique piece of machinery . . . the key to providing a better life for those who live in the cities and . . . a way of improving community relations. Although the urban problem is not one which, in itself, centres on race, large numbers of our coloured citizens live in our older cities.'

In 1974 the Labour Party returned to government. After an initial statement by Alex Lyon, Minister of State in the Home Office under Roy Jenkins, that 'huge resources' would need to be diverted to 'areas of intense urban deprivation', the government reverted to 'pilot schemes' which were to cover whole local authority areas. These were called Comprehensive Community Programmes. They were to be based on the principle that self help or community schemes were not enough, and that local and central government resources must therefore be redirected to those most in need. The emphasis however was on the redirection of resources or their better organisation, rather than on any overall increase in resources. 'Trial runs' were to be set up in Gateshead, Wandsworth and the Wirral. Meanwhile the Home Office's Urban Deprivation Unit sponsored the setting up of the Greater London Council's Deprived Areas Project, based in Islington and Tower Hamlets. And the Department of the Environment announced Area Management Trials. *Gilding the Ghetto* says of these programmes that:

> 'Both are designed to find ways of managing urban problems more effectively, not by changing policy but by determining who or what services have highest priority. This is a far cry indeed from Seebohm's insistence that: "concentration upon priority areas is not in our view an alternative to extra resources — it assumes their existence".'

Taken together, this array of poverty programmes and schemes cost around £10 million a year. As *Gilding the Ghetto* puts it:

> 'Even Roy Jenkins who as Home Secretary was later to take charge of many of the poverty initiatives said in a book he wrote in 1972: "There is no simple remedy for poverty. But it could be massively attacked if we carry through certain policies . . . substantial spending *will be required* . . ." [his emphasis] . . . and he went on to recommend . . . an eightfold increase in spending on the urban programme. Yet nothing happened . . .'

Liverpool had more than its share of poverty programmes. Over the same period unemployment in Liverpool more than doubled. The studies produced by the various poverty initiatives usually pointed with insistence to the need for more spending on housing. The number of houses built in Liverpool, and the number of improvements carried out, declined steadily from year to year. As *Gilding the Ghetto* comments:

> 'The poverty initiatives then have clearly not made any great impact on inner-Liverpool's real material problems. All they have done is to restate, usually in academic terms, what the people who live there have known for a long time. If you live on Merseyside you have a better than average chance of being made redundant, being on the dole for a long time, living in slum conditions, being evicted, and forced to wait over six months for hospital treatment. Your children are more likely to die in infancy, or when, after getting no nursery schooling, they finally get to school, of being in larger classes in worse buildings, only to emerge finally onto the dole. Over 10,000 people leave Liverpool each year as a way of avoiding these problems. Those who are left can debate them in the neighbourhood councils and area

management experiments left behind by the "poverty projects". But, as they well know, talk is not going to make any impact on the worsening situation that faces them.'

One of the main products of these schemes was numerous written reports. Most of them were critical of the governments which sponsored them. In a strange quirk of the system, many of them were nevertheless published at the expense of these governments. For example the printing and publication, together with lavish illustrations, of *Gilding The Ghetto*, whose criticisms of the government and especially the Home Office were particularly explicit, were paid for by the Home Office. At the bottom of the last page, in very small print, there is a bit of an understatement: 'This report does not necessarily reflect the views of the Home Office or any of the local authorities'. Alex Lyon, Minister of State at the Home Office in the Labour government of the day, said in Parliament on 29 July 1974 that CDPs:

> 'are not a means for chanelling money into areas of need. They were designed to put teams of articulate young people into areas where the population, though deprived, was inarticulate, to help those people to express their own sense of grievance and to put pressure on the authority to do something about the situation.'

The problem was that the demands that the 'articulate young people' made were usually incompatible with the goals of governments, and could not be accommodated within the existing social and economic order.

Probably the great majority of their reports was highly critical, in particular, of governments' failure to mobilise more resources. Communities, most of the reports concurred, could not reasonably be expected to 'pull themselves up by their bootstraps', and any amount of reorganisation of local services was unlikely to make up for the basic problem of lack of resources, industrial decline and unemployment. Some of them concentrated on the latter problems, to the exclusion of the more narrowly 'social' concerns they were supposed to have. For example the Final Report No.2 of the Birmingham CDP, entitled *Workers on the Scrapheap*, consists of an analysis of the decline of industry and relatively well paid jobs in the area and justified this emphasis as follows:

> 'The arguments we are going to develop . . . connect the problems of Saltley and of the inner city with the problems of the British and international economy, instead of trying to deal with them separately as some special branch of social work.'

And it added:

'It is not a problem which can be solved by the residents of the area pulling themselves up by the bootstraps in an orgy of self-help and community associations.'

A report by the CDP Inter-Project Editorial Team, entitled *The Costs of Industrial Change*, described the issues as follows:

'The original brief of the Community Development Programme rested on some dubious assumptions. Poverty, bad housing and so on were, it implied, residual flaws in a society that had solved all its basic problems. There was also the 'blame the victim' element in the Programme's conception: poverty and deprivation were allegedly the fault of individuals, and 'deprived areas' places where there happened to be particular concentrations of people with the special characteristics that made them poverty-prone. The solutions then were supposed to lie in self-help by the poor.

'But far from coming up with cheap and easy solutions to poverty, the CDP's action and research work has led to a rejection of these framing assumptions. Having investigated the problems in detail and tried the self-help trail it became clear that the problems of these areas were firmly tied to much more basic structural problems in society and that the solution does not consist in the poor pulling themselves up by their bootstraps, but in sufficient political will being directed toward fundamental and far-reaching social change.'

The reports, like this one, often raised or hinted at questions about the nature of the existing political and economic system and its effects on inner city poverty. The Liverpool Inner Area Study, published in November 1974, comments as follows:

'A number of issues emerge from this description of inner area characteristics and the work carried out by Inner Area Studies. The chief one is the poverty and neglect of the area and its people in every sense. To a great extent this poverty is a reflection of inequalities in society as a whole. Clearly the scale and character of the problem is too great for policies concerned solely and specifically with inner cities to be effective. Any fundamental change must come through policies concerned with the distribution of wealth and the allocation of resources.'

Similar ideas were expressed in the CDPs' *Forward Plan for 1975/6*:

'Poverty is seen to be a consequence of fundamental inequalities in our present political and economic system, and the conditions which working class people experience are a consequence of these inequalities . . . To rectify this situation requires fundamental changes in the distribution of wealth and power . . . the development of working class action and pressure on the widest possible front . . .'

And 'senior members' of the research team of the Southwark CDP, Stephen Hatch, Enid Fox and Charles Legg, in a book entitled *Research and Reform: Southwark CDP 1969-1972* which was distributed by the Home Office's Urban Deprivation Unit in 1977, wrote as follows:

'the Home Office documents tended to diagnose deprivation as due to malfunctioning or inadequacy of services or people; hence the emphasis on integration, co-ordination and communication. However, the project . . . stressed involving the people living in the area in schemes flowing from their own perceptions of need . . . what if the people living in the area wanted changes that would involve more than improving the existing system? Or what if the cause of deprivation was seen as inequality, the product of a social structure that would not yield to action within the project area?'

Some of the many people engaged in the 'profession' of community work which flourished in the 1970s in different local authority departments or community development units had similar ideas. As one of them, Di Parkin, put it (in a personal comment on this chapter):

'I can remember working as a community worker for a social services department on a North Tottenham estate and feeling (as desperate, ground down, multiply oppressed women came into the project) what a con it was. I thought "What you need madam is the socialist revolution but I don't have it in the filing cabinet", so I gave them cups of coffee and somewhere to sit, someone to listen to them and it felt like trying to empty the sea with a leaking teaspoon. Maybe now I might see more that being someone who listened, was actually rather important.'

The writers of *Gilding the Ghetto* produce some hypotheses on what governments' expectations of the poverty programmes may in reality have been. They note that the state under capitalism has a dual role: it must ensure the profitability of private capital, and it 'has to deal with the consequences of the way that capital operates and ensure that the working class accept these consequences'. It must also ensure that capital has available to it a healthy workforce, able to reproduce itself. All of this implies spending on welfare. But from 1968 onwards the government felt compelled by balance of payments crises to make cuts in public expenditure. Therefore, as *Gilding the Ghetto* states:

'It was imperative for [the state] to act on the welfare problem but it had to do so in a way that wouldn't place any further burden on public spending. New forms and techniques had to be devised to carry out the state's old role . . . Seen in this light the poverty programme takes on a new logic.'

One of the government's acts in the 1970s was to increase public spending on 'law and order' by the Home Office. It was also the Home Office which initiated most of the early poverty programmes. This, said the authors of *Gilding the Ghetto*, was no coincidence and suggested that the programmes' rationale was closely related to the Home Office's main role, that of social control and the prevention of crime. The report's title was in fact taken from a remark at a conference in 1969 made by a Home Office official, Miss Cooper, who is reported to have said:

'there appeared to be an element of looking for a new method of social control — what one might call an antivalue, rather than a value. "Gilding the ghetto" or buying time, was clearly a component in the planning of CDP . . .'

Already in the 1960s governments were worried by the 'breakdown of the family' and the loss of social control which this implied; the Ingleby Report, for example (entitled *Children, Family and the Young Offender* and published in 1965) states that:

'The causes of delinquency are complex, and too little is known about them with certainty. It is at least clear that much delinquency — and indeed many other social problems — can be traced back to the inadequacy or breakdown in the family. The right place to begin, therefore, is with the family.'

Communities, on the other hand, might provide a method of securing law-abiding behaviour which could substitute for the family. Thus the CDPs, according to *Gilding the Ghetto*, were intended to 'use the "community" as a focus for mobilising informal social control mechanisms, rather than the individual or the family in isolation'. There was a belief that: 'Small amounts of money spent on family and community support might prevent much larger sums being wasted later on extra police and new prisons'. The CDP activists were approached by 'the local constabulary', who were however quickly rebuffed. In addition, the presence of black immigrants was considered a danger; as Alex Lyon stated in Parliament on 29 July 1974:

'The problem is complicated by the fact that a great many of those who suffer in these areas of deprivation are black and immigrant and, therefore, add to the deprivation felt by the indigenous population of these areas. They add newness, inadequacy of language and the cultural differences which go to make up racial discrimination within our inner cities.'

The government was also aware of the possibility that inner city riots of the type that had occurred in the United States, for example in Watts in Los Angeles, might also occur in Britain. Its main, and misguided, response to the perceived threat of racial violence was to restrict immigration (see above). But it also adopted some limited initiatives to legislate against discrimination, it set up the Community Relations Commission and the local community relations councils, and its poverty initiatives usually contained projects such as language centres, hostels for Caribbeans, and play-schemes for both black and white children. Thus, says *Gilding The Ghetto*, 'While the main emphasis went on keeping more blacks out of the country the home situation was being kept in hand', and:

'It is clear that the Home Office involvement in the Urban Deprivation Programme reflects much more than concern for the welfare of the poor in this country. For the state, urban poverty means crime, juvenile delinquency, and in cities with large immigrant communities, potential race riots. The Home Office programmes represented to a large extent an attempt to breathe new life into the crumbling institutions of the family and the community in order to mobilise cheap, informal social control mechanisms. If the development of "community identity", "self respect", "parental authority" and "self-help" could not stem the tide of vandalism and racism, the traditional law enforcement agencies, the police and the courts, would have to solve the problem. But it would be at much greater cost and would also represent a set-back for the governing idea that Britain can remain an orderly, self-disciplined society, free of violence, discrimination and crime without fundamental changes to the existing economic structure.'

The government's hope was, as Derek Morrell, the Home Office official mainly responsible for CDP put it at a meeting to discuss setting up the Coventry project, that the CDPs would 'help the people of Hillfields to frame realistic aspirations and enable them to obtain the means to realise them'. Working class people had to be convinced that their problems were not the inevitable result of their class situation and the requirements of capital but of other things which they themselves ought to take responsibility for, and that therefore they should make 'realistic' proposals for reform, rather than more radical demands. *Gilding The Ghetto* comments:

> 'The theories current at the time centred on the notion of the "culture of poverty", the idea that people inherited poverty, not because they were victims of the process of industrial decline but because there was something about them, their lifestyle, their values, that made them unable to take advantage of the opportunities available to them.'

A Home Office press release of 16 July 1969 pronounced that people suffered from 'ill health — financial difficulties — children suffering from deprivation — inability of the children to adjust to adult life — unstable marriages — emotional problems — ill-health and the cycle begins again'. Deprivation, according to such views, is transmitted like some hereditary disease; whole areas are infected by it. Nowhere in any of the Home Office's official statements was there any mention of industrial decline and unemployment. The indicators of success set for the CDPs were improved family functioning, personal care, childrearing practices, education and support for young children; increased incomes were not among them. As *Gilding the Ghetto* puts it, the Home Office apparently wished to promulgate the belief that: 'The people themselves are to blame for the problems caused by capital': 'in the final analysis the "deprivation initiatives" were not about eradicating poverty at all, but about managing poor people'.

In the CDPs and other such programmes, academic sociologists were enlisted to provide the justifications for these ideas, expected to measure and analyse the 'cycle of deprivation' and 'social pathology', and to prescribe solutions which could be accommodated within the prevailing social and economic order (rather as economists had already been successfully enlisted to devise acceptable prescriptions for the functioning of the capitalist economy). They were to be assisted in this task by the notion, embodied in the designation of numerous disparate, small areas as 'pockets of special deprivation', that the problem was a problem of a minority and could be solved in isolation. The majority of the working class population was thus deemed to have no problems, and certainly no problems which they might share, and unite in struggling against, with these isolated deprived people in small pockets of the inner cities. However the sociologists who were hired for the poverty programmes mostly failed to meet the expectations governments had of them. The 'absurdity of the pathology model', say the writers of *Gilding the Ghetto*, was 'implicitly or explicitly rejected by the staffs of all the EPAs, CDPs and Inner Area Studies'. Many of them saw the issue as one of struggle between social democracy and revolutionary socialism. They refused to accept that the former had solutions for the problems of inner cities and industrial decline. Eventually the CDPs were closed down; the last local projects closed in 1978. The experience ended in disarray, having not only done little or nothing to improve the situation of people in inner cities, but having also failed to meet some other parts of the largely hidden agenda of the governments which promoted the poverty programmes.

The 1977 White Paper

By the mid 1970s both the Labour government and the Conservative opposition were showing signs of learning from at least some of the comments made in reports by the CDPs and Inner Area Studies. Statements by ministers referred to the effects of the national economy and industrial decline on cities. For example the Labour Secretary of State for the Environment, Peter Shore, referring to 'inner area decline', stated in Parliament on 17 September 1976 that:

> 'The causes lie primarily in their relative economic decline, in a major migration of people, often the most skilled, and in a massive reduction in the number of jobs which are left . . .
>
> 'Just as we are all now aware that the future of the nation is inextricably bound up with the fortunes of our manufacturing industries, so too is the future — and the wealth — of the inner areas. We shall need to see what can be done to stem the tide of manufacturing jobs moving out, and the possibility of reversing it.'

These concerns culminated in the Labour government's 1977 White Paper *Policy for the Inner Cities*, which formed the basis for the Inner Urban Areas Act of 1978. This was a broader programme which included economic and environmental as well as (continuing) social objectives, and talked about the causes of economic decline and the need for jobs. The Act provided powers for local authorities designated by the Secretary of State for the Environment to give grants and loans for land, property and environmental improvements. The introduction to the White Paper stated that it 'owes a great deal to the studies and experiments of recent years', which it lists, including 'above all the three Inner Area Studies'. It began by setting out the 'problem': 'Many of the inner areas surrounding the centres of our cities suffer, in a marked way and to an unacceptable extent, from economic decline, physical decay and adverse social conditions'. It argued that the economic decline of cities had to be reversed and that it was necessary to 'reduce, and possibly in some cases to end, the loss of people and jobs from the cities as a whole and the inner cities in particular': 'This means making the cities more attractive for employers and more attractive for people to live and work in'. Among the measures proposed was an improvement in housing, including new building for private ownership to change the housing 'mix'. Responsibility for the Urban Programme was transferred from the Home Office to the Department of the Environment and the Welsh Office, although the Home Office was to remain responsible for race relations. The White Paper expressed the hope that policy would be adopted in a unified manner and on an area basis, building on the results achieved by the Comprehensive Community Programmes. The government considered and rejected the idea of using 'new town style development corporations to tackle inner areas', preferring instead to rely on local authorities which were 'democratically accountable bodies'. It said that the latter would need to work in partnership with central government and voluntary bodies and, reverting to the idea that the inhabitants of inner cities should pull themselves up by their bootstraps, that: 'Involving local people is both a necessary means to the regeneration of the inner areas and an end in its own right . . . Self help is important and so is community effort'.

The White Paper also enunciated the policies which were to dominate the politics of urban renewal from then onwards: local authorities must become 'entrepreneurial' and should 'stimulate investment by the private sector'. Existing firms and businesses were to be 'preserved', and new ones were to be encouraged 'by making available suitable cheap premises or sites for small businesses'. The local authorities were enjoined to 'administer all their powers, including those for housing, planning and the environment, so as to facilitate the growth of employment in inner areas'. In addition, the White Paper states, they were to be given new powers to:

'(a) make loans to firms on commercial terms of up to 90 per cent for land purchase and for the erection or improvement of industrial buildings — whether or not the authority owns the land or buildings;

'(b) establish Industrial Improvement Areas where local authorities can carry out, or assist owners to carry out, the conversion of buildings to create new employment, improvements to access and improvements to amenities;

'(c) provide in the partnership areas an initial rent-free period in the letting of factories; and '(d) give help in the partnership areas with the high cost of site preparation for industry in inner area locations.'

The Urban Programme was therefore extended to cover industrial, environmental and recreational provision as well as social projects. Its funding was quadrupled, from under £30 million a year to £125 million a year in 1979/80. The White Paper stated that the funds must not be spread too thinly and proposed therefore to offer 'special partnerships to a strictly limited number of authorities'. It argued that these should be in 'the big cities' because they had lost population and jobs to a greater extent than elsewhere, and because they had suffered big and disruptive changes in their physical fabric, for example through slum clearance. The White Paper therefore announced that partnerships would be offered to Liverpool, Birmingham, Manchester/Salford, Lambeth in London and 'the Docklands authorities who are ready to start a major programme of urban renewal for the Docklands area'. In addition, there were to be Inner Area Programmes, which were expected to devise overall policies for their areas and to redirect existing resources to those most in need, although they might hope subsequently to receive some 'special assistance'. The list was subsequently extended to include, in descending order of priority and available powers, seven 'Partnership' areas, 15 'programme' authorities, and 19 'other districts'. In Partnership areas, committees or 'Partnerships' were set up, with representatives of local and central government, the health authorities, the police, the private sector, voluntary groups and others. The Partnerships had no executive power. They were based on the hope that people working for these various organisations could involve the local community and devise an agreed strategy for parts of urban Britain. Consensus and cooperation would ensure success. This assumption turned out to be optimistic.

The new recognition that the suffering of inner cities was linked to industrial decline and job losses came at a time when there was little public money available to do anything about it. The spending on special programmes for inner cities, although much increased, was still small in relation to the problems. It was usually cancelled out, and often exceeded, by the cuts being made in public expenditure overall, even in the areas which were to benefit from 'positive discrimination' (see also below). There was little direct spending to create permanent and productive jobs in the public sector. Instead, there was heavy reliance on the attraction of private investment through public funding for the rehabilitation of premises and the provision of buildings and infrastructure. A central goal of the policy was thus to cause private industry, through bribes and subsidies, to invest in one place rather than another. There were many similarities between this policy and previous attempts to redirect industries through regional policies and Industrial Development Certificates, with the difference that this time the redirection was intended to be into rather than out of existing large urban areas. These regional policies had had limited effect, often subsidising moves which capital would have made anyway. The new incentives likewise did little to determine the locational decisions of large firms, although they may have affected the decisions of smaller firms at the margin. And they could not increase the total amount of private investment in the British economy, since this is determined primarily by the government's macro-economic policies.

A book by Aram Eisenschitz and Jamie Gough, entitled *The Politics of Local Economic Policy* (which refers mainly to the consensus politics of the late 1980s but is nevertheless relevant to the general question of local policies to attract private investment) points to the 'zero-sum' nature of many local economic initiatives. These may, at most, poach investment from elsewhere. Even when, as was the case with the left Labour-led Greater London Council in the early 1980s, such initiatives eschew the attraction of inward investment, the promotion of local firms may nevertheless displace others. The justification for the process might be that discrimination is reversed. But this is seldom clear. The displaced employment may be within the same area, outside the area but held by local people, held by local people who are *more* deprived, or in other *more* deprived areas. When the firms promoted are what Eisenschitz and Gough call 'Bootstraps' type firms — community businesses, cooperatives or small start-ups — the effect may be worse: good working conditions are replaced by bad ones, and by self-exploitation. The competition between localities may lead to the over-provision of expensive infrastructure; new roads, housing, schools may need to be built to accommodate the new workforce and traffic, or may even be built in advance, in the desperate attempt to attract firms. The fact that there is competition at all may mean that the areas needing most get least. To the extent that the competitive bidding has an effect, it is liable to mean that the authorities which can afford to spend most on advertising and public relations, and are therefore likely to be those least in need, get most from the limited private investment pool.

In addition, subsidies were paid by the state to private enterprise through a succession of national bodies: the Conservative-created National Economic Development Council and National Economic Development Office (NEDC and NEDO), the Labour government's 1965 National Plan, the Industrial Reorganisation Corporation set up in 1966, the strengthened NEDC and the National Enterprise Board (NEB) in the 1970s. These various forms of intervention and subsidy did not entail any significant increase in the state's ability to control the movements of private capital, either into or out of cities. When the Labour government took office in 1974 it had proposed more powerful forms of public control over the behaviour of capital, recognising that previous policies had had little effect on the anarchic decision-making processes of the private sector. Its manifesto had promised 'an irreversible shift of power towards working people'. It contained proposals to nationalise key companies in each manufacturing sector in order to set standards of 'social responsibility' for other companies to follow, to be backed up by 'planning agreements' with the remaining companies to ensure that priorities were met; to set up a new National Enterprise Board to provide financial assistance, establish public enterprises and enforce the planning agreements between government, unions and employers; and to give trade unions the right to have information on the forward strategies of large companies. These proposals might have given the government some control over the restructuring of capital and its ability to abandon communities at will. But they came to nothing. Tony Benn, who had been the only Labour minister to make any real attempt to implement them, was shifted out of the Department of Industry. Planning agreements were made voluntary. The subsequent 'voluntary' planning frameworks agreed with a few firms, most notoriously the £64 million planning agreement with Chrysler which failed to stop Chrysler selling the company to Peugeot in 1978, were generally flouted. The NEB's powers to purchase shares in companies were not compulsory and were strictly limited by the need to obtain the consent of the Secretary of State for Industry and by a low level of funding. The NEB's role became primarily one of promoting industrial efficiency and profitability and assisting in the reorganisation of industry; it 'was transformed', as Huw Beynon and Hilary Wainwright put it in *The Workers' Report on Vickers*, 'into an instrument for carrying out rationalisations which private capital did not have the strength to impose'. During Benn's time as minister he also provided some support for the shop stewards' combine committee at Lucas Aerospace; these stewards struggled to persuade the company to adopt alternative plans to make socially useful products, for which they believed there was a market, rather than close plants on the grounds that the market for their military products was absent; but Benn's successors failed to support them (this experience was described in detail in a book by Hilary Wainwright and Dave Elliott entitled *The Lucas Plan: A New Trade Unionism in the Making?*). The private sector and its representatives in the Confederation of British Industry were, as always, vociferously opposed to any public or workers' control over profitable companies (as opposed to the nationalisation of loss-making industries essential to private profitability). The NEB was unacceptable to the Conservatives even with its limited and largely negative role, and they abolished it after they took office in 1979.

Nevertheless both Labour and subsequent Conservative governments persisted with the idea of attracting the private sector to invest in particular areas. And at a local level some of the more left-wing Labour-controlled local authorities, especially in the period from the late 1970s to the mid 1980s, attempted to take up the more radical versions of these ideas, including those initially promulgated by the 1974 Labour government. The Lucas Aerospace experience in particular had a powerful effect on parts of the left and on the politics of some Labour local authorities.

The Greater London Council

The Greater London Council was the most prominent of these. In 1981 a left-wing group of councillors, led by Ken Livingstone, obtained majority control of this metropolitan council. They retained this control until the GLC was abolished by the Thatcher government in March 1986. The GLC represented, in a sense, the last flicker of revolutionary left politics before the long dark night of Thatcherism and the triumph of the ideology of the market eclipsed them, for the time being. They were exhilarating times for the left which, possibly for the first time, controlled a substantial section of the state, with large resources at its disposal. The previously remote and secluded corridors and grandiose chambers of County Hall were taken over and opened up. They were occupied by a heady mixture of Trotskyists, Stalinists, anarchists, trade unionists, community, women's movement and black activists, left academics, and subversives of various types. Some of these were recruited as 'officers' in the GLC, some were people with whom these new officers were working, some were spectators. Much of the GLC's activity was flamboyant; its new officers had a gift for publicity and dramatisation and they produced a newspaper and glossy publications and ran festivals, the last of which had an attendance of a quarter of a million people. In deliberate provocation, the Council set up a huge sign on County Hall, opposite the House of Commons, displaying the latest unemployment figures. The GLC was much disliked by the government. As Norman Tebbitt, then a member of the Conservative cabinet, explained in March 1984:

> 'The Greater London Council is typical of new modern divisive socialism. It must be defeated. So we shall abolish the Greater London Council.'

Years later, in a broadcast on *London News* on 15 January 1996, Lord Howe, former deputy prime minister, expressed his 'sadness' about the abolition of the GLC, stating that:

> 'It's a consequence of the battle that we had to fight with loony left socialism in a number of the key cities of the country.'

But the GLC was popular with Londoners. At the mid-term elections its majority increased, dashing presumably the hopes of the government that the GLC might wither away without forcing the government into the embarrassing situation of abolishing an elected authority.

The new GLC administration's very detailed manifesto centred on economic policy; 71 of its 157 pages were devoted to industry and employment. The manifesto promised that the GLC would use its various powers both to create jobs in London and to improve working conditions. The GLC publication *The London Industrial Strategy*, in a foreward written by Michael Ward, chair of the Industry and Employment Committee, starts off, in reference to the Conservative government's 'monetarist' economic policies, as follows:

> 'When the history of Britain's experiment with monetarism comes to be written, the contrast between unmet needs and vast human and financial waste will be the theme.
>
> 'The financial waste of London's unemployment is now two and a half billion pounds a year in benefits and lost taxation alone. To include the value of lost output, this figure could be more than doubled.
>
> 'The human waste is the loss of precious skills of our unemployed engineers, builders, carers and curers. It is also the waste of those who have never worked and may never do so.
>
> 'The needs confront us every day: housing and hospital waiting lists

increasing; roads, bridges and sewers crumbling; poverty and decay.

'Our strategy is to use wasted resources to meet needs. Elected, publicly accountable authorities must intervene to replace the anarchy of the market economy with justice and fairness. London now has the worst concentration of unemployment in the developed world: we need planning to bring jobs and prosperity.'

The GLC also promised to pursue its objective of creating useful jobs with the participation of working people and to strengthen their control over resources and policy. As the manifesto put it:

'We shall set out to increase the element of democratic control over industrial decisions: control by elected authorities and control by working people in their workplaces.'

The GLC had resources which were larger than those of any other local authority, but nevertheless small in relation to the problems. It had a revenue budget of £800 million a year. It had lost much of its housing stock and some of its powers; its remaining statutory spending responsibilities were concentrated on transport, the fire brigade, waste disposal and the arts and recreation; it also had staff working on land and planning issues and scientific and other services. The manifesto proposed to graft economic policy onto these other functions partly by using the '2p rate', the additional amount which councils were allowed to raise for general purposes, under Section 137 of the 1972 Local Government Act. It undertook to set up a separate, 'arms length' organisation, the Greater London Enterprise Board (GLEB) with powers to invest in the private sector; to improve conditions within the Council; and to use the GLC's purchasing and grant giving powers and its pension funds to intervene in the economy of London. The funds raised through the 2p rate were used mainly for industrial investment through the GLEB; GLEB received an annual allocation of £30 million out of the £38 million raised in this way. A new unit of economists, the Economic Policy Group, was set up.

The GLC, of course, set itself an impossible task. Socialism in one town was likely to be even harder to achieve than socialism in one country. Much of what the GLC did was intended to serve as an experiment, a model on which the Labour government which was confidently expected to win the next election could build. The GLC produced some impressive rhetoric, as well as some reality. It claimed that it would operate 'in and against the market': it would invest in the

111

private sector and also attempt to change it. Its goal was 'the restructuring of industry in the interests of labour' rather than of capital, in other words both to make industry more profitable so as to retain jobs, and to secure improvements in the nature of those jobs. Its new economists and others, once they were recruited, developed what were called 'sector plans' for parts of London's industry and economy, for the clothing and print industries, for the food industry, for offices, for furniture, the docks, retailing, cultural industries, domestic work and childcare, homeworking, health care and so on; most of these plans, together with ten-point recommendations and estimates of potential job creation, were published in *The London Industrial Strategy* in 1985.

The sector plans were intended, in part, to determine the policies of GLEB. GLEB operated with a multiplicity of different and often conflicting goals. It had to secure the survival of the firms it invested in, it was supposed to promote production for need rather than merely for profit, and it was supposed to strengthen trade unions, improve working conditions, increase the control of the workforce over management decisions through exemplary forms of industrial democracy, and promote equal opportunities. The last of these objectives, for example, could potentially conflict with all of the others: not only could it impose costs on the firm as a whole, but it might have to be enforced against the wishes of the existing workforce (as did occasionally happen). In practice of course the first objective, that of ensuring the survival of firms, had to dominate. And GLEB was not very successful even in this objective. As was the usual problem in such attempts at partial public control under capitalism, GLEB had no powers of compulsory acquisition. The management of successful companies was unlikely to be interested in the relatively small sums of money available from GLEB, especially since these came with strings, and in any case would have been in a strong position to resist such strings. The intention that GLEB should invest only in large or medium firms was, again, thwarted by its small resources and also by the lack of strongly unionised medium-sized firms in London. It ended up investing overwhelmingly in very small firms; in 1985 little more than a dozen projects, out of a total of around 200, had more than 20 employees, and the largest had only 200. These firms, were, in addition, precarious. Often the firms and in particular the trade unionists who approached GLEB were threatened by closures; several of GLEB's firms were bought from the receivers. Their managers were usually incompetent, often also hostile to the objectives of GLEB, and sometimes dishonest (to the surprise of some of the less worldly-wise of the GLC's and GLEB's officers). GLEB nevertheless continued to try to work with managers who the workforce well knew could not be trusted, partly because it had extreme difficulty in finding adequate replacements for them. Both in GLEB and in the firms that it funded there was a serious shortage of 'red experts', willing or able to work 'in and against the market'. By 1985 GLEB had virtually full ownership of around half of its larger projects; a further quarter of them were cooperatives. Thus the idea that GLEB, by investing small sums in a large number of firms, could spread its influence more widely and effectively than if, for example, the GLC had adopted a policy of setting up wholly-owned municipal enterprises, was largely negated. In addition GLEB was unwilling to make investments large enough to secure the survival of these firms. Especially after responsibility for GLEB was taken over by the boroughs in 1986, many of them collapsed.

In any case securing the survival of some firms was not enough, in the thinking of the GLC, to justify its activities. In the chapter on 'Industrial Democracy: the GLEB experience' in *A Taste of Power* (an attempt at self-appraisal, which drew on the experiences of those who were subjected to the attentions of the GLC and was written by its former officers after the GLC was abolished), we argued that:

'Industrial democracy is central to the purpose of GLEB. Although much emphasis has been put on the objective of creating jobs, it could be argued that, in a recession and without increases in overall demand, jobs created or saved by GLEB will be at the expense of jobs elsewhere. The justification for GLEB's existence must primarily be that the jobs it creates and saves are better than jobs elsewhere and, perhaps, that jobs in certain parts of London are disappearing at a catastrophic rate and at a high social cost. An important part of this justification is that they provide an experience of workers' control.'

The intention was that workers' control should be built on strong trade unions and in particular that trade unions should extend their control over company decision-making. Reflecting the original ideas of the 1974 Labour government, the GLC's 1981 manifesto had stated that:

'Any intervention by GLEB in respect of its investment functions would be conditional on three-way talks, leading to agreement, between GLEB, the enterprise and the unions concerned covering in particular future patterns of employment and investment in the enterprise. Such local Planning Agreements would form part of the London Industrial Strategy.'

'Enterprise planning', as these agreements came to be called, was supposed to grow out of trade union organisation, as an extension of collective bargaining. As we wrote in *A Taste of Power*:

> 'It was hoped that trade unionists confronted by threats of closures and redundancies would, as the Lucas Aerospace workers had done, move from defensive trade union positions to proposing alternative production plans for saving jobs, meeting social needs and introducing new technologies under trade union control. These plans could then be supported by GLEB.'

However, in spite of much rhetorical assertion, the plans did not work out as intended:

> 'Except in a few cases, and then only in a limited way, the original idea did not bear fruit. The idea of democratically determined enterprise plans rapidly lost its central position in GLEB's practice and theory. Few enterprise plans, in the sense of fully worked out business plans based on the involvement of the workforce, exist; those that do tend to bear little relation to reality. Instead, GLEB came to emphasise the idea that enterprise planning is a process, which involves the progressive extension of trade unionists' control over economic decisions.'

Some GLEB officers and managers of GLEB firms did make considerable efforts to engage the workforce in management decision-making. In some cases they did so because they believed that this was actually a good way of managing and securing the survival of firms. GLEB and GLC publications contained a great deal of rhetoric about 'tapping the gold in workers' minds' and argued that the workers were those most capable of understanding production processes and how to improve them. GLEB did also, on occasion, strengthen and sometimes create trade unions in the firms that it invested in. This attitude was not consistent. In one case in particular GLEB management, and GLEB-appointed managers, rode roughshod over the trade unions and imposed redundancies with minimal consultation with either the workforce or their trade union representatives. In other cases, partly because of the nature of the London economy, GLEB invested in firms in which there were no trade unions, but it then struggled, often successfully and against the opposition of obstructive management, to introduce and then support them. In some cases the intervention of GLEB officers strengthened the position of existing trade unions. In a few cases they did succeed in extending the role of trade unions and their involvement in decision-making; this was generally more successful than GLEB's other methods of trying to extend workforce control, such as the appointment of worker directors on company boards. GLEB also supported a number of cooperatives, in which the role of trade unions was limited, although again, in at least one of these, GLEB intervention secured the establishment of a trade union where it did not exist before.

The objective of improving working conditions was similarly made hard by the nature of the firms that GLEB invested in. In some of the firms there were improvements, but in others workers took cuts in real wages, accepted more flexibility, agreed to the loss of over-time and/or worked harder. They did so because they wanted to keep their jobs, but also to some extent because the involvement of workers and their trade unions in management decision-making led them to identify with the problems of their firm. This is an outcome which many workers and trade unionists fear. When the GLC and GLEB talked about 'tapping the gold in workers' minds', they were using language similar to that used by Japanese managers and those who try to emulate them, and which basically means that employers want to exploit workers even more intensively than is achieved by more traditional management methods: to have the full use, not just of the workers' hands, but of their minds as well. Nevertheless there was a difference between what was happening in GLEB's case and the situation in which private management promotes workers' involvement to enlist their cooperation, since in most cases the gains were not being privately appropriated, or not to the same extent. Mainly for this reason, unions such as the AUEW and SOGAT actively supported GLEB's involvement. Particularly in some GLEB-supported cooperatives, there was a strong desire to ensure that trade unions existed and were strengthened in order to defend the interest of the workforce against pressures for greater productivity and self-exploitation. But there remained the concern that, as is classically the case in cooperatives, workers in GLEB-funded firms were open to such pressures simply because they had begun to identify with, and appreciate, the new more democratic structures of their firms. As *A Taste of Power* comments, 'Much the same issues would arise under socialism'.

There was undoubtedly a considerable extension of workers' involvement in decision-making processes in GLEB-funded firms. Particularly in order to make this effective in matters such as finance and accounts, future marketing strategies, new equipment and so on, there was a need for more training and more time. Although there was also, at times, some lack of interest on the part of workers, there was enough evidence that workers and their trade unions welcomed the opportunities provided by an expansion of democracy in the workplace to make many people feel that the experiment was worthwhile, and that it was a considerable loss that it was cut short by the abolition of the GLC. In *A Taste of Power* we offered the following overall justification for the experiments in industrial democracy conducted by GLEB:

> 'Any process of building socialism must involve the democratic control of the economy by the working class. The extension of democratic control within the workplace will be part of this process. It is unlikely to take place overnight. It is therefore important for workers and the labour movement in general to gain experience about the problems of running industry in advance of any radical changes of ownership, and GLEB has made a contribution to this experience.'

In its other areas of activity the GLC displayed the same concern, not always adequately met, that the trade unions, the workforce and the public should be involved in policy. In transport, one of the GLC's main areas of statutory responsibility, it attempted to work with trade unions as well as the management of London Transport to provide an expanded and better service. Its 'Fares Fair' policy, which involved big cuts in fares, was extremely popular and led to a considerable increase in the use of public transport. When the government disallowed this fares policy, public transport use dropped again; eventually the government took control of public transport from the GLC, thus contributing perhaps to the now widespread dissatisfaction with the state of public transport in London and its lack of strategic direction. In public services such as health provision, the GLC was critical of the lack of control by the users of the services and advocated more democratic structures. Its Popular Planning Unit supported a People's Plan for the Docks, drawn up by GLC officers and local community groups, which advocated totally different uses for the abandoned docks than the ones which eventually took over (see below). Recognising that the fate of many of London's workers was linked to the outcome of struggles elsewhere, the GLC supported and funded attempts to make it possible for trade unions to cooperate across frontiers, in the film-processing industry and the motor industry for example.

The GLC's commitment to the ideas of democracy, control of policy-making by Londoners and open government did however raise dilemmas. As the introduction to *A Taste of Power* puts it:

'The manifesto commitment to economic democracy was extremely vague about who was to be involved and how. A lot of questions immediately emerged, and were answered in practice, unsystematically and in a hurry. For example, which parts of the community were to be involved in policy making, since one cannot involve seven million people individually? How, most seriously, were those people who were the least organised, with the least power, to be involved? How was people's control over their working lives to be increased, and did this imply the transfer of resources to groups in the community and the unions? If so, what happened if those groups used resources in ways which went against Council policy? What sort of commitments should be asked for in return for these resources? Should the GLC officers work with shop stewards and trade union activists, or only with trade union officials?'

The GLC's officers struggled with these questions; the outcomes of some of these struggles are related in *A Taste of Power*. In an attempt to de-centralise control, it made grants to a large number of community, women's, black, national and international trade union, refugee and other organisations and movements which, as the preface to *A Taste of Power* puts it, were 'outside conventional party politics'. These grants, while usually welcome, were also sometimes criticised for creating dependency and in some cases for the interference which GLC support brought with it, for example in its promotion of equal opportunities policies. A large number of these organisations failed to survive the abolition of the GLC. Some took this as an indication of their lack of grass roots support. This was perhaps unfair, since the reason for GLC support in the first place had to do with the lack of access to resources of those with 'the least power' in capitalist society, and this was what the GLC set out, however unevenly, to remedy. The GLC's support for these and other causes was, moreover, considered threatening by the government. It provided an alternative model in the capital city which was dangerously attractive to many of the people who suffered under capitalism.

From 1985 onwards the GLC was preoccupied by a long campaign to save itself from abolition. Its campaign was conducted mainly in the media and through established political and legal channels. The GLC had for a time high hopes of the House of Lords, which appeared ready to condemn its abolition as unconstitutional and anti-democratic. Livingstone lost the support of much of the left with his insistence that the struggle should be conducted on these levels and his opposition to any activist resistance to abolition, such as strikes, occupations and refusal to cooperate with government plans, which might have disrupted the hand-over of control and made the GLC, rather than the government, open to accusations of causing chaos in London government. Attempts by its officers to organise active opposition to abolition foundered in disunity. When the GLC was finally abolished, with the other metropolitan authorities, in March 1986, it went out with a whimper, in a state of anger and demoralisation. Its partial successor, the London Strategic Policy Unit, set up and funded by the London boroughs in theory to keep its ideas alive until the next Labour government re-established a central strategic authority for London, accomplished little. Many of its officers are now dispersed among local authorities, struggling to survive in the disillusion, cynicism, 'new realism' and adaptation to cuts which now pervades these places. The other metropolitan authorities were abolished at the same time as the GLC. They had adopted, in a variety of ways, some similar policies. In Sheffield, which had had solid Labour administrations for many years, the metropolitan council, also now abolished, did not go down the GLEB road but attempted to promote economic development and democracy directly through the council itself. In the West Midlands, on the other hand, the also abolished metropolitan authority set up the West Midlands Enterprise Board which had a more commercial orientation, and less commitment to goals such as workers' control.

The GLC's socialist, radical and democratically-orientated policies won public support and admiration to a remarkable extent. With the abolition of the metropolitan authorities, some of their functions were taken over by government-appointed bodies or Quangos. Others passed to local borough councils. With few exceptions, these local councils were much less capable of carrying out left-wing policies in ways which were effective and popular, or indeed left-wing at all. In particular, their support for economic development was even more constrained by lack of funding than the GLC's. It appeared inevitable that these local councils could support only small businesses. This support was generally speaking a caricature of what a socialist local economic policy might be. Small sums of money were given out to firms with usually minimal attempt to ascertain whether the firms were unionised or what their conditions were like, let alone any persistent attempt to improve them or to insist on trade union rights, equal opportunities policies or any other improvements for the workforce. For example in 1987 the London Strategic Policy Unit produced a report, *Sewing Up The Pieces: Local Authority Strategies for The Clothing Industry*, requested by the London boroughs which funded it. The research showed that, especially in the boroughs of Hackney and Tower Hamlets which funded large numbers of small clothing firms, council officers knew little and did less about working conditions in these firms, many of which in any case went bust. Small grants from councils sometimes merely enabled one firm to lower its prices and put another one down the road out of business. Less than a handful of larger firms, mostly in Islington and Haringey, allowed trade union access let alone membership; in most London clothing firms joining a trade union led to the sack. Conditions, of course, were bad. Sometimes councils claimed that their support of such firms was justified by the fact that they were 'ethnic businesses'. This usually meant that they were supporting the severe exploitation of black workers by other members of their own community.

Other policies of a more radical nature, such as the declaration of nuclear free zones or the promotion of rights for women, black people and gays and lesbians, tended to be tokenistic and ritualistic and do little more than expose the councils to scurrilous attacks in the gutter press.

Conservative governments and the erosion of local control

Mrs Thatcher, when she won elections for the third time in 1987, announced in her triumph that 'The inner cities' would be 'next'. Perhaps she believed that, like the GLC, they could simply be abolished; a blot on the face of Conservative free enterprise Britain which had to go. The Thatcher attack on the inner cities and all that they stood for in fact began soon after she first took office. The Conservatives embarked on a process of centralisation of power and erosion of local accountability. Not only did they abolish the metropolitan authorities, they also attacked the funding and independence of local authorities in general. Their intention was both to cut public spending and to undermine the influence of Labour-controlled authorities, many of which are in inner city areas and have suffered particularly severe cuts. Although spending on special schemes for inner city areas continued, local authorities have to put in bids for it rather than receiving the money as of right. The amounts spent in this way have been exceeded many times over by the amounts withdrawn from councils' general spending programmes, on housing for example. In addition, a major Conservative innovation was the removal of control over spending under some of the programmes from local authorities to bodies run by central government-appointed businesspeople and officials.

The Conservatives did not, as some feared they would, immediately end the Urban Programme, although they did so in 1995. But they added the usual plethora of new measures. At the end of *Progress on Cities*, a publication produced in 1989 by the Cabinet Office and the Central Office of Information, 35 'Government Measures' were listed. Among them was the Urban Development Grant, introduced in 1982, which has funded private sector projects. This was followed by City Grant and Derelict Land Grant which, like many of the government's programmes, concentrated on the physical improvement of inner city areas. In 1985 the government set up City Action Teams (CATs) which, according to the Department of the Environment, were to 'provide for the regional directors of the Departments of the Environment, Employment (including the Manpower Services Commission) and Trade and Industry to work together in developing and implementing their policies and programmes in the Partnership areas'. This was followed in 1986 by the setting up of Task Forces, which in spite of the usual fanfare involved expenditure of only £8 million a year. There was also Estate Action, another Department of the Environment programme which provided money for 'run-down council estates' and supported 'local estate-based management'. The Home Office set up a programme entitled Safer Cities. The Department of Trade and Industry 'sponsored' English Estates to work with the private sector to provide managed workspace for new small businesses. There was much concentration on training. Between 1980 and 1990 central government spending on training nearly tripled in real terms to £2.7 billion per year. The continually changing training schemes were overwhelmingly for young people and the long term unemployed. Many were make-work; some provided low level skills; few led to jobs. Unemployed people could spend years going from one government scheme to another and many were pushed into the various training schemes or onto the Enterprise Allowance, the small weekly sum available to promote self-employment, in what amounted to the beginnings of a shift from welfare to 'workfare'. The Manpower Services Commission (MSC) and its successors the Training, Enterprise and Education Directorate, the Training Commission and the Training Agency provided funding for local training projects. These were succeeded by the Training and Enterprise Councils (TECs), run by government-appointed business executives and staffed by government officials, supposedly to make training and business advice more responsive to the needs of business; by 1993 there were 82 TECs in England and Wales and 20 similar

Local Enterprise Councils in Scotland. There was also a proliferation of enterprise support and advice agencies, run variously by local government, the private sector, central government and voluntary agencies; the government's current attempt to bring these together in Business Link, or 'one-stop shops' seems merely to have added to the confusion and rivalry. Of the new programmes which were outside local authority control, in addition to the TECs, the most notable were the Urban Development Corporations (UDCs) and Enterprise Zones, which were set up from 1981 onwards and took a growing proportion of urban funding (see below). In 1991 the government announced a new 'flagship' programme, City Challenge, under which partnerships of local authorities, business and the voluntary sector were to bid against each other for part of Urban Programme funds (see below). In 1993 it set up a new Urban Regeneration Agency (URA), to 'subsume' the Department of the Environment's Derelict Land Grant and City Grant programmes and to take over English Estates. The URA was subsequently re-named English Partnerships. It was described by the inner cities minister John Redwood, in an interview in the *Financial Times* of 18 September 1992, as planned to be 'a sort of roving UDC' to deal with remaining small areas of land 'which could be better used' and intended to 'trigger private sector investment' and have 'compulsory purchase powers where needed to assemble land for development', with resources of up to £300 million a year; unlike in UDCs, planning powers were retained by local authorities which the minister hoped would 'cooperate' but which would lose their powers 'in exceptional circumstances' (if they did not cooperate?). City Challenge was then suspended, and partly replaced by a new scheme, Capital Partnership, under which local authorities could bid for a fund of £20 million to help those of them that had assets to sell them off. In 1993 the government announced an initiative to bring all these various schemes together into a 'Single Regeneration Budget' (SRB), to include resources valued at £1.4 billion and administered under 20 separate programmes by five government departments (Environment, Trade and Industry, Employment, Education and the Home Office), and also to integrate the regional offices of four departments (Environment, Trade and industry, Employment and Transport) in ten new Integrated Regional Offices to administer this budget. The government announced that the essence of the new programmes was the devolution of responsibility, thus falling in line with the current advocacy of the virtues of 'difference' and local variation, and abdicating responsibility for a strategic vision.

121

The money available under the SRB is not restricted to the existing urban programme areas, and could in theory be spent wholly in rural areas. As in City Challenge and other government programmes, its allocation is to be based on a competitive process. It is not clear how the winners, or the balance between need and potential, will be determined.

In 1988 the Conservative government launched, with the usual fanfare, what it called its Action for Cities campaign. Reviewing progress a year later in the preface to *Progress on Cities*, Mrs Thatcher claimed that:

> 'we were embarked on a great enterprise which would carry our towns and cities into the 21st Century in much better shape. That enterprise is now well under way.
>
> 'Visit our major cities and you will find a new confidence and a new sense of purpose. Derelict land is being cleared. New roads are under construction. The private sector is investing in housing, factories, offices and shopping centres. Most importantly, people are getting jobs and unemployment is falling fast.
>
> 'This economic recovery is already bringing people the new hope for the future which is central to Action for Cities. And the government is helping them to fulfil that hope. Better training is available for those without jobs. It is easier to set up your own business. New education policies will help raise the performance of inner city schools. Council tenants are being given a choice of landlord. Crime is being tackled and security on housing estates is being improved. And, increasingly, businessmen and others are giving these policies the local backing which is crucial to turning these opportunities into achievement.
>
> '. . . Things are truly looking up for our inner cities.'

Others took a different view. Thus for example the Town and Country Planning Association, in its report *Whose Responsibility?: Reclaiming The Inner Cities*, published in 1986 (admittedly two years earlier, but little has since changed) its own review of progress since 1979. It stated that:

> 'overall conditions in Britain's inner city areas have deteriorated steadily and at an accelerating rate. We conclude that central government has failed to appreciate the savage effect which its economic policies have had on the inner city areas. We regard it as nothing short of calamitous that the limited funding made available by government for the IAP [Inner Areas Programme] has been exceeded many times over by the reduction in funding for main programmes caused by cuts in public expenditure.
>
> . . .
>
> 'What kind of priority for inner city areas is it that creates a situation

whereby the funds made available under the Urban Programme have been massively exceeded by the funds lost through reductions in Rate Support Grant and Housing Subsidy? In the case of Inner London, for example, a recent report prepared for a GLC conference on inner city policy showed that in the period 1979/80 to 1983/4 Inner London gained £261m in Urban Programme funding while losing £865m in RSG, and a sizeable proportion of the £791m of housing subsidy lost to London (1981/2 prices). Partnership and programme authorities elsewhere have in recent years suffered similar imbalances between what they receive through the IAP and what they have lost through cuts in RSG and housing subsidy. Manchester City Council, for example, gained, in real terms, an extra £9m via the urban programme between 1980/81 and 1984/85 while losing some £100m in RSG settlements within the same period.'

Since then, the government has continued to cut the sums allocated both to special urban programmes and to local government main spending programmes. The Urban Programme was run down even before its abolition. In 1992, for example, the government announced that its urban spending was to be reduced from £987 million in 1992-93 to £806 million in 1995-96 and that, within this total, the Urban Programme was to be cut by 66 per cent; even the budgets of some Urban Development Corporations were to be cut; only the Urban Regeneration Agency was to have increased funding. In 1995 the government announced that the funding of the new Single Regeneration Budget was to be cut from £1.44 billion in 1994/95 to £1.35 billion in 1996/67. In addition, although from the late 1980s onwards there was some political convergence between the government and Labour-controlled local authorities, the onslaught on local government main spending programmes has continued. At the end of 1994, for example, the government announced what amounted to further swingeing cuts. There was to be a 2.2 per cent rise in 'total standard spending', or the government's estimate of what local government should spend (which is used as the basis for grants to local government), from £42.58 billion in 1994-95 to £43.51 billion in 1995-96. The Association of County Councils estimated this 'increase' would in reality amount to a cut of 3.3 per cent in cash terms. This was because in 1994-95 councils actually spent £44.42 billion. In 1995-96, if spending on all services was frozen and extra responsibilities for 'community care' were taken on at the expected cost, their spending would rise to £45 billion. But the government was expecting them to spend about £1 billion *less* than they were already spending — before inflation, pay rises, the expected increase in the number of school age children, the compulsory increase in spending on the police or their additional 'community care' responsibilities were taken into account.

Local authorities have done little to resist this onslaught. In an earlier period, the Labour councillors of Clay Cross had refused to implement the Conservatives' 1972 Housing Finance Act, which required higher rents to be charged for council housing, and were barred from public office as punishment for their stand; although they were saved from imprisonment by the Labour election victory in 1974 they were not reinstated at the time. This was one of the few examples of resistance. In the 1980s, the Militant-dominated Labour council in Liverpool initially won a legal victory against the government in its refusal to set a budget which fell within the limits imposed by the government. Labour-controlled councils then met on several occasions to organise united resistance to cuts, under the auspices of the Association of Local Authorities (ALA), the Association of Metropolitan Authorities (AMA), and the Local Government Information Unit (LGIU). The majority view of these Labour-led councils, argued for by Ted Knight of Lambeth and others, was that, rather than setting a deficit budget, they should refuse to set a rate at all until the government made concesssions; at the time there was no legal requirement for councils to set a rate by a certain date. But the Conservatives offered selective financial inducements to councils to cave in and comply with the restrictions, starting with Livingstone's GLC. The GLC had to set its rate before the London boroughs in order for the rate precept from those boroughs to be calculated and it was unwilling to act in isolation. From then on the government was almost completely successful. Several councils, especially those which had been rate-capped in July 1984, attempted to varying degrees to defer setting a rate, but most gave up after a relatively short period of resistance. One of the more determined attempts at resistance was in Hackney. In March 1985 Hackney borough council passed a strong motion refusing to set a rate until the government provided more money. Hackney was taken to court by an SDP candidate and lost, on the grounds that its motion amounted to a de facto decision to set a deficit budget and was therefore null and void. A minority of Labour councillors in Hackney then voted with the Liberals and Conservatives to set a balanced budget. Hilda Kean, the Labour leader, and other senior councillors resigned, stating that they had campaigned against cuts and were not prepared to implement them. They were then sued for alleged losses incurred through deferring a rate, but eventually were required to pay the relatively small sum of £500 each. The Labour councils in Liverpool and Lambeth managed to hold out somewhat longer, and came to be virtually alone in their attempts at resistance. Most of their councillors lost office. Their example was marred by the existence of allegations of corrupt practices in both places, in particular against Ted Knight in Lambeth and Derek Hatton in Liverpool. In Lambeth the banned councillors were replaced by new left wing councillors who, because they were inexperienced, found it hard to combat the corruption which was allegedly rife among senior officials in the council (many of whom, according to another senior employee, had Masonic connections), thus perpetuating the council's poor reputation. Some other councils attempted to find ways round the restrictions with ingenious financial deals, most of which came to grief, hoping to be bailed out by a Labour election victory; when this did not occur, they ended up making yet deeper cuts. Elsewhere individual councillors, members of local Labour parties and even some district Labour parties argued, unsuccessfully, that Labour councils should refuse to implement Conservative cuts and if necessary resign, or allow the government's auditors to take over. In Oxford the district Labour party voted against setting a legal budget but was disregarded by the Labour group. Some individual councillors refused to comply, and some suffered considerable financial and other forms of hardship as a result. The majority of Labour councillors argued that they should not break the law. Most no doubt believed that there were still useful things to be done if they remained in office, and hoped to find ways of countering the Conservative restrictions. But some also justified their position in part by claiming that, if they had to make cuts, they would make them in better ways than the Conservatives would. Such claims are dubious, and some suspected that the main concern of some of these Labour councillors was to remain in office. There is little doubt that, if a sufficiently large number of Labour-controlled authorities had united in refusing to implement Conservative cuts, the Conservatives would have found it difficult to take them over, or to have all of them run by public auditors. They would then perhaps have been forced to make concessions and provide more funding, so as to avoid making cities ungovernable

Virtually the only successful resistance to Conservative policies on local government was the struggle against the Poll Tax, or Community Charge as the government called it. But this resistance was conducted without the official approval of Labour councils or the Labour Party, although some individual Labour councillors supported it. The Poll Tax was levied at a flat rate, with partial exemptions for people on social security and students. This meant that the rich who had previously paid high local authority rates on their houses saw their local taxation greatly reduced, while for example couples and individuals on low incomes or one income suddenly found their local taxation doubling, or more than doubling. The government hoped that by imposing the tax equally on all individual adults it would make clear the link between local expenditure and their pockets, and that they would then vote against high spending (Labour) councils. Instead it provoked widespread anger and hostility against itself. Unlike other Conservative policies, such as unemployment, which affected a relatively small number of people directly, the tax had a direct effect on millions of working people, as well as students and unemployed young people. There were numerous demonstrations against the Poll Tax, including a large one in London which was put down with considerable violence by the police. Probably the most effective activity was the campaign for non-payment. Huge numbers of people, including many who were previously exemplary law-abiding citizens, refused to pay, and many went to court to explain why they were not paying. A few people were sent to prison for non-payment and others had their possessions removed. The tax became uncollectable, and much of it has still not been collected, in spite of large increases in council employment for the purpose. For once the poor had a weapon of considerable power. The tax contributed to Thatcher's removal and was eventually abandoned by her successor John Major.

Labour councils, on the other hand, confined themselves to verbal opposition, from which they gained little, and did their best to collect the Poll Tax. In general they meekly remained within the limits imposed by central government, set legal budgets, and took the blame for implementing Conservative cuts. Perhaps paradoxically, their failure to take a strong stand against Conservative policies, and the resulting perception of the voters that they were responsible for providing a declining level of services, made them more vulnerable to Conservative accusations that they were squandering money on 'loony left' policies. They thus became increasingly discredited.

Inner city policies and the private sector

At least from the 1970s both Labour and Conservative central and local governments have pursued policies of support for private business. Local authorities have competed with each other to attract private investment to their areas. But Conservative governments since 1979 have set particular store by their attempt to bring about the replacement of public spending by private spending. For the Conservatives the idea was central to their strategies for urban regeneration.

The government hoped that business leaders would come to see themselves as responsible for the health of their communities, and that they would be induced not only to invest for profit, but also to play a growing philanthropic role. After the riots in Toxteth in Liverpool, Michael Heseltine, then Secretary of State for the Environment, took a group of business executives on a tour of the area. The message was that it was up to them to ensure that the same thing would not happen again, by investing in the area. In one of the government's more recent 'flagship' schemes, City Challenge (see below), the private sector is expected to play a leading role in devising and implementing plans for regeneration, in partnership with 'the community'. The Training and Enterprise Councils are set up as companies and led by business people, dragooned into service by the government, though largely staffed by civil servants. In November 1993 the government announced a new scheme, entitled 'City Pride', which was to seek business help in visualising the future for London, Birmingham and Manchester and was to bid for a share of urban development funds. London First, the private sector body set up in 1992 'to promote strategic thinking in the capital', was expected to be prominent in drawing up City Pride plans for London.

The government's hope that the private sector might be persuaded to perform a social role, and thus reduce the need for public money, clearly, like several other policies pursued by the government (for example immigration controls), does not fit with its proclaimed adherence to free market ideology. Thus for example Samuel Brittan, in a critique of this aspect of government policy in an article in the *Financial Times* of 1 February 1993, quotes Milton Friedman:

'Few trends could so thoroughly undermine the very foundations of our free society as the acceptance by corporate officials of social responsibility other than to make as much money for their shareholders as possible.'

Brittan felt obliged to add that Friedman was well aware that 'the profit maximising game, if it is to be in the general interest, requires a complex background of property rights, law, and above all mutual trust', and that the east European countries were discovering this. But, he said,

'What Friedman was really getting at, however, was the doctrine that business has to contribute to good causes, such as urban renewal, support of the arts, or the out of hours welfare of its own employees . . .

'The point is . . . that it is up to individual citizens to decide how much to contribute. Insofar as they favour collective action, such action should be through duly constituted political processes and not through managers setting up as taxing authorities over the funds of shareholders.'

Businesspeople themselves have, not surprisingly, not always been particularly enthusiastic partners (or taxers of their shareholders). But there has been some business response to the government's urgings. Organisations such as Business in The Community, whose chief executive is Prince Charles, argue that it is in the enlightened self-interest of private companies to promote the welfare of their communities; in its publication *Business in the Cities*, for example, Business in the Community states:

'There are huge costs to industry of ignoring urban and rural decay . . . The lack of alternatives tends to stimulate street crime, drugs and social malaise . . . Business leaders cannot stand back and wait for others to act; government cannot successfully tackle these problems alone . . . For business to hold back is to risk much: in direct costs, in social costs, in foregone markets and in business survival . . . Acting together, in partnership, in local communities is the only way to break into the vicious cycle of city decline; and it is the crucial prerequisite for long term future business growth.'

Business in the Community has, for example, set up 'Opportunity 2000', an initiative to promote more openings for women in management. Some individual companies have set up 'community affairs programmes', contributing to educational schemes for example. A survey conducted by Opinion Leader Research, reported in the *Financial Times* of 20 October 1993, found that over 80 per cent of those polled considered that 'a reputation for being socially responsive and responsible is becoming a competitive advantage'. Sir Allen Shepherd, chairman and group chief executive of the drinks company Grandmet, is reported in the *Financial Times* of 2 July 1992 as believing that 'community involvement' now represents 'a core element of corporate responsibility in . . . the new age of consumer-driven capitalism. Customers are increasingly looking through the front door of the companies they buy from. If they do not like what they see in terms of social responsibility, community involvement, equality of opportunity, they won't go in'. Grandmet hopes 'to give a lead in helping combat the growth of an underclass by promoting the concept of self help', in part by helping people get jobs. Grandmet employees are encouraged to join in: 'Sir Allen says: "It's a big part of career development. I like to see people in the trenches, not stuck in the back office. It's better than a thousand management courses. It's playing the game for real". There is no compulsion on staff to participate but the chairman is not unhappy for employees to believe that taking part will do no harm to their career prospects.' Stanley Kalms, chairman of the electrical retailers Dixons, was reported in the *Financial Times* of 8 November 1993 as believing that business had a responsibility to do something about crime, pointing out that: 'ironically, many of the maxims of Baroness Thatcher's "enterprise culture" are being applied to breaking the law. "The crime industry is a major profession, turning out new products at a rate of knots", he says'. Kalms proposes not only that retailers should set up 'joint security squads to patrol high streets', but also that they should support training activities, on the grounds that 'there is a direct connection between education — or the lack of it — and crime': 'industrialists should not sit on their hands while their businesses suffer from . . . a breakdown of law and order'. Businesspeople have been fairly active in the Training and Enterprise Councils. Some have contributed to non-profit trusts, such as the North Kensington Amenity Trust and the East London Partnership. In many places, they have agreed to hold discussions with local authorities about their attempts to regenerate run-down industrial areas. They have clearly felt it in their interest to improve their local authority's chances in the City Challenge competition (see below) by putting their names to the bids. On the other hand, once the City Challenge bids were successful, some of the business leaders began to withdraw or scale down their undertakings to invest. At a conference on City Challenge at the University of Westminster in December 1992 Tony Hawkhead, Chief Executive of the East London Partnership, stated that, although East London Partnership members 'willingly provided much of the private sector support for Tower Hamlets' successful application as a pacemaker bid last year', nevertheless: 'Perhaps the most obvious misconception was the conclusion of some of the local authority and community partners that the private sector was there simply to provide free cash — a sort of milch cow. That was not a conclusion shared by the private sector!' He added that: 'We are committed to regeneration, but we depend on the government . . . we need an end to the recession . . . there is a great and growing demand for finite private resources'.

As well as hoping that businesses will help deal with the social and economic problems of inner city areas by investing in them, governments have offered them considerable inducements to do so. Businesses have usually been willing, or eager, to take the proferred subsidies. These may or may not have affected their decision to invest in a particular area. Of the three Japanese motor-companies which have invested in Britain, Nissan received large government subsidies to invest in Sunderland, but Honda built its plant near Swindon and Toyota built in Derbyshire without regional aid from the government. Other companies have engaged in a game of bluff. Ford, for example, said that it would move Jaguar production to the USA if the government did not offer it a subsidy to stay in Britain. The government did not dare call its bluff. On a more local scale, there is much evidence that once, for example, an Enterprise Zone or a City Challenge area is established, firms will move into it from neighbouring areas in order to obtain access to government subsidies. As a book edited by MacGregor and Pimlott entitled *Tackling the Inner Cities* makes plain, 'While echoing the Government's "partnership" theme in its rhetoric, and paying dutiful lip service to the principle of *laissez-faire*, the coded message of the CBI (Confederation of British Industry) is an urgent demand for more government funding, not less'.

In Manchester two academics, Jamie Peck and Adam Tickell, carried out a fascinating series of interviews with local business people. In a paper produced in 1993, entitled *Business Goes Local: Dissecting the 'Business Agenda' in Post-democratic Manchester*, they argue that one of the main interests of business was in supporting the government's agenda of undermining the power of the town hall and by-passing its supposedly bureaucratic procedures — with the help, of course, of central government:

> 'Called to arms by neoliberal ideologues and by members of the royal family, business leaders have joined the battle for Britain's cities. But who is the enemy? Judging from the way in which their troops have been deployed — in local business lobbies and in newly-created arms of the non-elected local state — the enemy would appear to be holed up in the town hall.'

This process resulted in the formation of a new business elite which came to control large sums of public money through non-elected local bodies. In an interview on Radio 4 Lady Anson, Chair of the Association of District Councils, said: 'There are now more and more appointed bodies locally who are taking over the powers of local government.

Nobody knows who they are, they don't know who they are accountable to, and yet they are spending, in fact, more money across the country than the whole of local government put together'. Two members of this business elite interviewed by Peck and Tickell described themselves as follows:

> 'You now find as you go round the various things [new agencies] to some extent a repetition of the same faces, which does get its name of the Manchester mafia . . . It's chairmen and MDs who turn up to these meetings. So it's real people, real decision-makers . . . Not just me, but the other people on that group, you'll see they're Sirs and the rest of it. They're Tory party supporters, and when they want a minister up, they tell the minister when they want him up. And they come, and they come. Tugging forelocks as well . . . That's power.'

On the other hand, Peck and Tickell argue, the agenda of these busy business elites was largely negative. They agreed with the government that local government was inefficient, wasteful and should have its power and scope reduced, and that the notion of universal welfare provision should be replaced by competition between localities for a share of whatever private investment and government funding might be available. But they had no strategic vision for the regeneration of their city. Thus, Peck and Tickell say:

> 'Business leaders active in local policy and politics in Manchester define themselves as people seeking tangible results. A leading member of the Manchester Mafia characterised this as a process of "getting hands on, jacket off, sleeves rolled up and down to the hard basics of what we're going to do and how we're going to do it". Yet while such hard-nosed pragmatism is useful in getting development projects underway — usually with the proviso that there will be, literally, concrete results — it is a *modus operandi* rarely consistent with the more esoteric questions involved in the formulation of an economic development strategy. Attempts to address these questions at monthly or bi-monthly meetings with key actors from the business community seem rarely to yield innovative results. In the words of one such committee member, when such questions arise, "I just look sort of blank and try to say something". More often than not, this "something" will be a plea to stop talking platitudes and "get on with it". In this way, the local business agenda is effectively reduced to the pursuit of grants and projects. A strategy it is not.'

They conclude that even the business desire to restructure the local state is limited: 'in the Manchester business community there seems not to be the time, the will nor the ability to "run the city". Dabbling aside, this is a job which most business leaders continue to see as an unrewarding "pain in the neck", a job best left to others'. In similar vein, in a leader on May 10 1993, the *Financial Times* praises the commitment of business leaders to the cause, but says they are in a muddle about what they should be doing:

'It was an insight of the Thatcher years that government should not try to do business's job. There is currently a risk that the opposite fallacy will become entrenched — that business is able to do the government's job.'

In reality, of course, the government's notion of reliance on the private sector for urban regeneration implies state intervention of another sort. Above all, it implies substantial public expenditure. The attraction of the private sector into run-down inner city areas, to the extent that it has occurred, has required public subsidies, in the form of land reclamation, the provision of infrastructure, training, business advice and the production of glossy publicity materials. The Urban Development Corporations, and especially the London Docklands Development Corporation, have epitomised this process.

UDCs and property-led development

A significant part of the government's project to 'rely on the private sector', and to undermine and by-pass Labour local authorities by replacing them with private sector 'enterprise', was the creation of Urban Development Corporations (UDCs) and Enterprise Zones (EZs). The government diverted much of the available inner city funds to these two programmes. In 1981, following the 1980 Local Government Planning and Land Act, two UDCs were set up, in London (the London Docklands Development Corporation, LDDC) and Liverpool; a further five UDCs were set up in 1987, four in 1988-89 and one in 1993, making a total of 12. They received large amounts of money. Between 1981 and 1990, total UDC funding was £1.7 billion (of which the LDDC received £700 million). Although money for UDCs was officially 'additional' to Urban Programme funding, it comes out of the same overall DoE budget for inner cities. Over the same period, Urban Programme funding declined in real terms. During the 1980s the relationship between the two types of funding moved progressively in favour of the UDCs. In 1990-91 the latter received more than twice the total grant for all 57 Urban Programme Districts. From 1990 this gap narrowed a little; funding for most UDCs has been declining faster than inner cities funding as a whole. In addition, 13 Enterprise Zones were created in 1981, and a further 14 by 1984. One of these Enterprise Zones is in the Isle of Dogs, under LDDC responsibility; it contributed approximately a further £130m in rate allowances and estimated capital allowances to the area between 1981 and 1987. In the LDDC's case, these large government expenditures were supplemented by the Department of Transport, which spent in 1981-87 a further £173 million on (inadequate) transport infrastructure for the LDDC area, including road improvements and the Docklands Light Railway.

The UDCs are accountable only to central government, from which they receive grants directly. They took over the planning powers previously exercised by local authorities, which were seen as a deterrent to private sector investment. The EZs give private firms greater freedom from planning regulations, exemption from Development Land Tax and Rates and 100 per cent capital allowances from corporation and income tax on capital expenditure on commercial and industrial property. There is much evidence that, rather than attracting new investment, they have merely caused firms to move from elsewhere, and often from nearby. The UDCs spent the DoE's grants mainly on clearing derelict land and preparing sites, on improving the environment for inward investors, and on public relations hype. They are almost entirely concerned with the physical regeneration of an area. They operate on the presumption that it is enough for the public sector to reclaim and refurbish derelict sites and then, provided the private sector builds on them, for whatever purpose, this in itself constitutes regeneration. The one policy constraint which the LDDC, for example, set itself in its 1987 Corporate Plan, was to 'see that each site is used to its maximum economic potential', in other words that any wider social and economic objectives were subordinated to the choices implied by the free market in land and property and to the search for profit. These choices often ran counter to local authorities' existing plans for the areas. A paper by Bob Colenutt and Sally Tansley, published in 1990, comments that 'office and housing developments for the West side of the Isle of Dogs were built on sites zoned for industry in Tower Hamlets's adopted Borough Plan', and:

> 'Most UDC areas had a pre-existing plan and some development in the pipeline; the plain fact is that very often this plan was either one that did

not suit the property market of the mid and late 1980s, or required a different
kind of government intervention to succeed.'

The UDCs were almost wholly unconcerned about what happened to
the people who might be living in the area. Although there was talk of
benefits 'trickling down', no attempt was made to measure any such
effect; in the DoE's Expenditure White Papers, the main measure of
UDC performance is merely the acreage of 'derelict, unused or seriously
underused land brought back into use'. The creation of employment
was not an important objective. Mr Butler, Under Secretary at the DoE
for its Inner Cities Initiative, told the House of Commons Employment
Committee in 1988:

> 'We do not see the UDCs as being primarily or immediately concerned with
> employment, they are about regeneration, and indeed the physical
> regeneration of their areas.'

Thus the policy was not so much about improving the situation of
people already living in an area, as about changing the nature of the
area altogether. As Heseltine put it in his book *Where There's a Will*, his
aim was 'to make the inner cities places where people would want to
live and work and where the private investor would be willing to put his
money'.

In most cases, the result of these policies was that new developments
mainly took the form of office building and luxury housing. The London
Docklands Development Corporation provides the most outstanding
example of these processes, and the one in which the government has
taken most pride. The changes to the area are indeed startling. The
area has sprouted a fantastical landscape of weird and wonderful, shiny
new buildings, serviced by a Heath Robinson railway winding through
this futuristic wonderland, and the surrounding wasteland, on stilts.
There was no overall plan and no aesthetic guidelines. Each building is
the creation of its own developers and architects and may stand isolated
among dereliction or the remnants of the previous life of the area. Some
of the new office buildings look as though they really are meant to be
temporary accommodation, ephemeral objects of fashion. Some have
been occupied by blue chip companies, most of which moved from the
City of London in search of lower rents and to avoid what appeared to
be a potential shortage of modern office accommodation in the City.

The LDDC, pressed on the issue of jobs, claims to have created over
20,000 of them between 1981 and 1990. But it also admits that two

thirds of these jobs were transfers from elsewhere. Of the third that were 'newly created' only 20%, or some 1,300, went to the mainly working class residents of the three Docklands boroughs, Tower Hamlets, Newham and Southwark. In other words the jobs were mostly for professional salaried staff, most of whom were in any case already employed by the incoming firms. Canary Wharf was supposed to create some 47,000 jobs. The consultants employed by the LDDC, Peat, Marwick Mitchell and Co., predicted that only 1,800 of these were likely to go to local people, with up to 70 per cent of these being in part-time activities such as cleaning. At the same time many local firms and industries which did employ local working class people have closed. According to estimates by the local authority-funded Docklands Development Committee, around 13,000 jobs were lost from the LDDC area during the 1980s, many of them from major manufacturing firms. Some of these were driven out by rising land prices. In other cases, the LDDC itself was directly responsible for the closures or removals, through using Compulsory Purchase Orders (CPOs) to clear sites. Colenutt and Tansley state that:

'According to evidence supplied to the House of Commons Public Accounts Committee in 1989, 84 local firms have been subject to CPOs of which 44 were successfully relocated. A further 123 firms have been removed to facilitate development of LDDC sites and 140 firms are affected by CPOs for the proposed Docklands Highway.'

Unemployment in the area actually rose. For example between October 1982 and September 1987, according to official Department of Employment figures (reproduced in a memorandum from the Docklands Consultative Committee to the 1988 House of Commons Employment Committee), the number of people unemployed in the three Docklands boroughs rose from 45,679 to 50,074.

Much of the £4 billion of private sector investment which the LDDC claims has been attracted to the area was for private housing. A National Audit Office report on UDCs, published in May 1988, made clear that the policy of promoting private home ownership, rather than addressing the needs of local homeless (or badly housed) people, was a deliberate policy of the government, which instructed the LDDC to provide sites for private house builders. The LDDC set a target of increasing the proportion of home ownership in the area from 4 per cent to 30 per cent, so as 'to encourage a different balance' and 'to attract the wide mix of residents needed to foster economic development'. On some sites the developers were required by the LDDC to provide a proportion of 'affordable housing', at around £40,000 per house, but this itself was out of the reach of local people subsisting on low wages or state benefits. In 1988 the LDDC, uniquely among UDCs, was forced by political pressures to bid for DoE funding for a contribution to 'social housing', through supporting new-build housing association projects and even making some token gestures towards the refurbishment of council estates; but some of the plans were dropped after 1990 as a result of the LDDC's financial problems. The effects, in any case, have been minimal, and they sometimes appear to have more to do with improving the view for the occupiers of new luxury housing than with actual benefits to council tenants.

These effects were contested by local people and by community organisations, and were documented in particular by the Docklands Consultative Committee. In addition, they began to be questioned in more official quarters. In May 1988 the National Audit Office published a report on UDCs which included some mild admonitions on the need to address 'social and environmental factors', some comments on local people's view that they should be consulted, some discussion of the issues of rising unemployment and the need for training, and the observation that 'Most of the new jobs in Docklands so far have gone to people from outside the area' (which meant, by and large, professional people). A House of Commons Employment Committee report, published in August 1988, was more critical. It noted that unemployment in the area was higher in 1988 than it was when the LDDC was set up in 1981. It stated that:

> 'it is not good for the health of a community for the original inhabitants of an area to see others benefiting, as they see it, at their expense while they suffer from increased road traffic, congestion, higher house prices and associated ills. Nor is it just.'

And:

> 'UDCs cannot be regarded as a success if buildings and land are regenerated but the local community are by-passed and do not benefit from regeneration. The Committee recommends that the remit for UDCs should be altered to provide a more precise definition of "regeneration". This should include employment and unemployment objectives, both in general and for the local community. It should also charge the UDCs with greater responsibility for ensuring that communities both in the areas covered by UDCs and in the neighbouring areas benefit from regeneration.'

The UDCs were forced to show more awareness of the problem of local discontent, and some of them appointed community liaison officers; the LDDC appointed a Community Affairs Director. The local authorities, for their part, became more accommodating towards the UDCs. In London, the Docklands boroughs of Newham and Southwark, which had boycotted the LDDC's board meetings, began to bow to the prevailing spirit of new realism. They and Tower Hamlets signed Social Accords over particular developments with the LDDC in the late 1980s, and they have moved from outright opposition to most of the LDDC's developments to attempts to negotiate some 'planning gains' on particular projects from the developers (see below).

However, the UDCs were by the early 1990s in serious financial difficulties, and their ability to provide any crumbs from the table has correspondingly diminished. The slump in the property market led them into growing financial crises, especially as many of them bought land at the height of the property boom. Billions of pounds of public money was spent in support of supposedly 'market-led' schemes which were a disaster even from the point of view of the market. Moreover, as Colenutt and Tansley comment:

'It is a myth that the market has regenerated UDC areas. Developers would not have been attracted in without large government subsidies, public sector land acquisition and reclamation.'

The UDCs have so far shown no sign of searching for an alternative to their property-led strategies. They are, however, no more than outstanding examples of developments which are widespread. In most British cities the replacement of local jobs and low cost housing by office building, luxury housing and large retail developments has been a notable feature of the 1980s and early 1990s. In many cases these are also assisted by public subsidies, which may have had the effect, as they undoubtedly did in Docklands, of attracting speculative property developments into one area rather than another. As David Widgery comments in his, sadly, valedictory book, *Some Lives! A GP's East End*:

'look round from the monumental folly of Canary wharf and see the humiliation of ordinary Londoners by the triumphal obelisks of commerce. But look too at the other linchpins of London's architectural identity: Piccadilly Circus, Soho, Liverpool Street Station and Waterloo Station, all remade in the Thatcher mould, newly clad in the gleaming impenetrable façades of modern North American commercial architecture with their

antiseptic malls, sterile piazzas, ghostly galleria and glacial curtain walls . . .
'"The inner cities next," announced Mrs Thatcher in her 1987 paroxysm
of third-term triumph in 1987: what she meant was the recolonisation of the
old proletarian-bohemian, artisanal-shopkeeping, Labour-voting areas of the
city centre by the values and the personnel of the Home Counties.'

There have been a few examples of successful resistance. On the South
Bank of the Thames, next to a typically opulent private housing
development festooned with golden balls, there remains an isolated
monument to the struggles of local communities: the old Oxo building,
retained and restored by Coin Street Community Builders. Their success
was due to a last-minute snatch of the property and surrounding land
by the Greater London Council, which put restrictive covenants on it
and sold it at a price which reflected these restrictions to Coin Street
Community Builders. The latter are converting the Oxo warehouse into
low cost rented flats for local people, workshops and other community
uses, and they have also built a small development of houses which has
been formed into a cooperative (rather than council housing) so as to
avoid them being bought and sold for high profits under the
government's 'Right to Buy' scheme. There are also a park by the river,
a market and some small shops. Coin Street is, however, the exception.

Consensus politics and the
re-incorporation of local authorities

Initially the encroachments of new developments, especially office
developments, were resisted by many Labour-controlled urban local
authorities. Coin Street's achievements were made possible by the
intervention of the GLC. The GLC had also attempted, unsuccessfully,
through its support for *A People's Plan for Docklands*, to protect some of
the original uses and populations in Docklands, and it had similar
policies for other areas in London. The local borough of Southwark,
just across the river from the City of London, for a period in the 1980s
also supported local campaigning groups in their opposition to new
'overspill' office developments, which destroyed local jobs and housing
and provided few new jobs accessible to local people. Southwark
council, like many others in similar situations elsewhere, regularly
refused planning permission for these developments, which the Secretary
of State for the Environment then regularly allowed on appeal. But by
the end of the 1980s Southwark borough council, again like other
boroughs, had changed tactics. Rather than opposing the developers'

plans, it attempted to make them pay for its agreement to them under what was termed 'planning gain'. The council thus saved the developers the time and expense of appealing against refusals and making their case in public inquiries, and in return the developers contributed, usually small sums, towards local objectives such as training programmes and recreational facilities. This phenomenon has now become practically universal. Local councils are now much less likely to try to use their planning powers to enforce zoning policies (for example to secure jobs and houses for local people rather than speculative office development), believing that it would be futile to do so against the Ministry of the Environment's determination to use its powers in favour of the developers, and pursuing, instead, a policy of cooperation with the developers to achieve some gains for local communities. This, in turn, ensures that only the highest value uses of a site are considered 'realistic'. Colenutt and Tansley say for example that:

> 'One site in Bristol, St Anne's Board Mills which the Council had zoned for job creation, has changed hands several times with the value of the 70 acre site rising from £6m to £30m between the announcement of the UDC and some months later. Now the Council says the only "option" for the developers is to build luxury homes.'

Local authorities had also by the late 1980s largely abandoned their earlier attempts to oppose the closure of factories and other big employers. In Oxford, for example, the city council's opposition to the closure of the Cowley car plants in 1989 was half-hearted. The Oxford and District Trades Council set up a campaign to oppose closure, the Cowley Against Closure Campaign (CACC). But, partly because this campaign was bitterly opposed by the trade union leadership in the plant, which in similarly 'new realistic' manner preferred to negotiate with management behind closed doors, Oxford City Council backed away from its initial support for a campaign against closure. Then, as we wrote in *The Factory and The City*:

> 'a year after the initial closure announcement, the Cowley trade unions asked the Labour-controlled city council to organise a "political campaign". There were therefore two separate "campaigns". But the city council and the senior stewards set up a restricted delegate body, the Cowley South Works Closure Committee (CSWCC). This committee spent much of its time trying to close down CACC and organising an "independent inquiry", chaired by Lord McCarthy. The inquiry, after months of self-imposed delay, pronounced that it was too late to oppose closure.'

139

Instead, the Inquiry proposed negotiations with British Aerospace, with its property company, Arlington Securities, which is building a business park on the site of the closed factories, and with Rover Group. It advocated alternative uses of the site that would provide local employment and training for former Rover Group workers. It recognised that business parks of the type normally built by Arlington Securities provided hardly any jobs likely to be suitable for former car workers, and those only after a five-year time lapse, and proposed that the council should negotiate with Rover and Arlington to achieve the early development of some light industrial units. The council, however, rapidly abandoned any attempt to implement even the recommendations of its Inquiry. Rover Group refused to enter negotiations with the council. Arlington Securities talked to the council, as it had always said that it wanted to, but conceded virtually nothing. The council obtained some small sums for a training programme, but no industrial units. Some 6,000 relatively well paid car manufacturing jobs were lost. The jobs in the business park, if and when they eventually appear, will largely be filled by commuters from elsewhere, as the fact that much of the site will be a car park, and that much of the construction work so far has been on new fly-overs and roundabouts, indicates.

By the late 1980s, partly as a result of negative perceptions of the Urban Development Corporations, and partly because local authorities themselves were more willing than before to cooperate with UDCs and the private sector, there was some questioning of the justification for undermining elected local authorities. In 1989, the Audit Commission published a report, *Urban Regeneration and Economic Development: The Local Government Dimension*, which applauded the new realism of many Labour-controlled councils and their willingness to work in 'partnership' with the private sector, and suggested that it was inadvisable for the government to ignore the importance of the role that could be played by elected local authorities in regeneration attempts. Some of the government's own initiatives showed signs of similar changes of attitude. In 1985, City Action Teams had been set up in each of the eight main Urban partnership regions to coordinate the activities of central government departments, local authorities, the private sector and the voluntary sector. In 1986 Task Forces were set up, 'to improve the targeting and enhance the benefits to local residents of money channelled through existing central programmes'. Some of those involved were reputed to have 'gone native', in the sense that they became sympathetic to the views both of local communities and of the local authorities. For example in Southwark, according to a 1988 council report, the Task Force engaged in 'substantial co-operation with the Council. In particular the Council has supported the creation of the Community Forum which affords North Peckham residents the opportunity to comment on TF schemes, and there have been some joint Council-TF projects . . .' The government's Training and Enterprise Councils (TECs), supposed to put businesspeople in charge of determining and meeting local training needs, were themselves working with local authorities and in some cases were critical of the failure to secure jobs for local people in the property-led 'regeneration' that was occurring. In 1988 a special report of the CBI London Region Urban Regeneration Task Force stated that there was a need for partnerships in which the government, local authorities, teachers, church leaders and local people would work together, with the private sector in the lead — and with government subsidies.

By the end of the 1980s all this had led to a substantial convergence of all parts of the political spectrum on a consensus in local economic policy. Thus Aram Eisenschitz and Jamie Gough, in their book *The Politics of Local Economic Policy*, argue that both the left and the right moved from seeing their respective local policies mainly as models of, or propaganda for, their national policies, to the notion that local scale and reliance on locally-generated activity, based on 'partnerships', had specific advantages. The possibilities for cooperation between the Conservative government, Labour local authorities and private business came to exist at a local level in ways which would have been impossible at a national level; the government's promotion of 'partnership' even with the private sector, let alone with the Labour Party, was a feature of its policies for local rather than central government. Eisenschitz and Gough put forward one possible explanation for this phenomenon. They argue that the consensus-orientated local politics of the late 1980s and early 1990s filled a gap in 'local socialisation', helping to provide the conditions and the collective mediation necessary for the profitable operation of capitalist firms at a local level. At the national level, neo-liberal policies reigned. For the government, the advantage of adopting the consensus notions of partnership at a local but not at a national level was that this could be done without re-opening a 'Pandora's box' of national demands.

The consensus now firmly endorses the long-held notion that the promotion of economic development and prosperity in one's local area means attracting private investment to it. This in turn results in a politics of competition *between* localities and collaboration *within* them. It provides an inducement to workers and left-led local authorities to collaborate with employers, curbs their pressures for resources, and diverts their attention from national issues and demands. Thus, Eisenschitz and Gough suggest: 'By highlighting localistic competition the Centre believes that local authorities can be kept in bounds without the Right's crude coercion'. All of this has given a new lease of life to the old idea that the problems people suffer are within their power to address, if only they are enterprising enough, form partnerships with the private sector and the authorities, and compete harder with other localities. However, even if some local jobs are created through what has been termed local boosterism, others will be lost. As Eisenschitz and Gough say, flatly, the claim that jobs can be created, as opposed to attracted from elsewhere, by local economic initiatives is 'unfounded'. Local policy lacks the monetary, fiscal and other tools available to national governments and is not allowed, for example, to create public employment. It has therefore to resort to 'spatial competition'. In a competitive system, as in the market, the gains are unlikely to go to those who need them most.

Bootstraps again: the community to the rescue?

At the same time as the reincorporation of Labour local authorities was going on, there were attempts to incorporate another 'partner': 'the community'. The community is a hazy notion. Neither the government, nor the Labour Party, which also appears to be espousing the now fashionable community cause, nor even community activists themselves, make much of an attempt to define what they mean by 'the community'. It is for example unclear whether some sections of the community, whether they are the most deprived or the most privileged, are considered more important than others; who represents the community; or how its views can be determined. Sometimes the views of 'the community', and particularly 'the black community', are equated with those of their male traditional leaders; the Southall Black Sisters, among others, have contested such a definition of their 'community'. Some notions of community are exclusive. The neo-fascist British National Party was elected in the Millwall ward in Tower Hamlets in 1993 on the slogan 'housing for the local community'; their intention was to exclude not the new rich in their luxury apartments, but black people. In a less vicious form, problems have arisen in Southwark, where most of the activists in the community and tenants' groups live in the north of the borough and are from the white working class, many of them with a background of work in the docks, which was a white preserve. They have been at times reluctant to accept that black people from further south in the borough should have access to housing in the north. In 1995, when Walsall council planned to decentralise its activities to neighbourhood committees, without any overall policy commitments and obligations such as to equal opportunities, its opponents talked of the risk of 'white neighbourhood' control of a neo-fascist nature.

The government's reasons for wishing to involve the community, whatever it may be, also vary. The government is more explicit about some of these reasons than about others. But one set of government ideas which *is* made explicit, and is expressed in particular in relation to the government's City Challenge scheme (see below), goes back to the ideas of the Community Development Programmes (CDPs) (see above). This is that communities could do much for themselves, through 'self help'. As Liz Walton, from the DoE's Inner Cities Grants Division, told a conference organised in 1993 by the National Council for Voluntary Organisations in Manchester, the government's aim is 'to restore people's confidence, make them more self-reliant . . . break down their apathy', develop their 'belief in their area' and enable them to 'help themselves'. Kenneth Clarke, then Home Secretary, gave a lecture to the Conservative Reform Club in 1992 in which, the *Financial Times* of November 25 1992 reports, he lamented the growth of an 'underclass' in decaying inner city areas and said that:

'The long term answer lay in a partnership between statutory and voluntary agencies and private companies and "active citizens" that would allow local communities — with government help — to find their own solutions: "It is enormously important that people work out how to do things for themselves and that they believe that what they get from their own efforts is really theirs".
"But changing the attitude of inner-city residents towards enterprise, work, choice and responsibility would take time . . ".'

The notion that 'communities' of poor people, if they try hard enough, can help themselves, and in fact ought to pull themselves up by their bootstraps, is a notion which harps back at least to the days of the CDPs and, longer ago, Samuel Smiles. If the government can inculcate this notion, it may absolve itself from responsibility for unemployment, poverty and other social ills. In a similar way, statements by the Conservative government and at times by Tony Blair, as leader of the parliamentary opposition, imply that vandalism and dilapidated estates can be attributed to the personal failings of single parents. If people are poor, the government asserts, they should not rely on the state as provider but should do something about it themselves.

With a certain inconsistency, the government appears also to consider that voluntary organisations and charities are desirable as providers (whereas the state is not), even though receiving money from charities need not imply any less dependency than receiving publicly-funded services. This is presumably because, for ideological reasons, the government believes in the virtue of private, individual, charitable and voluntary activity, rather than state or collective action. The government also no doubt wishes further to undermine and weaken local authorities, which are not only part of the state, but also Labour-controlled. It may wish, by involving 'the community', to provide legitimisation for its ideological and economic goals, including 'market-led' development, and to divert community and campaigning groups from other more subversive goals. The most vociferous and organised opponents of many of the new government-promoted and private development schemes were local community groups. The LDDC was fought by the Docklands Consultative Committee and others, the massive development proposed at Kings Cross in London was opposed by community groups, the office developments in Southwark were opposed by the North Southwark Community Development Group (a federation of 27 groups, many of them tenants' associations). Others exist around the country. The experience of the LDDC and other UDCs and private developers may have led the government to the conclusion that it was best if such groups could be 'involved' from the outset, brought to accept the developers' plans, and engaged in discussions and negotiations, as the local authorities increasingly have been, about how 'the community' might benefit from the spin-off from such developments.

The government's apparent recognition of the value and importance of 'the community' of course has positive aspects. It implies some recognition of the rights and responsibilities of individuals, of the under-valued capabilities of ordinary people and of their ability, given the chance, to make better decisions about, for example, the use of resources to rehabilitate their housing estates or their area than any local or central bureaucracy can. It has an appeal rooted in the struggles for improvements in their surroundings of community and tenants' organisations. But the community organisations that exist now are a pale shadow of those that existed in the 1960s and 1970s (see above).

There is much evidence that community activism, like other forms of political action and resistance, flourishes in times of relative prosperity, and that poverty and, above all, unemployment have powerfully debilitating and demoralising effects, submerging people's creativity in the battle for mere survival. Many community organisations have failed to survive the withdrawal of funding from the GLC and other cuts in local authority support. Others depend on funding from local authorities which are now less radical than they were, and less willing to allow them independence in the way that the GLC, for example, tried to. Much of the local authority and government funding for voluntary organisations is to enable them to carry out core welfare functions previously carried out by the state, rather than campaigning for improvements in public policies. They are in danger of becoming in effect quangos, with even less accountability to local people than local authorities. A report by the Joseph Rowntree Foundation, published in 1995 and entitled *Mixed Fortunes*, found for example that the income received by 17 charities providing welfare services had risen by more than half in the last five years and that most of the extra money came from contracts with local authorities; these charities received more than half of their income from the state, felt they were in danger of turning into quangos, and spent some of the (static) funding they received from other sources on accountants and lawyers. Many of the community organisations that have survived from earlier more radical days, with or without local authority support, have dwindling membership, with a few resolute people struggling on. On the whole, they fall easy prey to the current blandishments of the government. They find it hard to resist the prevailing ideology of 'new realism', the onslaughts of Thatcherism and the 'market', and the apparent impossibility of radical alternatives.

A book entitled *The Crisis of London*, edited by Andy Thornley, provides a perhaps representative example of the current attitudes of many supporters of community action. The authors say in their introduction that they have a 'policy orientation', 'reflected in the decision to draw upon the knowledge and experience of people who are working to influence London's future'. But in their concluding chapter, called 'A Vision for London', they say they cannot put forward much of a vision because they are against 'expert blueprints and rigid utopias'. They favour, instead, a 'citizens' perspective', to be 'built up from the variety of different groups in the population', and based mainly, as George Nicholson's chapter advocates, on the views and democratic participation of people in particular localities or communities. These ideas suffer, as much of the current advocacy of the importance of the 'community', 'localities' and 'a sense of place' does, from a failure to define what these concepts mean, whose views are important, and how they might be ascertained. Variety, 'difference' and 'localness' are assumed to be good, without explicit justification. The ideas are common to many other current academic books which take up the fashionable themes of 'place' and 'localities'. Places are described, with little attempt to derive generally applicable theories from the detailed study of local areas. The authors of *The Crisis of London* acknowledge, briefly, that there may be 'other groups', such as women and black people, who share experiences of deprivation which are not locally specific. There is no mention of class, although it is possible to infer, from many of the things they say, that they *are* mainly concerned about people who are exploited under capitalism.

In general, the position taken by the authors of *The Crisis of London* is not that the market, or capitalism, need to be replaced, but that they are working badly — and work better in other parts of Europe. Michael Edwards (who in his chapter on redevelopment proposals at Kings Cross says that the main aim of the academics who worked on these issues at University College London was 'to provide some research support to local community groups, councils and the wider public . . .') is the only contributor to use the word 'socialist', and he is also one of the few to make his political argument explicit:

> 'my argument is not an extremist one. The contradictions and (from almost everyone's point of view) incompetence of London's land use and transport planning, of railway strategy and of labour-force policy generate raised eyebrows all over Europe . . . our particular mess is probably worse than you could find in Paris, Milan, Madrid or . . . Berlin. I am not arguing merely that the incremental chaos of London is anathema to socialists, but that it constitutes a pretty self-destructive form of capitalism too.'

This chapter has a fascinating analysis of the struggles between developers and local inhabitants and councils at Kings Cross. The developers, as elsewhere in the book, come out better than the government. They have a bit more vision and creativity. Their greed, Edwards argues, is only the 'normal greed' of capitalism: 'If we find their project socially unacceptable it must be a general objection to what gets produced under capitalism — and perhaps a criticism of the particular framework within which they operate in Britain'. But such political clarity is seldom replicated elsewhere, in this book or in the many other current publications on the problems of inner cities.

Perhaps the authors, like other participants in current academic debates, are influenced by the vacuities of postmodernist theorisations. No policies can or need be advocated or struggled for, because anything goes. As David Harvey wrote in *The Condition of Postmodernity*:

> 'postmodernism, with . . . its penchant for deconstruction bordering on nihilism, its preference for aesthetics rather than ethics, takes matters too far. It takes them beyond the point where any coherent politics are left, while that wing of it that seeks a shameless accommodation with the market puts it firmly in the tracks of an entrepreneurial culture that is the hallmark of reactionary neoconservatism. Postmodernist philosophers tell us not only to accept but even to revel in the fragmentations and the cacophany of voices through which the dilemmas of the modern world are understood. Obsessed with deconstructing and delegitimising every form of argument they encounter, they can end only in condemning their own validity claims to the point where nothing remains of any basis for reasoned action. Postmodernism has us accepting . . . all the fetishisms of locality, place, or social grouping, while denying that kind of meta-theory which can grasp the political-economic processes (money flows, international divisions of labour, financial markets, and the like) that are becoming ever more universalising in their depth, intensity, reach and power over daily life.'

Like others, including the government, the authors of *The Crisis of London* turn to 'diverse community groups' as though they might somehow provide solutions. It is not clear why. They acknowledge that community groups suffer from lack of money. They propose that planning powers should be used to secure lower land prices for socially useful developments. But elected local councils tried this and failed. There is no reason why, if some of the anyway inadequate powers and resources of local councils were handed over to local community groups, the latter should do any better. If they had more resources, there is also no particular reason why they should be any less remote and unaccountable than local authorities are accused of being; and they are not even elected. There is, moreover, little that local communities can do about their most overwhelming problem — the lack of jobs — without changes at a broader level. To achieve such changes requires radical action, rather than acceptance of government money for a few small projects. This the critics of the Community Development Programmes in the 1970s well recognised. Their successors in the 1980s and 1990s seem to have forgotten that lesson.

City Challenge

The government's renewed orientation to 'the community' was embodied in one of its latest 'flagship' schemes, City Challenge. City Challenge is now apparently out of favour; in November 1992 Norman Lamont, then Chancellor of the Exchequer, announced that it would be suspended for at least three years, and the funding allocated to it did not fully meet even the existing potential commitments. However from time to time ministers say that they would like to revive it. The programmes themselves run for five years from their initiation in 1991 and 1992, and account for around 16 per cent of Department of the Environment funding for inner cities.

City Challenge embodies one idea, in particular, that now pervades many of the government's programmes: potential recipients must bid against each other for the money. It was set up as a competition between Urban Programme authorities, and it concentrates a sizeable chunk of inner cities money in 31 small areas. There have been two 'bidding rounds' in this competition, in 1991 and 1992. The expected third round was formally cancelled, or postponed, at the end of 1992. The bids were prepared by local authorities, who were thus fully involved in the process. In the first round the government invited 15 of the 57 local authorities which have Urban Programme status to bid for a five year programme. 11 of these, described as the 'pacemakers', were 'successful'. In the second round, in 1992, the government invited all 57 to bid; 54 of them did so. 20 of them were 'successful'. The money allocated for each of these 31 local authorities was £37.5m, spread over a five year period, or £7.5m per year. There is no provision for inflation.

City Challenge was not, even formally, described as additional money. It came out of (or, as the jargon has it, was 'top-sliced' from) overall inner city funding, which is itself declining. Just over £1 billion is planned to be spent over the six years covered by the two rounds of City Challenge bids. City Challenge funding is itself not large, for example compared to the, even more concentrated, funding for UDCs; as Les Southern, chief executive of Middlesborough City Challenge, pointed out at a conference organised by the National Council of Voluntary Organisations in Manchester, 'We have contiguous boundaries with the UDC. I have £7.5 million, they have £60 million'. Yet, at the time it was initiated, City Challenge took around a third of the money available for inner cities (excluding UDCs). It will be confined to a little more than half of the 57 Urban Programme areas, which themselves do not cover all of the areas suffering from deprivation and industrial decline. Within these areas, the City Challenge bid in Lambeth, for example, covers 25 per cent of the borough's population, or less than 60,000 people. North Kensington's City Challenge area contains just under 25,000 people, less than 20 per cent of the borough's total population (a large proportion of whom, of course, are far from being deprived). Government spokespeople sometimes say that the purpose of City Challenge is to show what can be done. If these programmes were pilot programmes, and were subsequently generalised to all of the areas suffering from decline, this would still not go very far towards the massive transfer of resources which would be required to make some real improvement in their situation. But there is in any case no indication that the government intends to more than treble its spending on inner cities.

City Challenge was announced by Heseltine, then Secretary of State for the Environment, in May 1991. Lucy de Groot, who was the lead officer responsible for Lewisham council's successful City Challenge bid, comments in an article in *Local Economy* in November 1992:

> 'When he returned as Secretary of State at the end of the eighties, Heseltine had seen the revolution he had made in Docklands and he knew it was fundamentally flawed, even before the collapse of Olympia and York. Physical regeneration, the stimulation of the private market, the creation of improved infrastructure, the scapegoating and marginalisation of local government was not enough.'

City Challenge is based on programmes drawn up by the local authorities, which also administer the funds. The old 'partners', the private sector, remain prominent, but additional 'partners' were introduced, in the shape of 'the community', voluntary and tenants' organisations, and so on. Since the local authorities' bids had to be submitted to central government which would determine the 'winners', their content and policies clearly had to please the government. The government, indeed, produced some guidelines: the local authorities were to outline a vision and five year strategy for the transformation of a defined area; they must do so on behalf of a partnership of organisations and individuals including the private sector and the community; they must demonstrate that their strategy would 'lever' private sector funds; and they must propose a way of administering the programme at arms length from the local authority. The selected areas had to present 'opportunities' as well as problems; therefore they tended not to include, for example, desolate, out of town estates, whose needs might be greater. Other ways of pleasing the government were clear. For example any successful proposals for improving council estates would probably have to include an undertaking that a variety of tenure systems would be introduced (in other words that there would be partial privatisation). The bid documents, naturally, follow these guidelines, and are in fact remarkably similar to one another. Many of the local authorities hired private consultants to produce their shiny documents. Tower Hamlets, for example, according to one of the consultants involved, spent several hundred thousand pounds on hiring a team of consultants for 7-8 months. Their 'bids' are presented in suitably up-beat PR language, and all use much the same vocabulary and marketing devices. The *Financial Times* of 18 September 1992 described Lambeth's bid, for example, as follows:

> 'its glossy, pro-business, cross-party City Challenge would have been inconceivable in the days of "Red Ted" Knight . . .
>
> . . .
>
> 'Lambeth's City Challenge programme is dressed up like a corporate plan. It begins with a "vision", specifies objectives, then outlines strategy with maps and statistics galore. The "vision" is 2,000 jobs, 8,000 training places, and turning Brixton into "the centre of multicultural entertainment and shopping in South London". Watch this space.'

The marketing hype was applied fairly uniformly across the de-industrialised cities and towns of Britain. It is hard to determine how the government made its choices. It presumably did not do so on the simple basis of need. But nor did it follow the recommendations of the consultants it hired to evaluate the bids, which awarded 'Borderline Fail' marks, for example, to the bid documents of Lambeth and North Kensington, both of which were later pronounced 'winners'. Direct demonstration of likely ability to 'lever' private sector funds was certainly an advantage. Thus Jon Aldenton of the Tower Hamlets Environment Trust suggested at the University of Westminster conference in 1992 that:

> 'It turns out much depended on who had the best lobby, did the right number of letters come from the private sector, and such like. We ended up writing private sector letters to the Minister saying if you approve the Dalston bid we will be investing £6.5 million of building society money in the area so please give them the money.'

A substantial number of representatives of the private sector did clearly feel it in their interest to improve their local authority's chances in the City Challenge competition by putting their names to the bids (although once the bids were successful, some of them began to withdraw or scale down their undertakings to invest). Some, but not all, voluntary organisations and tenants' associations also decided to participate in this process. Since Urban Programme funding is no longer available and City Challenge is currently the main source of money, many of them feel they have little alternative. The local authorities' bid documents usually list the private, voluntary and community organisations which are said to have contributed to evolving the plans they contain, and describe the ways in which consultations and publicity were carried out. But many community organisations complain bitterly about the failure of the local authority to consult them adequately and the lack of opportunity for them to put forward projects. Given that there was a period of from (according to different council officers' statements) only six to ten weeks between the time when the local authorities were formally invited to bid and the deadline for submitting their bids, the projects included in the bid document had in effect to be projects which had already been designed and worked up. This meant that most of them were council projects or at least projects which were awaiting funding, usually previously submitted by established organisations such as housing associations and large voluntary organisations. After a bid had been accepted, councils had a further six months to draw up Action Plans. These were expected to be an elaboration of the bid documents, with more detailed figures and projections, and there were relatively few changes from the original bid documents and the projects listed in them.

Thus for example in the Conservative-controlled borough of North Kensington and Chelsea, which was a successful competitor in the second City Challenge round, the process was as follows. Once the council had decided to bid for City Challenge funds it contacted, according to council officers, over 250 community, voluntary and tenants' and residents' organisations that the council knew of. It wrote them letters saying that a City Challenge bid was being prepared and that the council wanted their ideas about what should be done to improve the area. It put an advertisement in the local 'free' newspaper, the *Kensington and Chelsea News*, and in the council's Community Liaison newsletter. It received large numbers of responses, including 110 written responses, which included applications for money, ideas for projects, and points about what was needed generally in the area. The major input was from large established organisations, such as the North Kensington Amenity Trust (NKAT), which made fairly detailed project submissions. In addition, the council looked at what ideas were around within the council's various departments. And it consulted the 'big players': the Health Authority, the West London Taskforce, the housing associations and 'of course' the police. The council offered to send its officers to talk about the bid. Two public meetings were organised by voluntary organisations.

Council officers then started the process of inviting bids and worked out a method of dealing with the proposals and ideas. They wanted the bid to represent what they optimistically termed 'the whole community'. So in March-April 1992 they set up a Partnership Group. This was chaired by a long serving Conservative councillor. The council chose representatives from voluntary organisations, tenants, police and the private sector. This body played a role in selecting projects for the bid. A majority, perhaps 60-70 per cent, were council projects; most of the others were NKAT projects. This, according to the council, was because of the limited time scale; the council felt that it was involving the community as much as it could. It also accepted that the community was at a disadvantage from the start; the council had full-time employees, but for the community a 'learning curve' was required. NKAT was one of the few organisations capable of responding in the short time period; it submitted fairly worked up proposals for two projects which were adopted as 'flagship' projects: the Westway Sports Centre and the St Ervans site re-development; it had of course previously done a considerable amount of work on both these projects, in the expectation of receiving funding from other sources.

The council heard in July 1992 that its bid was successful. It had to produce the Action Plan by December. This 'involved putting flesh on the ideas in the bid' and was 'hard work', according to the council. A council officer was appointed to direct this work; another four council officers and one official from the West London Task Force were seconded to write the Action Plan; all these council officers are still seconded, in theory part-time, to the City Challenge office. At the beginning the council spent £5,000 on employing a consultant from Price Waterhouse but this turned out to be unhelpful. The council wrote the actual text. It used an outside firm to produce a City Challenge booklet and design its lay-out and presentation. The Partnership Group met again after the bid was put in in April. It had to make a presentation to 12 civil servants and give them a tour of the area. Four of the group made the presentation: a tenants' representative; the police chief superintendant (who 'produced a gun'); a representative of Virgin Communications; and the local MP. Another presentation was made to the inner cities Minister, John Redwood, this time by the leader of the council, its chief executive and the representative of Virgin.

In Brixton, where Lambeth City Council's second round bid was also accepted, a similar process occurred. The council went through the usual procedures of consulting and informing local community groups and others on the proposed content of the council's bid for City Challenge funds. Many of those active in the City Challenge process nevertheless felt that the bid document and the Action Plan were drawn up with little consultation, let alone control by the community. Council and City Challenge officers agreed that nearly all the projects in the Action Plan were taken off the shelf, mostly the council's shelf. But they argued that this was because the government allowed little time (an argument with which Department of the Environment officials disagreed). They also argued that the projects had already been out to consultation under the council's normal procedures, which of course implied that City Challenge did not improve on the previous situation. In addition, the council was bound by the DoE's requirement that the projects should attract funding from elsewhere, especially the private sector, in other words that there should be 'leverage' of private sector funds. This meant in particular that most of the large projects which the council decided to put in its bid were the ones which had a projected private sector input. Nearly a quarter of Brixton Challenge money was to be given to the private developers P&O, as a subsidy to secure their contribution to the redevelopment of part of the Brixton central market.

The DoE told the local authority 'winners' not only that the ideas in the bid must come from the community, but also that their implementation had to be administered by a 'hybrid body', at 'arms-length' from the council. 'The community' was to be formally represented, along with the local authority, business and central government, on the board of this special City Challenge body; in other words it was to be represented directly, rather than through its local elected councillors. Thus Ruth Le Guen, head of the DoE's Inner Cities Grants Division, stated (in a summary of her presentation circulated at a conference at the University of Westminster in 1992) that: 'Initiated by local authorities, implementation and further development of all plans will be overseen by a partnership board, with representation in all cases from the public and private sectors and the community, but with variations in the size and breadth of representation from these groups'. Usually these City Challenge bodies have been set up as private limited companies, with boards which meet approximately monthly to oversee their decisions and staffs of varying sizes and compositions. Their chairs and chief executives have often been council officers, sometimes councillors, sometimes business people; in one case the chief executive came from a community organisation. The boards themselves vary both in size and composition. But they usually include the chair, the chief executive, councillors, representatives of the private sector and of statutory bodies such as the Health Authority, the police and the TECs, and representatives of 'the community'.

Thus for example North Kensington City Challenge company was set up as a company limited by guarantee, with a chief executive, a board of directors, an executive board and staff. It has an office in NKAT property under the Westway. The council advertised for the chief executive's job. It was largely responsible for the selection process, with some input from the Partnership group, and it appointed an accountant who had previously worked with councillors; his appointment was subsequently confirmed by the City Challenge board. Later three other senior staff were appointed from outside the council; a sergeant was seconded from the local police. A year later, in November 1993, a Community Development Officer was appointed; he had previously been active as a tenants' representative on a local housing estate and believed in the potential for community participation in decision-making. The company's staff has put most of its efforts into making sure that the money has been spent on time, and has been successful in this. Its staff have however been criticised for being remote and failing to communicate; until the Community Development Officer was appointed, none of them had much community experience or background. The North Kensington City Challenge board's meetings are held in public, and their documents are publicly available. Observers are freely admitted. North Kensington board meetings have been held in different places, including sometimes in the main council offices, south of the City Challenge area. Not all of the directors attend. Some of the community directors in particular, who are paid no expenses and are expected to read large amounts of paperwork often available only shortly before the meetings, have found it difficult to attend. Some have also stated that they feel intimidated and outnumbered by council insiders and officials, and few of them speak at the meetings.

In Brixton the City Challenge company was also set up as a private limited company. Its first chief executive had previously worked in the council's housing department. As elsewhere, there was a marked, and much criticised, absence of local people among the company's paid staff. Unlike in North Kensington, board meetings are held in private and board papers are available only to members of the board. Company officers plead commercial confidentiality as a reason for holding closed meetings and refusing to allow the public to read board papers, responding to requests for information with the statement that: 'This is a private company'.

In the subsequent stages of the City Challenge process, local authorities have been given continuing responsibilities, some of which, of course, contribute to their unpopularity. They act as the formal conduit for City Challenge funds. Projects approved by City Challenge boards must then be approved by the local authority, which retains responsibility for ensuring that the money is properly spent. Thus in theory at least the local authority retains a right of veto on projects approved by the board. In North Kensington, as elsewhere, there have been tensions in the company's relationship with the council. There are five councillors out of the 24 directors on the City Challenge company's board, including the chair. The council's community liaison officer plays an active role in board meetings, explaining what is and is not possible from the council's point of view. Meetings of the council's City Challenge sub-committee take place immediately after the board meetings. Up to now these have been a formality. But at one executive board meeting, for example, there were quite acrimonious discussions on a particular voluntary sector project, with the chair and the council officer insisting that the project needed further appraisal, and the company's officers, a Labour councillor and a private sector representative united in favour of an immediate decision to fund it; the issue was put to a vote, which was in any case unlikely to be conclusive. The council's argument was that it had longer experience of the nature of community organisations and other potential recipients of funding than City Challenge company officers and some board members. In general, while the company's officers have wanted to secure some leeway to depart from the Action Plan drawn up by the council, in particular so as to be able to accommodate new ideas produced by the community and others, the council has warned that commitments have already been made (both to the voluntary sector and to departments of the council) and that this may not be possible. This experience is repeated elsewhere, and often causes much anger among community representatives in particular, who feel that they are simply being used as window-dressing for programmes which are decided elsewhere and which there is no possibility for them to change. In Brixton in particular the relationship between the community, the City Challenge company and the council has been particularly bitter and conflictual.

The reincorporation of the local authorities into the process of distributing public money to the inner cities is in any case likely to have a limited effect on the policies that are pursued. The government has manoeuvred rather cleverly. It long ago succeeded in reducing local authorities to agencies for carrying out cuts, and thus adding further reasons for local people to dislike them. Nearly all of them have yielded to the pressures of new realism and now actively attempt to encourage inward investment by the private sector. Under City Challenge, the government retains centralised control over local authorities' strategies for their area. Even after projects have been submitted and approved in the bid documents and Action Plans, any spending above a certain amount has to be submitted to the DoE for final approval, and the project documents must contain detailed information on projected outputs and spending. The funding is not secure for the full five years; City Challenge companies have to go through twice-yearly appraisals to secure continued funding. The main pressure from the DoE is felt by some City Challenge officials to be to spend precisely the required amount of money, neither more nor less than £7.5 million a year. But the government has also indicated that funding will not be renewed if insufficient attempts are made to involve the community. In insisting that the community must be separately represented in the City Challenge institutions, the government was implicitly restating its belief that (usually Labour-controlled) local councils are unrepresentive. It is a view with which many would agree, including people who have long campaigned against local authority bureaucracy, failure to consult, unresponsiveness, corruption and, more recently, new realism, cuts and other failings. The government is now seen as the generous provider of the (smaller) sums of money available through the much publicised City Challenge. And in addition, it has stipulated that 'the community' must be formally consulted and involved in the process. All this has led to some peculiar reversals of political perceptions. Thus at a conference organised in Manchester by the National Council for Voluntary Organisations (NCVO) to discuss City Challenge, some community activists were not only critical of Labour-controlled local authorities, but, on occasion, suggested that the central government might be more receptive to their ideas and help them in their battles with these authorities. For example local activists from Manchester's City Challenge area in Moss Side and Hulme asked the DoE representative why the government did not force the local authority to listen to the views of the community and 'deny them the money if they don't'. The official's reply was that this was not a role the DoE could perform: 'we cannot prescribe centrally'.

The attempt to redefine local democracy, separately from the existing system of electing representatives to local councils, is obviously not straightforward. The City Challenge companies were supposed to be the vehicle for increasing the participation of the community. But quite apart from the question of the extent to which these companies can affect decisions made by the government and the council, the question is also how the representation of the community on the boards of the companies is to be determined. This question has been resolved in a great variety of ways. In North Kensington, as elsewhere, the council took responsibility for organising the selection of the company's directors. The government's expressed view, according to council officers, was that there should be equal representation on the board for the local authority, the private sector and the community, in other words that there should be eight representatives for each of these. The pressure locally in North Kensington was for there to be much higher representation for voluntary organisations; the government said no, that would cut out the private sector. In the DoE's letter approving the bid, the government also said it wanted more 'ethnic' representation. This, according to the council, helped it in its relationships with the Partnership group; there had always been pressure from the community for more 'ethnic' representation. The council wrote to the Partnership group, which was originally selected by itself, inviting its members to become directors. But in the event there was an almost complete turnover from the Partnership Group. British Rail, British Gas and European Passenger Services are not represented on the board. None of the voluntary sector representatives are the same, and there are no tenants' representatives as such. The Council of Churches refused to accept the person appointed by the council, and carried out its own selection process. In the end, on the 24-member board, the council says that it 'erred on the side of more community representation'; 11 of the directors, in the council's view, 'directly represent the community'; the council claims that it was 'pushing it a bit with the DoE'.

The directors on the North Kensington City Challenge board whom the council says represent the community were elected from 'forums'. Most of these were set up by the council. Council officers claim that the idea of setting up forums originated with themselves. There were six directors elected from two 'community forums', two representatives from 'voluntary organisations which provide services to the community' and three representatives from an 'ethnic minority forum'. In addition there are: one director from the church, who the council suggests represents the community, and who is a Christian (although in theory he could be Muslim); five councillors, three Conservatives and two Labour; the chief superintendant from Notting Hill police station; and one representative from the Health Authority. Finally there are five directors from the private sector: one representative from a housing association (the Kensington Housing Trust); two representatives nominated by the Chamber of Commerce, one the director of a Bodyshop franchise in the Portobello Road, and the other the owner of a small business; and two representatives from CenTEC (Central London Training and Enterprise Council), one from Virgin Communications, the other from a small recruitment and PR firm. The board is chaired by a Conservative councillor.

The North Kensington community forums are open to anybody resident or working in the area. Again, observers are freely admitted. Two forums were established, East and West of Ladbroke Grove. After the bid was successful and before the first board meeting, the council held a series of meetings 'to start the debate about how the community wanted to select its directors'. For the first of these, it engaged a firm of architects with experience of community consultation exercises; these consultants 'facilitated' the first meetings of the two community forums, on the West and East sides of Ladbroke Grove. The council was not happy with their efforts, and dispensed with their further services. The forums were then organised by the council's community liaison officer and chaired by the council's chief executive. The second set of public meetings discussed the detail of organising elections; there was said to be consensus on the mechanics of organising elections, that there should be hustings and nomination forms; but disagreement on who should be eligible to vote. The council's view was that it was desirable that people should stand and vote as individuals because people who are for example chairs of voluntary organisations 'are not always representative and the majority of people don't belong to organisations'. In the end, in both forums, those eligible were all those over 18 who live and/or work in the City Challenge area. The meetings on the East side were chaired by 'a member of the community'; on the West side they were chaired by the council's chief executive and by councillors.

The elections to the two North Kensington community forums took place in December 1992. There were again two separate meetings on either side of Ladbroke Grove. At both meetings the election process was run by the council, with ballot boxes, voting papers, and verification of the electoral role and of proof of employment in the area carried out by council officers. On the East side, about 12 people stood. The meeting was well attended; most were residents, only a few were people employed in the area but living outside it. Each candidate gave a five-minute presentation. The voting continued for an hour. The three candidates elected were clear winners and were, according to the council, 'independent'. The election meeting on the West side was more subdued and took place in a church; there were fewer candidates and fewer people attending to vote. According to one council officer the results were 'quite refreshing'; the people who were elected were not from voluntary organisations (apart from the Law Centre); the council officer knew four out of the six people elected from the two forums, but 'they were very much new people'. Of the six, two men and one woman were from the Moroccan community (one of these was unemployed, a former hospital worker and active trade unionist; one was a council employee; one was an employee of the Moroccan Cultural Centre); one was from the Law Centre in Golborne Road; one was from a tenants' association; and one was a social services worker. In spite of the fact that the process was organised by the council, there were complaints that there were too many Moroccans on the board and a local Catholic priest claimed that the elections had been 'rigged': Moroccans, he claimed, had been 'bussed in from other areas'. The reality seems to have been that the Moroccan community organised for the elections (one of the first occasions on which it has done so), whereas the tenants' organisations and others failed to do so. There were also complaints that the publicity was inadequate. The council employed a private company to distribute letters giving notification of the meetings and the elections, and they were not distributed around all of the estates. The Labour Party on the West side claims that it organised to ensure that its candidates were elected; both the Moroccan directors elected from the West side are members of the Labour Party.

After the elections took place, the council's officers continued to act as the forums' secretariat. The job was not taken on by the City

Challenge company, which provided no administrative back-up for the forums' meetings, although when in late 1993 the City Challenge company eventually appointed a Community Development Officer, the intention was that he would take over their organisation. The forums have elected only directors of the company; they have no officers, no funding and no office. Meetings have been infrequent, in spite of requests from at least one of the directors for them to be held more frequently. In the autumn of 1993 the forums decided to set up a joint steering committee, open to anybody who wished to attend from either forum. This committee was supposed to meet a few days before the board meetings to discuss the agenda and papers and advise the directors. It produced a paper which was critical, among other things, of the company's failure to keep the community informed of its activities.

In North Kensington a voluntary sector forum was already in existence, set up and administered by the two Social Councils which exist in the North and South of the borough. These meet every other month. It was therefore possible to establish a small sub-group of the northern forum (the Notting Hill Social Council). The local authority had limited involvement, but an officer from the council's community relations section helped with the formal process of electing the two directors just before the board meeting. Both are from large established organisations; one is the director of the North Kensington Amenity Trust and the other is the secretary of the Notting Hill Social Council, both of which have offices under the Westway. In 1993 the two directors wrote a memorandum, reflecting the views of the forum that communication between the City Challenge company and the voluntary sector was not as good as it should be and that the relationship needed improving. North Kensington's 'ethnic minority forum' was set up specifically for City Challenge purposes. It was organised by another officer in the local authority's community relations section, who set up a meeting to organise elections. The meeting discussed how the elections were to take place and which communities would be represented, and was well attended. After some discussion it agreed there would be one representative each from the Moroccan, Caribbean and Asian communities. The directors have been criticised by some for not being regular attenders or large participators at board meetings. The forum has held some subsequent meetings. At its meeting in November 1993 there was an attendance of one, but previous meetings were better attended.

In general the representation of the community achieved through these processes had, at least until late 1993, been more formal than real, with members of big voluntary organisations as active as they had always been in their relations with the council, and newcomers hesitant about attempting to intervene. One of the major deterrents to their active intervention was their recognition of the limited scope for change in the programmes to be financed. They also believed that, mainly because of the emphasis on private sector funding and financial constraints, many of the larger projects would be irrelevant to the needs of local unemployed, low waged and/or black people. They found the staff of the City Challenge company unapproachable. The latter were overwhelmingly involved in the technicalities of getting the projects and funding organised, and had few contacts with local people. They were, however, quite open in their dealings with the public and sympathetic, at least in theory, towards their goals and needs.

In Brixton on the other hand the members of the City Challenge board representing the community were elected by, and as, representatives of organisations. As a means of securing formal community representation on the board of the Brixton Challenge company, the council set up two community forums, a tenants' forum and a private sector forum. These forums were not open to individuals, but to members of accredited organisations. They elected representatives to act as board members, and also officers: chairs, secretaries and treasurers. The meetings were called, administered, minuted and sometimes chaired by officers of Brixton Challenge, and the elections were organised by them. Many of the forum members expressed a great deal of hostility towards the City Challenge leading officers. This was partly because the forums encountered an extreme unwillingness by some of these officers to allow their activities to be monitored or to give out information. The concerns expressed by numerous people at the forums were not only that they could have little say in what was being done, partly in their name, through City Challenge, but also that they were finding it hard even to obtain information. The forums spent much of their time criticising the Brixton Challenge team's unwillingness to give them information to enable them to make judgements on existing plans, asking for more information, contesting the confidentiality of board meetings, and criticising, for example, the failure to inform forum members of recruitment opportunities and the almost total absence of local people in the Brixton Challenge office. Brixton Challenge officers were also defensive in their relations with outside researchers and observers and attempted to prevent the attendance of observers at forum meetings.

In addition the Brixton City Challenge forums were frustrated by their perception of their inability to affect decisions made by the council and the board. Several forum participants argued they were being 'used', that they were merely 'window-dressing' to legitimise plans that had already been sewn up elsewhere, and so on. In response Brixton Challenge officers suggested that, although the Action Plan was in a sense binding, there would be opportunities for the community and other forums to insert new projects because there would be 'slippage'; some of the existing projects would 'fall by the way'. The forums however did not show much sign of trying to work out how to take advantage of this rather hypothetical possibility. They were on the other hand critical of some individual projects, especially on the grounds that they might lead to the displacement of local businesses and even homelessness. They also expressed a good deal of doubt about the chances of Brixton Challenge producing any significant number of new local jobs. Brixton Challenge's engagement of a firm of consultants to administer a voluntary Code of Practise on local employment for firms participating in Brixton Challenge projects was viewed with a great deal of scepticism. The hostility towards Brixton Challenge was not universally held. There were people in the forums who argued that the process provided opportunities for a community input and pleaded for these opportunities to be taken and, for example, for the forums to organise jointly to take advantage of them. A few forum members and officers defended the board and the Brixton Challenge team, and said that they are doing a good job and were themselves hampered by lack of resources. Most of the elections were hotly contested. Quite a few community activists appeared anxious to obtain positions in the forums and on the board. The question is whether they were wasting their time.

The government, for its part, continues to press for its chosen ideological goals: for privatisation, for market-led strategies, for a 'mix' of housing tenure, for support for enterprise and small businesses, and so on. Ruth Le Guen (see above) listed the 'threefold aims' of City Challenge as 'to attract wealth to the area', 'to secure benefits for residents', and 'to pilot more effective ways of managing urban renewal'. The biggest change is in the second of these aims; in her speech she expanded on this, saying that City Challenge, 'unlike the UDCs', would 'be targeted from the outset on disadvantaged residents', and that it was based on the recognition that certain areas suffered from multiple deprivation, that there was 'no automatic trickle down' of benefits from regeneration, and much alienation of local people. The aim, therefore, was both to improve the area, *and* to ensure that residents benefited from the improvement, for example through helping them to get jobs in the new developments, both in their construction phase and subsequently, and providing training to enable them to do so. Thus, under the heading 'inward development', Ruth Le Guen listed 'linking developments through contract rules with training opportunities for residents: but must not put off developers'.

But the aim of attracting wealth, or inward investment, from outside the area remains the first objective. If wealth *is* attracted in from outside, this may be a mixed blessing. Although City Challenge is said to be 'targeted' at existing *and* 'disadvantaged' local residents, the goal of changing the population 'mix' remains. As Ruth Le Guen put it, 'the housing mix needs to be changed so that those who make it, stay in the area', and, *in addition*, she said, 'the yuppies must be attracted in', so that they provide the wealth which will lead to regeneration. Supposing City Challenge is successful in its own terms, there is therefore no certainty that local residents will not, yet again, find their place taken over and transformed through the usual forms of gentrification. Their streets may be sanitised and emptied, dragooned into the heavy livery of post-modernist architecture (whose supposed variety is quite superficial). The big chains may take over from local shops and the small workshops and subversive unseemly factories may be driven out. They themselves may be pushed yet further to the margins.

It is conceivable, although not on current evidence very likely, that the City Challenge process might have the effect of raising the level of organisation, self confidence and political awareness in communities. But if it did, it of course remains to be seen how the government, and City Challenge boards, would react if the community's demands were not what they hoped for and could accommodate. These new representatives of the community might possibly demand changes in the general orientation of government policies for the inner cities. Supposing the community organisations on the boards of City Challenge companies got together and demanded that public money was spent not to subsidise 'market-led' investment for the wealthy, but to provide facilities and housing for those who cannot pay, and jobs which are unionised and well paid, would they be listened to? Or will the whole exercise turn into a glorified form of planning gain, with community representatives fighting each other to win some rather small amounts of funding for their particular projects, in return for raising no objections to the state provision of subsidies for the 'market-led' developers to invade and take over their place? There are indications, from the experience of City Challenge so far, that the latter is more likely to be the case. The result of the process may be, as the government perhaps intended, that the valuable time of community activists is taken over by the elaborate processes of applying for City Challenge money and competing for influence and posts on its various bodies. The chances of effective resistance to the government's destructive policies may thus recede yet further into the future.

CHAPTER 7

Protest and resistance

Resistance, however, is needed. Cities were built around jobs and the jobs have gone. The current policies of governments are making the recession deeper and the situation of those who still have jobs more precarious and harsher. Local authorities have less and less money with which to do anything to resolve the major problems of cities, such as homelessness and a crumbling and increasingly unsafe environment. The 'special programmes' for inner cities, however great or small the influence of members of 'the community' is on these programmes, will not change this reality. At most, they may attract small amounts of investment from one part of the city to another, add a few superficial post-Modernist adornments, and create a few cultural or sports centres which are often inaccessible to the unemployed and the poor who live in the area. The problems of cities require, as the community activists pointed out in the 1970s (see above), more radical solutions.

It may be that capitalism will have another boom. Socialists, like right-wing realists, are pessimistic on the chances of resolving the current crises in the world economy, and especially of ending mass unemployment, under capitalism. Nevertheless some believe that it is premature to write off the possibility of returning to something like full employment even under the prevailing economic system. In the past capitalism has swung from boom to slump and back again. There is no inevitable reason why changes in technology should imply the employment of fewer people; in the nineteenth century, the Luddites were proved wrong, at least in some of their arguments; not all jobs can be mechanised, new products arise and there are many unmet needs. In their book *The Politics of Local Economic Policy* Eisenschitz and Gough raise doubts on the 'fatalistic' view that there is some kind of inevitable and permanent 'jobs deficit' or 'surplus population' because 'the volume of consumption is fixed or rising only slowly, and . . . technological change does not itself help to stimulate economic expansion'. This they say is a 'weak theorisation of high unemployment'. The main obstacle to full employment is the same as it has always been under capitalism: the attachment of governments to the notion that deflation is the only way of resolving capitalism's recurrent crises of over-production. It is reinforced by the view that the working class can only be controlled, and have its aspirations curbed, by unemployment. In periods of growth, government policies change and the strength of the working class grows again. If something like full employment returned, much would change. Full employment would dramatically improve the immediate material situation of the people who live and suffer in inner cities. As the right well knows, the power of the working class and its traditional methods of struggle would again increase, and would again force the ruling class to concede some reforms to improve the situation of workers and of the cities they live in.

This does not mean that capitalism ought to survive. Its disadvantages do not go away in periods of growth and relative affluence. It is a system based on greed and the never-ending accumulation of capital (and often useless material goods). There is an inexorable and inherent need for capitalist firms to expand, to search for new markets and new consumers and to develop new tastes for yet more commodities. Capitalism's drive for profit creates injustice, waste and violence. It has potentially disastrous effects on the environment and, through arms sales for example, contributes to wars and swelling numbers of refugees. The market breeds inequality and leads to the exploitation of most people by a few wealthy individuals and big corporations. This happens within countries and also between them. Capitalism has only worked, in the sense that it has provided relative comfort and an absence of starvation, in small parts of the world. In Third World countries, all of which are increasingly integrated into the capitalist world market, malnutrition is widespread and starvation persists. In the 'advanced industrialised countries' of Europe and North America, poverty was not eliminated even during the periods of boom. During recession, homelessness and even hunger are again on the increase. The squandering, waste and the promotion of excessive and unplanned consumption inherent to capitalism's unceasing drive for new markets threaten most parts of the world and create pollution and squalor. The 'freeing' of financial markets has created unpredictable, violent and potentially catastrophic surges and collapses in stock markets and exchange rates, and has sucked ordinary bank depositors and savers into a kind of international gambling system, haphazardly controlled by unaccountable young men and a few women pressing buttons on computers. Above all, high consumption levels, for some, in the industrialised countries lead to the over-exploitation of the land and peoples of the Third World and the spread of starvation and deserts.

In the 1990s there has been something of a backlash against the excesses of the 1980s, free market ideology and Thatcherism. In Britain privatisation is beginning to get a bad name which derives mainly from the financial bonanzas which the directors of the privatised industries have awarded themselves. Directors' salaries and Conservative sleaze are publicised and criticised. The property slump turned even many middle class homeowners into holders of negative equity, or of mortgages whose value exceeds that of their houses; it added some of them to the growing mass of repossessed and homeless. On 24 December 1993 the *Financial Times*, the newspaper of the financial establishment and committed defender of capitalism and the free market, nevertheless published a leader called 'Capitalism at Christmas' which ought to be reproduced in full but which said in part:

'. . . Never in 2,000 years has the doctrine of the free market spread so widely across the globe. Communism has been buried, socialism is in deep retreat, and even the hardiest proponents of social democracy are beset by doubt. Adam Smith has vanquished Marx, immobilised Keynes, and turned many thoughts away from Jesus . . . democracy and pluralism, two important doctrines associated with capitalism, are being taken up with less enthusiasm, and in fewer countries, than the system of wealth creation that is now everywhere regarded as the most effective that humanity has yet devised.

'No known alternative stands ready for the choosing. . . . The result of the Uruguay round is likely to be an acceleration of production, a greater accumulation of man-made assets, and an entrenchment of the market as the dominant economic force on the face of the planet.

'It remains, however, an imperfect force. Even the middle classes, who have benefitted most from economic growth, are wrestling with unease. Those in jobs fear that they may lose what they have, while those outside note that however rich the super-rich may get, large-scale unemployment persists. Lower down the income scale the picture is far worse. The 1980s created losers as well as winners, as can be seen on the pavements of cities across Europe and the US. In many cases the poor have become poorer, relatively in some countries, absolutely in others. About two-thirds of the world's population have gained little or no substantial advantage from rapid economic growth. In the developed world, the lowest quartile of income earners has witnessed trickle-up rather than trickle-down . . .

'. . . the true spirit of the festival requires that those who desire an economic success built upon something other than foundations of much misery and deprivation engage in the search for policies which are both hard-headed and ethical. Human economic history has not ended with the triumph of the free market. It has hardly begun.'

Others, in the same newspaper and elsewhere, have argued that social democracy is in danger and that the ruling classes of the rich countries may end up offering their citizens little other than repression, xenophobia and the exclusion of foreigners, corralling themselves into ghettos. The government appears, however, able to brush aside with impunity the protests of social democrats and liberals, even when they are members of the political and financial elite, against its increasingly racist and anti-liberal measures. In the history of capitalism, long slumps have sometimes ended, and been replaced by booms, only after wars. Wars did not stop in 1945; they carried on, usually far from Europe; but they now seem to have intensified, and are fuelled by immiseration and new nationalisms. After the last big slump, the war was preceded by fascism. The Thatchers, Portillos and other right-wing Conservatives, the law and order fanatics, the racists and increasingly brutal policemen may be portents of worse to come. Marx, for his part, warned that the alternatives facing us were socialism or barbarism.

It is of course not just community activism which has lost its capacity for resistance (see previous section). The left in general is in retreat. However much the left tried and still tries to disassociate itself from what happened in the Soviet Union and Eastern Europe, the collapse of Stalinist regimes in those areas has weakened its capacity to argue for socialism and win support. The onward march of the ideology of the market appears irresistible. With a few exceptions, 'left' intellectuals accommodate to it. Little by little, the language of public ownership, workers' control, class, revolution, even socialism, disappears. Left academics have drifted off into the highways and byways of post-Fordism and post-modernism, sterile debates and intellectual games which lead to no action. Post-Fordist ideas tend to lead, instead, to acceptance of notions of a reformed capitalism, responding 'flexibly' to consumer demands, and the replacement of the organised working class by 'flexible' individual workers and class collaboration. To the extent that post-Fordists call for action, they may advocate cooperation between employers and workers for the enhancement of their firm's productivity and profits and/or the competitive position of their locality; they point

TERESA HAYTER

repeatedly to the consensual model of the 'Third Italy', but find it hard to discover replicates of this very particular situation elsewhere. Post-Modernist ideas, on the other hand, tend to negate altogether the possibility that there might be goals towards which it would be worth struggling. Large numbers of what David Harvey has called FRUMPS (formerly radical upwardly mobile professionals), especially academic geographers, intone the new liturgy that 'Place matters' and 'Everywhere is different', as if that meant anything at all other than, perhaps, a denial of the importance of theory which is nevertheless clothed in pseudo-theoretical jargon and long words.

The Labour Party retreats, step by step, Conservative measure by Conservative measure. Its leader, Tony Blair, has adopted the mantle of law and order, and he and members of the shadow cabinet proclaim their toughness on crime and their hostility towards those who are forced to live rough on the streets. Most of the far left organisations which retain their commitment to Marxist and Leninist ideas have lost membership and support. Their hope of winning a base among organised workers has diminished with unemployment. Unemployment has enabled the Conservatives to impose legal restrictions on trade unions and get away with it. Few workers are currently willing to break the law, and face the immediate threat of the sack, in order to take strike action for their wages and conditions, let alone for broader and longer term goals, as they did when trade unions were first established. When workers do take industrial action, they tend not to be supported by their leadership, which argues that support for such action would put union funds at risk (to the point that it becomes hard to see what union funds might be for). This has been the situation of the brave struggle of Liverpool dockers for more than a year. In France at the end of 1995, workers and unions provided yet again proof of the potential power of mass strike action, and won not merely victories for their own members, but more general gains for the working class, the unemployed and the poor. But their example has not yet been followed in Britain. The labour movement has moreover made little effort, and had little success, in recruiting or organising the unemployed, the casually employed and the impoverished residents of inner cities. With good reason the latter are overwhelmingly sceptical of politics and politicians, and sometimes appear to be more open to the courting of the far right than they are to the traditional left. They have one really effective means of making themselves heard: rioting. But the rioters usually make no political demands, and they confine themselves to their immediate

169

neighbourhoods. They are a product of alienation, rather than of any form of optimism or belief in the possibility of change.

Other methods of struggle are being found, which keep alive traditions of struggle, protest and direct action. There exists an amorphous, heterogeneous and growing movement of people whose common defining characteristic is non-violent direct action. Even Arthur Scargill, president of the National Union of Miners, arguing in November 1995 for the setting up of a Socialist Labour Party, recognised their importance:

> 'Today, radical opposition in Britain is symbolised not by the Labour and trade union movement but by the groupings such as those which defeated the Poll Tax, the anti-motorway and animal rights bodies, Greenpeace and other anti-nuclear campaigners, and those fighting against opencast mining.
> 'These are now the voices of protest and direct action, reminding us that only through direct — including industrial — action and defiance of unjust laws can we achieve real advance, whilst a moribund Labour Party and trade union hierarchy pleads with citizens to accept and submit to those laws.'

He added that:

> 'The environmental and community activists are doing a good job, but, inevitably, their aims are "single purpose" with no clear political perspective. It is a tragedy that the Labour Party is not at the centre of coordinating and organising such campaigns.'

This direct action movement is of course not new; it has progenitors in particular in the peace protests and squatting movements of the 1960s, 1970s and 1980s and especially the long-lasting women's protest against US missiles at Greenham Common. But it has received a powerful boost from mainly green ideas. It has, so far, little direct relationship to the problems of inner cities. In some cases its adherents appear to have little concern for the problems and needs of working class people. Animals may be considered more important than people. Sometimes the protests have the support of the rural gentry, anxious to preserve the aesthetics of the countryside. Occasionally the green protestors fail to disassociate themselves from the far right. Nevertheless it is a movement with very wide, cross class support. It has in particular the support of many young people, including unemployed and homeless people and the urban dispossessed. Some of the protests against road building have taken place in cities. The protest against an M11 link motorway took place both in the middle class area of Wanstead and in the densely populated working class area of Leytonstone, in East London; local residents joined the protests against the destruction of houses and trees. In Glasgow, there was a long-running direct action protest against a proposed motorway through Pollock Estate, a public park near some of the worst inner city housing in Britain, which had been donated by a philanthropist to the people living there; the action succeeded in preserving a small corner of the park for public use. Some of the direct action involves squatting, again in the poor neighbourhoods of cities, either to house homeless people or to create free community facilities for the unemployed and others. Many new age travellers are not only attached to a rural life and to idealistic notions of freedom from material possessions, but have also escaped from homelessness and unemployment in cities. Young people, both black and white, have demonstrated in large numbers against racism and racist attacks, and against, for example, the British National Party headquarters in South London. Near Oxford, protestors camped for several weeks outside the Campsfield Immigration Detention Centre in opposition to the imprisonment there of refugees and other black people; some climbed over the perimeter fence or adorned it with banners in ways reminiscent of the actions of Greenham women, some of whom joined them. Non-violent direct action has been used against banks and Third World debt and, most dramatically, the sale of British Aerospace planes to Indonesia. The Conservative government's 1994 Criminal (In)Justice Bill, criminalising squatting, trespass and many forms of protest, including potentially demonstrations and public meetings, united squatters, homeless, new age travellers, road protestors, ravers, hunt saboteurs, trade unionists and the far left in the political form of demonstrations and marches, followed by speeches, which was entirely new to many of them. The marches themselves were sometimes without leaders and planned routes in ways which, in turn, were new and perplexing to the police. At the end of 1996 in Liverpool, Reclaim the Streets activists had planned a street party on a Saturday when dockers had organised a demonstration. They decided to join forces under the slogan 'Reclaim the Future' and marched together to a rally addressed by dockers, Arthur Scargill, Hillingdon Asian women strikers, green activists and others. The activists announced a 'mass action' at the docks on Monday. When dockers and dockers' wives (organised as 'Women of the Waterfront') turned up at their usual early morning hour for the picket and raised their eyes from their tasks of collecting wood and getting stoves going, they saw a line of young people standing on the roof of the administration block and others up cranes, inside the docks complex ('goodness knows how they got in'). The dockers, most of them in their fifties, were passionate in their enthusiasm for the support given to their strike by 'the young people', and joint actions continue.

Much of the protest action is exuberantly creative. Protestors have bought old JCBs, painted them in bright colours and abandoned them in the middle of road works. At the road protest at Solsbury Hill near Bath, protestors built a giant bulldozer in maple poles, then set light to it and did somersaults through the flames. At Twyford Down, another roads protest near Winchester, people threw themselves in front of bulldozers. Protestors in Reclaim The Streets campaigns in Camden in London, in Oxford, in Brighton and elsewhere have blockaded and taken over streets and organised street cafes, complete with waiters in black suits and bow ties, and street parties. In London protesters met at Liverpool Street, travelled on the Central Line to Shepherds Bush and took the police by surprise, stopping the traffic on a section of motorway and hiding under the skirts of giant puppets to drill holes in the road and plant trees in them. The campaign against the M11 created a phenomenal display of sculpture and works of art, as well as incredible structures with more immediate defensive purposes. The campaign proclaimed independence from the British state and applied to the United Nations for nation status, first for Wanstonia and then, when they were evicted from Wanstead, for Leytonstonia. Protestors, there and at Newbury and other road protest sites, sit up trees and cranes and on roofs, string nets across streets and between trees, and encase themselves in concrete. At road protests against the A30 by-pass in Devon, protesters built a fortified camp, enclosing defensive underground pits and vegetable plots, at 'Trollheim', and an elaborate and potentially lethal network of tunnels at the nearby Fairmile camp. Groups such as Small World make videos of the protests and show them at festivals and elsewhere.

Protestors have been subjected to strong reaction from the state. They have been arrested in large numbers and have been beaten up both by the police and by private security guards. The latter, who are sometimes paid as little as £1.60 an hour, are gaining a reputation for unregulated violence and criminal backgrounds. The 2nd Quarter 1994 edition of *East Ender — A Journal for Regeneration by Conservation — Not Redevelopment* reports for example in an article on the No-M11 campaign that:

'It was a little after 7.00 in the morning of Monday 13 June when local residents near the Gainsborough Road end of Fillebrook Road were awakened by cries and shouts for help from their neighbours, residents of *Leytonstonia* — the independent free area which seceded from jurisdiction of the British government on 26 January . . .

'Camping in trees in the Rainbow Fluffy Forest and in benders on the ground near Leytonstone Henge, several people were asleep when they were subjected to violent assaults in a raid by employees of two security companies accompanied by chain-saw wielding contractors' vandals.

'Much of their property was damaged including clothing, bedding, tents, and guitars. Other musical instruments were smashed and many suffered kicks, sprains and punches to the head and body as they tried to gather their wits to defend themselves. One man was dragged out of his sleeping bag before he had a chance to get dressed. Later he was arrested by police for "indecent exposure". All the people were thrown off the site illegally despite protests and access to their damaged possessions was not allowed until several hours later when money, diaries and other personal possessions and papers had disappeared.

'The alarm was raised immediately. People from adjoining and neighbouring property and members of the press came over to see what was happening and tried to help. They found no police nor was there any official from the bailiffs' or sheriffs' office present.

'There was little local people could do to prevent the criminal assaults against mostly defenceless young people by this gang of common thugs and vandals.

. . .

'Later, upon request to Chief Inspector Stobbs of Leyton police, a police presence was provided in the garden to protect residents from the threat of further attacks against them.'

At the Solsbury road protest, security guards smoked people out of trees with fumes from burning tyres. When one of the protestors at Campsfield Detention Centre climbed on a roof inside the prison, she was dragged off by a Group 4 guard and an ambulance had to be called. The most vicious reprisals have been against the young people who went into the docks in Liverpool in 1996, perhaps because an alliance between direct action and traditional labour movement struggles is seen to have considerable subversive potential. When the protestors left the docks, the dockers and their wives escorted them in an attempt to protect them from the police but were unable to do so; the police came in their vans and seized the young protestors, beating them up so badly that five of them were hospitalised. The beatings inside the vans were so severe that they were audible and visible (the vans shook) to the dockers outside. Neither the protestors nor the dockers had previously experienced such treatment.

Occasionally the protestors succeed in their immediate objectives. A few roads have not been built. More have been delayed, with their costs spiralling. Direct action has helped to win the argument that more roads create more traffic, and more asthma. Spectacularly, Greenpeace direct action, combined with consumer boycotts and the protests of other European governments, forced Shell into a humiliating abandonment of its project for the deep sea disposal of its oil rig the Brent Spar, and infuriated the British government. But the protestors often have no clear overall objectives. They are angry about many things and about many aspects of British government policies. They condemn racism, war, the exploitation of the Third World by banks and governments, consumerism, homelessness, the police and the Conservative government, as well as the destruction of the environment. But they are also sometimes scornful of intellectualism and of all forms of organised politics, including those of the left. An article in *The Guardian* of 7 May 1994 quotes an attack by 'Andy' on 'politics' as follows:

> 'This is not privileged Britain at play. It's nothing to do with the chattering classes, or people wittering about crises in the Conservative party, socialism or nuances of government. It's positive people doing things for themselves and others and having a good time.
>
> 'Squatting groups are joining travellers, who are joining anti-road groups, who are ravers, who are vegetarians, who are all angry. People wear a lot of hats these days.'

Some of this protest has elements of a kind of post-modernist nihilism, a product of the hopelessness experienced by many young people whose entire conscious lives have been dominated by Thatcherism, unemployment, cuts in the welfare state, growing racism, attacks on civil liberties, and the fear of nuclear war. A little like those who riot in inner cities, some protestors express their anger almost spontaneously, without any particular political agenda. Nevertheless they express a powerful, and growing, protest against the status quo.

Many of the participants in direct action are greens, or inspired by green ideas. Many greens, and other protestors, do have ideas about long term goals. Greens have one overriding one: to save the planet from destruction. They argue that there must be overall reductions in consumption, at least in industrialised countries, on the grounds that current levels of consumption are unsustainable and will lead to the destruction of the planet. They believe that there should be less growth and less production of useless material goods. Many greens are hostile to central organisation and believe in the importance of local democracy, self-organisation and small self-governing communities. To the extent that they are influenced by traditional politics, some greens and other protestors are influenced by anarchist ideas. Many greens advocate a 'return' to the land and to lives of rural simplicity, avoiding the use of machinery and other energy-consuming inputs as much as possible and relying on sustainable sources of energy and methods of growing food. They believe, to varying degrees, in the goal of self sufficiency in local, usually predominantly rural, communities. In theory the world could accommodate its entire population on cultivable plots of two hectares each, from which people could gain most of their means of subsistence; some greens advocate such a transformation. Others put forward Morrisonian ideas for the 'greening of cities'. Thus a writer in the September 1993 issue of *Community Recharge: the North Kensington Newsletter* ('Free/save 30p (don't buy The Times!)') stands on a bridge in North Kensington, observes a heron and suggests that:

'I'm not the only insanely optimistic urban hunter-gatherer out there prospecting. The greening of the city is but a short imaginative leap away. . . . Foxes have been regularly sighted on BR's burgeoning unprivatised wilderness near Westbourne park . . . scrawny clusters of blackberries overhang Portobello Road . . . mauling passers-by, a ruderal domain reminding us of impending Ectopia . . .

'Tomorrow belongs to us . . . Flash forward . . . I deliver my freshly harvested perpetual spinach to Portobello's free range barrow folk by bicycle rickshaw. Above us, marijuana crops sway gently on the rooftops of the Autonomous Zone of North Kensington and North Paddington, all but the flowering tops used for making paper and clothes for export to the rest of Britain.

'The peoples' pub sells top quality home-brewed beer at rock-bottom prices, efficiently run bottle-banks and re-cycling projects generate vast profits, Community-run betting shops complete with Gamblers Anonymous meeting rooms and relevant therapists, eschew horse racing and bet on a new alfresco sport where energetic locals compete by riding exercise bikes linked to dynamos, charging up banks of 12 volt batteries, providing cheap, independent electricity.

'All rent, mortgages and property deals no longer exist. The homeless settle in the luxury dwellings of the Foxtons catalogue, and artists, musicians and inventors convert any vacant office and warehouse space not being utilised for dope production into spacious studios, venues and playgrounds.

'No one is malemployed. Police wear green uniforms and protect local urban farmers from bandits and outsider bailiffs and bureaucrats . . .'

Recharge, falsely accused of having displayed a cannabis plant in the window of its office, had already had its door smashed in by the police.

There are obvious inconsistencies in some of these ideas. Self sufficiency is difficult to sustain. Few people reject all of the products of large-scale mechanised production. Much of what is now produced in factories, and in cities, is useful. There are advantages in large-scale production of certain things. There are advantages, cultural, practical and possibly environmental, in people congregating together in cities and towns. A return to the land of all of the half of humanity who now live in cities would be difficult and probably undesirable. Though doubtless few greens would recognise this, they could be seen as advocating the formation of a privileged green elite, dependent in spite of its protestations on a more or less out of sight proletariat for which it has no sympathy or understanding. In Oxford, for example, greens were unwilling to recognise that hardship would result from the loss of car workers' jobs. It is difficult to convince them that it matters whose vehicular access to the city centre is blocked; it appears physically easier to block the access of working class people from East Oxford and Blackbird Leys, which is a goal long desired by much of the university, rather than the access of the middle classes from North Oxford; therefore the former is what is campaigned for. Greens tend to have little interest in matters of class and do not differentiate between industrialism and capitalism, refusing to accept that environmental disasters are related to the greed and disempowerment inherent in capitalism. They may assume a universal human interest in environmental matters, unaffected by levels of poverty or inequality in access to resources. In addition, not everyone is physically capable of producing food, or willing to revert to the backbreaking realities of peasant existence. Many, especially the young, appreciate the freedom, creativity and excitement of cities. It is true that there is, in various parts of the world, some voluntary exodus from cities. This is in the present situation largely a middle class phenomenon. Land is expensive. Even once it has been acquired, some form of external, non-agricultural income is likely to be needed or desired in order to secure access to goods produced elsewhere, especially if those who cultivate the land eschew the destructive effects of commercialised farming. In Britain this external income may be the dole, but the dole is paid for largely by taxing those who do the hard and dirty work, in manufacturing and extractive industries and town-based services, and to a much lesser extent their employers. Officially-supported projects to resettle people from cities as farmers, for example during the second world war in Britain and, currently, a few rural employment-creation projects in France, have a patchy and limited record. In the Third World, people leave rural areas and travel to cities, either in their own countries or in the industrialised countries, not because they seek excitement or even wealth, but because subsistence in rural areas is difficult or impossible. The shanty towns of Third World countries are swollen by people who are desperate for a livelihood, who live in hopes of an industrial wage, or who survive as best they can from providing services to the rich or merely to those who have a wage. The alternative to semi-starvation in cities is actual starvation in the countryside, together with increasingly severe degradation of over-exploited soils and forests.

Much of this could of course be changed. The peoples and land of the Third World should not be exploited for the over-consumption of the inhabitants of the industrialised countries, and a return to greater self-sufficiency and food production for local consumption in the Third World is advocated by many. Clearly there is scope, throughout the world, for using the land, including the land in cities, in different ways, for example for growing food for local consumption. Greens are of course right to warn of the risks of environmental damage and to argue for curbs on destructive forms of growth. It is also true that there are problems with the argument, often put forward by socialists at least in the past, that production and technological innovations are in some general way a good thing. Many socialists, as well as greens, believe that we should aim to produce and consume less, and certainly to waste less. They also believe that work should be shared. For example everybody should perhaps take turns in doing the work necessary to satisfy some basic level of human needs. Marx advocated a society in which the necessary work of production was shared; people could then work in the morning, and 'go fishing' in the afternoon. It might be that the production of basic necessities could most efficiently and quickly be carried out in large mechanised factories. People could share this work. They would then have more time to do the things they wanted to do.

Socialists have sometimes been unwilling, at least in the past, to talk about blue-prints for the future, or to define what they mean by socialism. Although, perhaps because of the beleaguered state of socialist ideas, there have recently been a number of attempts to devise such blueprints, these have often capitulated to the ideology of the market. Because of the experience of Stalinist regimes, they have been coy about central planning. Currently many 'socialist' economists advocate some form of 'market socialism', or 'managed social market capitalism', which would be little different from capitalism. Other socialists, including the members of some Trotskyist groups, stick to the ideas of nationalisation, common ownership, and central planning. These ideas retain their importance. Socialists believe in the public ownership of the means of production, including the land but also, as a minimum, all major enterprises and infrastructure. They believe this is necessary in order to make it possible for people in general, rather than individual capitalists, to decide in a democratic way what should be produced and how it should be produced. And they believe that production needs to be planned to ensure that it meets people's real and democratically-determined needs, including their need for jobs and an adequate income, as well as to avoid environmental destruction. While socialists increasingly recognise that greens are right to warn of the unsustainability of current patterns of growth, they argue that these patterns of growth are created by the capitalist 'free market' and cannot be changed unless capitalism is defeated and production is planned. They are likely to argue for some increase in certain types of production, as well as the reduction of others, to meet the many unmet needs that currently exist. Any decision to produce and consume less, and to share the work required to produce whatever is considered necessary or desirable, requires planning. The market does not accomplish such goals and cannot do so. Each individual firm is driven by its imperative to expand and to find or create new markets for new products. Private firms cannot consider the long-term interests of the planet and its inhabitants; their need is for immediate profits. The planning of production ought to be decided through a democratic process, involving as many people as possible.

There are some among both greens and socialists who agree on the necessity of overthrowing capitalism. They may also agree on some of the basic tenets of the socialist vision of the future. Where socialists often differ from greens is that the former believe that democracy, and planning, must be on quite a large scale if they are to have any real meaning or effect, and that the division of humanity into small isolated and self-sufficient units would, in addition, entail great loss in cultural, social and economic terms. Many socialists accept that there have been problems with central planning and that ways must be found to ensure that democratic participation is real, and also suggest that planning can operate with varying degrees of detail at different spatial levels so that, for example, at a local level there is much scope for increasing local democratic control. At the same time some greens and other supporters of small-scale local democracy also recognise that democracy has little meaning if it is so local that nothing much is affected by it. Thus, for example, the authors of a booklet published by a Red-Green Study Group, *What on Earth is To Be Done* (a title which refers to a pamphlet by Lenin), state that both the greens and the socialists in their group agree that equality is an important fundamental goal, however much or little is produced. They argue that it should not be the poor who bear the brunt of any attempt to reduce the damage done to the environment by humans. In addition, they argue for the importance of genuine forms of democracy. Thus:

> 'Ecological sustainability and participatory democracy both point in the direction of a decentralisation of power. However, questions of social justice in access to resources, individual and group liberties, as well as the geographical spread of ecological problems, all indicate the necessity of centres of decision-making, coordination and rule-enforcement across and between communities, up to and including the global scale.
>
> 'It would therefore still be necessary to address the problem of maintaining democratic accountability at these wider levels of decision-making and enforcement. Global and local sustainability and social justice will continue to be central objectives in any future society. This means that, contrary to some socialist and anarchist visions, collective decision-making institutions will still be needed to regulate our impact on the environment and ensure fair distribution of goods.'

They add that:

> 'in a world where natural and technological resources are unequally distributed, existing inequities will persist and even grow unless there are democratically accountable centres with substantial redistributive powers . . . Organisational forms need to be developed which, while allowing a maximum of decentralisation of decision making and participation, not only discourage a fragmentation of society into a multiplicity of local and particular interest groups, but positively enlarge the arena of common concerns.'

Even the goal, widely held among greens, of greater rural self sufficiency, if it was to be on a scale large enough to make much difference, either

179

for the people who now live in cities or for the environment, would require, as a first simple or not so simple condition, a revolution in the ownership and use of the land. Land which is now owned, in Britain and elsewhere, by big landlords and companies would have to be redistributed on a massive scale. Some such outcome has been mooted, in a partial way, by protestors in Britain. In April 1995, when protestors attempted to occupy George's Hill in Surrey (the site of Gerrard Winstanley's utopian community of the 1640s and now a golf course and private estate), they set up a land rights movement for Britain, called The Land Is Ours. Subsequently they occupied a site by the river in Wandsworth in London owned by Guinness and destined for a supermarket, and built small houses, mostly from scrap materials, and started gardens; they were evicted after several months of occupation. The Land Is Ours' programme includes the use of ex-industrial sites for social housing and, in the countryside, the use of planning powers to enable settlers to live on their own land and to secure new sites for travellers; subsidies and planning powers to help small-scale, high employment, low consumption land uses, such as smallholder organic agriculture; the protection and reclaiming of common spaces in towns and countryside; and restraints on developers. These are short-term, transitional demands which might go some way in the direction of helping the situation of the millions who are now stranded without employment, adequate housing or means of escape in towns and cities. Others continue to argue for the full nationalisation of the land.

The question remains of how to implement any such visions. There need to be not only some objectives to work towards, but also some means of first winning power and then meeting these objectives. In Britain now, direct action is potentially a powerful weapon for change. But the protestors are on the whole suspicious of programmes and manifestos, as well as, unsurprisingly, cynical about existing political processes. Many of them hope, in a rather nebulous way, to achieve a change in the climate of ideas. This is clearly essential for any project of more general change; otherwise, for example, the advocates of full democratic participation in a future society might find themselves forced to accept destructive outcomes, such as a continuing increase in car ownership. A change in the climate of ideas is perhaps capable of achievement through direct action and other forms of campaigning. But changing ideas will not overcome the powerful existing forces of capitalism and the state.

Socialists, on the other hand, have a particular view of the way to move towards their goals. They believe that the main agents of change must be organised workers, whose ability to withdraw their labour gives them the power to challenge capital. Although Eurocommunists and some others assert that 'the working class is dead' and that mass production has been replaced by small scale flexible production making strike action ineffective and improbable, this is largely a myth; the process of concentration of capital continues, and people are also employed in large numbers in the public sector and in the privatised utilities. In addition, when socialists engage in 'single issue' campaigns and in electoral politics, they do so not just for the sake of the immediate objectives of these campaigns or from a belief that democracy can in reality be achieved through parliament, but to help build up the strength and organisation necessary to defeat capitalism and to work towards socialism. Outside Europe and North America, socialism and revolutionary politics have, moreover, retained more vigour, both in cities and in rural areas. Land occupations and struggles over the ownership of land, usually under the banner of socialism, are widespread. In north-east Brazil for example, peasants have been struggling against oppressive and violent landlords, and attempting to occupy land, for decades. Land reform, in the sense of the transferring of the ownership of land from private landlords to cooperatives or collective ownership, has been a central demand of many of the liberation and revolutionary movements of the Third World (and would diminish the need for further migration to cities and even perhaps bring about a return to the land on a considerable scale). In Russia and in some Third World countries the old ruling class was overthrown by revolutionary struggles. The outcome was not socialism. But it nevertheless produced changes in a socialist direction some of which were of great value to those who were previously exploited and oppressed.

The looming crisis of the environment is what inspires many, especially young, people to political action. But what also makes action, above all, necessary, is the desperate impoverishment of many of the half of the world's human population who now live in towns and cities. The ideas of the green activists will be of little use if they do not take account of their problems, as, to some extent and perhaps increasingly, they do. Socialism has grown from the radicalism nurtured in cities, and it continues to provide the best hope for their future.

Bibliography

Amnesty International (1994) *Prisoners Without a Voice: Asylum-Seekers Detained in the United Kingdom*, London: Amnesty International British Section.

Audit Commission (1989) *Urban Regeneration and Economic Development: The Local Government Dimension*, London: HMSO.

Balls, E. and P. Gregg, (1993) *Work and Welfare: Tackling The Jobs Deficit*, London: Institute for Public Policy Research.

Benwell Community project: Final Report Series No.2 (1978) *Permanent Unemployment: Is This the Best Future We Can Offer Our School Leavers?* Newcastle-upon-Tyne: Benwell Community Project.

Benyon, J., ed. (1984) *Scarman and After: Essays Reflecting on Lord Scarman's Report, the Riots and Their Aftermath*, Oxford: Pergamon Press.

Beynon, H. and Wainwright, H. (1979) *The Workers' Report on Vickers: The Vickers Shop Stewards Combine Committee Report on Work, Wages, Rationalisation, Closure and Rank-and-File Organisation in a Multinational Company*, London: Pluto Press.

Birmingham Community Development Project, Final Report No.2 (1977) *Workers on the Scrapheap*, Oxford: Birmingham Community Development Project Research Team, Social Evaluation Unit, Oxford University.

Butcher, H. *et al.* (1992) *Local Government and Thatcherism*, London: Harvester.

CDP (1977) *The Costs of Industrial Change*, London: CDP Inter-Project Editorial Team.

Cabinet Office and Central Office of Information (1989) *Action for Cities: Progress on Cities*, London: HMSO.

Campaign to Close Campsfield (1994), 'Secret State', London: *Index on Censorship*, No.6.

Campbell, B. (1993) *Goliath: Britain's Dangerous Places*, London: Methuen.

Cochrane, A. (1989) 'Restructuring the Local State: the Case of Local Government', in Cochrane, A. and Anderson, J. (eds) *Politics in Transition*, London: Sage.

Cochrane, A. (1993) *Whatever Happened to Local Government*, Buckingham: Open University Press.

Cockburn, C. (1977) *The Local State: Management of Cities and People*, London: Pluto Press.

Cohen, S. (1988) *From the Jews to the Tamils: Britain's Mistreatment of Refugees*, Manchester: South Manchester Law Centre.

Cohen, S. (1992) *Imagine There's No Countries: 1992 and International Immigration Controls Against Migrants, Immigrants and Refugees*, Manchester: Greater Manchester Immigration Aid Unit.

Cohen, S. (1993) *Workers' Control Not Immigration Controls*, Manchester: Greater Manchester Immigration Aid Unit.

Colenutt, C. and Tansley, S. (1990) *Inner City Regeneration: A Local Authority Perspective*, Manchester: Centre for Local Economic Strategies (CLES).

Community Development Projects (1977) *Gilding The Ghetto: The State and The Poverty Experiments*, London: Community Development Projects.

Davis, M. (1990) *City of Quartz*, London: Verso.

De Groot, L. (1992) 'City Challenge: Competing in the Urban Regeneration Game', in *Local Economy*, volume 7.

Department of the Environment (1988) *Improving Urban Areas: Good Practice in Urban Regeneration*, London: HMSO.

Department of the Environment (1992) *DoE Annual Report 1992: Government Expenditure Plans 1992 to 1994-5*, London: HMSO.

Docklands Consultative Committee (1988a) *A Memorandum on Employment and Economic Activity in London Docklands — The Impact of the LDDC. Submitted as Written Evidence to the House of Commons Employment Committee by the Docklands Consultative Committee, February 1988*. London: Docklands Consultative Committee, February.

Docklands Consultative Committee (1988b) *Urban Development Corporations: Six Years in London's Docklands*, London: Docklands Consultative Committee, February.

Docklands Consultative Committee (1988c) *National Audit Office Study of Urban Development Corporations: The Response of the Docklands Consultative Committee.*

Docklands Forum (1988) *Economic Change in Docklands: Draft Report.*

Docklands Forum (1989) *Does the Community Benefit? What Can the Private Sector Offer? Lessons from London's Docklands.*

Duncan, A. (1992) *Taking on the Motorway: North Kensington Amentity Trust, 21 Years,* London: Kensington and Chelsea Community History Group.

Eisenschitz, A. and Gough, J. *The Politics of Local Economic Policy: The Problems and Possibilities of Local Initiative,* London: MacMillan.

Fielding, T. and Halford, S. (1990) *Patterns and Processes of Urban Change in the United Kingdom,* London: HMSO.

Giles, C. and Johnson, P. (1994) in *Fiscal Studies,* August issue, London: Institute of Fiscal Studies.

Greater London Council (1985) *London Industrial Strategy,* London: Greater London Council (available from Spokesman Books, Bertrand Russell House, Gamble St., Nottingham NG7 4ET).

Harvey, D. (1989) *The Condition of Postmodernity,* Oxford: Basil Blackwell.

Hatch, S., Fox, E. and Legg, C. (1977) *Research and Reform: Southwark C.D.P., 1969-1972.* London: The Urban Deprivation Unit, The Home Office.

Hayter, T. (1981) *The Creation of World Poverty,* London: Pluto Press.

Hayter, T. and D. Harvey, eds (1993), *The Factory and The City: The Story of Cowley Automobile Workers in Oxford,* London: Mansell.

Healey, P. *et al.,* eds (1992) *Rebuilding The City: Property-led Urban Regeneration,* London: Chapman and Hall.

Heseltine, M. (1987) *Where There's A Will There's A Way,* London: Hutchinson.

Home Office (1993) *Asylum Statistics: United Kingdom 1992,* Home Office Statistical Bulletin 15 July 1993, London: Home Office Research and Statistics Department, 50 Queen Anne's Gate.

House of Commons Employment Committee (1988) *The Employment Effects of Urban Development Corporations,* London: HMSO.

Jacobs, B.D. (1992) *Fractured Cities: Capitalism, Community and Empowerment in Britain and America,* London: Routledge.

Joseph Rowntree Foundation (1993) *Building for Communities,* York: Joseph Rowntree Foundation.

Joseph Rowntree Foundation and the Department of Social Policy and Social Work, University of Manchester (1995) *Mixed Fortunes*, York: Joseph Rowntree Foundation.

Lawless, P. (1989) *Britain's Inner Cities*, London: Paul Chapman Publishing.

London Chamber of Commerce (1992) *London's Economy: Trends and Prospects*, London: London Chamber of Commerce.

London Strategic Policy Unit, Economic Policy Group (1987) *Sewing Up The Pieces: Local Authority Strategies For The Clothing Industry*, by T. Hayter, L. Digings, M. Cook and L. Chambers, London: London Strategic Policy Unit.

MacGregor, S. and B. Pimlott, eds (1990) *Tackling The Inner Cities: The 1980s Revisited, Prospects for the 1990s*, Oxford: Clarendon Press.

Mackintosh, M. and Wainwright, H. (1987) *A Taste of Power: The Politics of Local Economics*, London: Verso.

Mackintosh, M. (1992) 'Partnership: Issues of Policy and Negotiation', in *Local Economy*, volume 7.

Malden, H.E., ed (1905) *The Victoria History of the County of Surrey*, London: Constable.

Merriman, N., ed (1993) *The Peopling of London: Fifteen Thousand Years of Settlement from Overseas*, London: The Museum of London.

Mumford, L. (1961) *The City in History: Its Origins, Its Transformations and Its Prospects*, Harmondsworth: Penguin.

National Audit Office (1988) *Department of the Environment: Urban Development Corporations*, London: HMSO.

Newham Docklands Forum and GLC Popular Planning Unit (1983) *The People's Plan for the Royal Docks*.

North Southwark Community Development Group (1992) *NSCDG 1972-92: 20 Years of Community Action*, London: North Southwark Community Development Group.

North Southwark Community Development Group (undated) *After the Docks — What?* London: North Southwark Community Development Group.

O'Malley, J. (1977) *The Politics of Community Action: A Decade of Struggle in Notting Hill*, Nottingham: Spokeman Books.

Di Parkin (1995), *Equality Audit on Street Cleansing and Car Park Service*, Leicester City Council.

Peck, J. and Tickell, A. (1993) 'Business Goes Local: Dissecting the "Business Agenda" in post-democratic Manchester', paper presented at the Ninth Urban Change and Conflict Conference, University of Sheffield.

Red-Green Study Group (1995) *What on Earth is To Be Done: A Red-Green Dialogue*, London: Red-Green Study Group.

Scarman, Lord (1981) *The Brixton Disorders 10-12 April 1981: Report of an Inquiry*, London: HMSO Commd 8427.

Shaw, K. (1993) 'The Political Economy of Urban Regeneration in the North East of England: the Rise of the Growth Coalition or Local Corporatism Revisited?', *Regional Studies* 27.

Socialist Workers Party (1978) *The Case Against Immigration Controls: Socialist Worker Pocket pamphlet No.6*, London: Socialist Worker Distributors.

Sutcliffe, B. (1994) 'Migration, Rights and Illogic', *Index on Censorship*, 3.

Taaffe, P. and T. Mulhearne, (1988) *Liverpool; A City That Dared to Fight*, Fortress.

Thornley, A., ed (1992) *The Crisis of London*, London: Routledge.

Town and Country Planning Association (TCPA) (1986) *Whose Responsibility? Reclaiming the Inner Cities*, London: Town and Country Planning Association.

Tym, R. and Partners (1984) *The Isle of Dogs Enterprise Zone: Monitoring Report to the GLC*, London: Greater London Council.

University of Westminster (1992) *City Challenge and Local Regeneration Partnerships: Second Conference Proceedings, November 1992*, edited by Alison Barker and Nick Bailey. London: The Planning Research Group, University of Westminster.

Wainwright, H. and Elliott, D. (1982) *The Lucas Plan: A New Trade Unionism in the Making?* London: Allison and Busby.

White Paper (1977) *Policy for the Inner Cities*, London: HMSO.

Widgery, D. (1991) *Some Lives! A GP's East End*. London: Sinclair-Stevenson.

Wilmott, P. (1986) *Social Networks, Informal Care and Public Policy*, London: PSI.